Critical Mass to Critical Action

A Study of the Process of Empowerment

Critical Mass to Critical Action

A Study of the Process of Empowerment

Professor G. Palanithurai

GYAN

The Publication of this thesis was financially upheld by ICSSR and the responsibility of the facts stated, opinions expressed or conclusions reached are entirely that of the author and ICSSR accepts no responsibility for them.

ICSSR Consultant

Dr Sheila Rai, 6, Shivaji Nagar Civil Line, Jaipur 302004

ISBN : 978-81-212-1326-4

Price : ₹ 424

First Published, 2016

Published by

Gyan Publishing House
5, Ansari Road
Daryaganj, New Delhi-110002
Phones: 9811692060
E-mail: books@gyanbooks.com

Printed at: G. Print Process, Delhi.

Cataloging in Publication Data—DK
Courtesy: D.K. Agencies (P) Ltd. <docinfo@dkagencies.com>

Palanithurai, G., author.
Critical mass to critical action : a study of the process of empowerment : report submitted to ICSSR, New Delhi / Professor G. Palanithurai.
pages cm
Includes bibliographical references.
ISBN 9788121213264

1. Panchayat—India—Tamil Nadu. 2. Employee empowerment—Government policy—India—Tamil Nadu. 3. Tamil Nadu (India)—Politics and government. 4. Indian Council of Social Science Research. I. Title.

JS7025.T3P35 2016 DDC 320.84095482 23

Contents

TO

THE DIVINE MOTHER

Acknowledgements

For any work an environment is necessary and a team is an imperative need. No work is possible without the cooperation of individuals who are in the system. In an academic institution a research culture is the requirement for a quality work. Research is not an isolated event. It is a way of life, a system, a culture and a process. Department of Political Science and Development Administration in the Gandhigram Rural Institute – Deemed University is known throughout the world for its work on decentralisation, grassroots democracy and grassroots development. The Department of Political Science and Development Administration was inducted into the UGC SAP activities because of its two decades activities in decentralisation and democratisation. It is not only a teaching department but also a committed research and outreach centre. Strength of the department lies in all the three dimensional activities namely, teaching, research and outreach activities. The Department of Political Science and Development Administration has got two outstanding academic programmes. It is not offering the academic programmes in a conventional mode and the degrees offered here are not the degrees offered in conventional universities. The Department offers an innovative M.A. Programme in Development Administration. It is a Five-year Integrated Programme. Yet another innovative, Two-year M.A. Programme on "Governance and Development" is being offered and it is supported by the UGC through its 'Innovative Programme'. To carry out quality research and outreach Programme we have created Rajiv Gandhi Chair for Panchayati Raj Studies. We carried out massive research activities mostly action research supported by various bilateral and multilateral agencies. They are, the Ford Foundation, UNICEF, UNDP, World Bank, State Planning Commission, Department of Rural Development, Ministry of Rural Development, Ministry of Panchayati Raj, Government of India, the Hunger Project, and various foundations in India and abroad. Within two decades we have operated projects worth about fifty million rupees. All our activities are in decentralisation, development and grassroots democracy. The above fact is mentioned here not to give self advertisement but to inform academic community that there is enough space to work in decentralisation. Decentralisation has not received the needed attention from the academic community as it ought to receive from the academic community and the research institutions. All the funding agencies have come to us only to work in decentralisation. It is because of the quality culture and commitment we have developed in our department over a period of time. Further, it is to be mentioned here that though in terms of faculty strength we are less in number. But we have developed a team culture and as a result a fine research environment has been created in our department. Periodically training programmes have been conducted for grassroots leaders in Rajiv Gandhi Chair for Panchayati Raj Studies and in turn they have enabled us to connect ourselves with the larger communities. Through our research activities we connect ourselves with policy community. Each and every research report carries one section 'policy recommendation'. We take it to the policy community for policy advocacy. In such a way we are well connected with stakeholders meaningfully. We have prepared Administrative Manual for Panchayati Raj functionaries in Tamil Nadu. Based on our work we have been asked to prepare model Panchayati Raj manual for the Ministry of Panchayati Raj, Government of India. Separately administrative manual has been prepared and published in vernacular for Tamil Nadu Panchayat leaders. It has gone for seven editions. I feel that it is a seminal contribution of our Department to the society. Because in the whole of our country only in two states Panchayat manual has been prepared and published. The department has got many projects related to Panchayati Raj.

This ICSSR project is one small assignment. The moment I initiated activities for this project, I was invited to be in Cologne University, Germany as a visiting professor for one semester. I left for Germany to take up this assignment. During that time my coordinatorship of this project along with my other projects have been handed over to my colleague Professor V. Ragupathy. He carried out all my project activities during that period. When I returned from Germany I came with a new assignment as we have signed MoU with German Universities. With great difficulty I manage the project as my work load has been increased. We are six faculty members to manage two M.A. Programmes, one M. Phil Programme and twenty Ph.D scholars' with more than 120 students. We have to make arrangements for village placement programme, extension programme, internship and other activities in the field as per the mandate of the academic programmes of the department. We are ably assisted by some of the JRF and other Ph.D scholars. Without their help we would not have carried out our academic works successfully. Apart from this we have to take steps for their placements. Since the passing out students from our department have got good assignments in various development and civil society organisations we are getting students for our M.A. Programme continuously. In Tamil Nadu, one cannot see one hundred and twenty students in the Department of Political Science in any University other than Gandhigram Rural Institute. For all the academic, research and extension activities my colleagues cooperated with me. Hence I have to thank my colleagues more particularly Professor V. Ragupathy and Research scholars namely, Ms K. Aruna, Mr P. Sathyaraj and Mr D. Sivakumar for their unreserved cooperation for my all academic activities. Our academic works were and are possible because of the very cooperative gestures of our authorities and for which I have to express my deep sense of gratitude to them. Finally, I record my thanks to ICSSR for its generous funding. I have returned part of the funding as my researchers have done some field work when they went for other project works in the field. I also register my thanks to the respondents for having sparred their time to respond to our questions during our interaction with them. I thank Dr S. Jaganathan, District Collector of

Namakkal for his valuable insights into the process of enabling environment for the effective functioning of Elected Women Representatives during our interaction with them. Finally, I register my thanks to my family members more particularly my wife Mrs Mala for her unrelenting support to all my academic research and outreach activities.

Professor G. Palanithurai
Rajiv Gandhi Chair for Panchayati Raj Studies, Department of Political Science and Development Administration, Gandhigram Rural Institute – Deemed University, Gandhigram – 624302

Chapter - I

Introduction

It is proved beyond doubt that, even in the western democracies, to promote women interests, the Women Elected Representatives can be trusted to a greater extent (Gargarella, 1992). The Elected Women Representatives whether they are of the west or the east, have different political priorities, policy concerns and perspectives on governance, development and administration (Phillips, 2000 and G.Palanithurai, 2004). But their concerns, policies, priorities and perspectives depend on the numerical strength of the elected women representatives in the authoritative bodies, which has been termed as 'critical mass'. It is a broad assumption partially confirmed in the world that when the critical mass comes to the authoritative bodies, it will perform the critical function. Critical function refers to in this study the tackling of household health, nutrition, well being of children, women, adolescent girls, problems of other marginalised groups, and democratisation of communities, organisation and institutions at the grassroots. To perform the above empowerment of Elected Women Representatives is considered critical and crucial.

In India, after the passing of the 73rd and the 74th Amendments to the Constitution of India, one million women have come to the Local Bodies as the representatives of the people. No doubt, they form a critical mass in the authoritative bodies (Theoretically speaking 10 per cent of the total numbers of any organisation or association form critical mass and, in India, their strength is more than one-third of the total strength of the bodies) in India at the local level. It is a question repeatedly asked as to whether the newly formed critical mass in the local bodies has performed the critical function, (Joti Sekhon, 2006, 101-102) since the conditions of women are unacceptable and women have been denied their rights and opportunities (Government of India, 1975). It is argued powerfully that to perform the critical function, the critical mass requires a critical support structure both internally and externally. Without the help of the support structure in the formative years the critical mass cannot perform the critical function. There have been a series of reviews and observations (Caroline Moser, 1989; Gita Sen, 1994) about the conditions of women based on which new schemes and programmes have been chalked out for the welfare of women throughout the world. Yet, one cannot see any significant impact as expected on the society in terms of gender equity. The marginalisation of the majority of women in the economy and the consequent neglect of women in decision-making and urban bias have led to a complicated situation in the general political framework of the society. It is also true that even the opportunities that have been provided to the women have not been properly used by them for their upliftment as they have been trained to be insensitive towards their own issues (Sakuntala Narasimhan, 1999, 44-45). Hence, against the above backdrop, the problems of women have to be addressed by the newly Elected Women Representatives. But the basic question here is to what extent the Elected Women Representatives are empowered and equipped to tackle the problems of women and other marginalised groups. This is the question to be investigated.

Review of Literature

Adequate literature is available in this area, but they mostly reflect the western experience (Paul Chaney, 2008; P. Norris and J. Lovenduski, 2001). In the South Asian context also one finds adequate literature on this area. But in those studies, though the conditions within which elected representatives are functioning are adequately explained, the implications of their presence have not been covered adequately (Damayanty Sridharan and Vesna Rodic, 2004). In Indian context, there are studies (G. Palanithurai, 2005, The Hunger Project, 2006, 2007, 2008; Panda, 2008; Nirmala Buch, 2006; Chathukulam and John, 2000) which have amply demonstrated the struggle and success of the Elected Women Representatives. They are mostly case studies and they are inadequate to generalise the results. There are other kinds of studies focusing on the leadership of the Elected Women Representatives (Celine Rani, 2004 and G. Palanithurai, 2008). These studies are confined to a few districts. In the same way, micro studies have also been conducted, but based on the above studies, one cannot generalise the conditions of Elected Women Representatives and the implications of the elected representatives' performance in the society. These studies have brought to light the potential available in the institutions to bring about transformation.

To overcome the problems and the gap in the literature, the Ministry of Panchayati Raj, Govt. of India has commissioned a study on Elected Women Representatives covering the whole country. It is about the status, position and conditions of the Elected Women Representatives in the local bodies in India (Ministry of Panchayati Raj, 2008). This study was also confined to the Gram Panchayat alone. This study has another inbuilt weakness that the entire analysis was made for the whole of India without taking into account the fact that the Panchayati Raj is a state subject and devolution process varies from state to state. Further, this study could not focus on the implications. The study "Experience of the Elected Women Representatives in Grassroots Institutions" (G. Palanithurai, 2004) brought to light the experiences gained by the elected women representatives while discharging their duties and responsibilities. They are drawn from their narrations while they were in refresher programmes. They are being analysed in the context of the women conditions in rural Tamil Nadu.

The study "Dalit Women's Rights to Political Participation in Rural Panchayati Raj" (Jayshree Mangubhai, Aloysius Irudayam SJ and Emma Sydenham, 2009) highlights the fact that despite reservations guaranteed under the 73rd Constitutional Amendment Act 1992 severe caste-class-gender obstructions operate to deny Dalit women the opportunity to enjoy the political power vested in them and to enable others to appropriate the women's ability to deliver more caste and gender responsive development outcomes as well as circumscribing the space for them to reshape underlying structural inequalities. This situation is compounded by the general failure of government and police officials to respond to cases of obstructions.

The study "Elected Women Representatives and Emerging Alternative Governance" (G. Palanithurai, 2005) has analysed the pattern of Governance emerged from the governance process done by the Elected Women Representatives in Tamil Nadu. This is part of a major research work done for the UNICEF. The whole exercise was done in the backdrop of the performance pattern of men representatives in rural local bodies. The distinctiveness in approaching the problems and issues is brought to light by the researcher. It provides enormous scope for analysing the reasons for their distinctiveness in handling power and discharging responsibilities.

The study on "Governance: From the Perspective of Elected Women Representatives" (G. Palanithurai, 2004) is an analysis of the performance of the Elected Women Representatives on some of the critical issues. Based on the case studies, he analysed the key perspectives with which the Elected Women Representatives have dealt with the social issues. Which are the issues being tackled by them from what perspective have been analysed and brought to light.

Yet, another study on "Evaluation of the Process and Performance of Women and Dalit Leaders in Gram Panchayat" (G. Palanithurai, 2005) focused on the performance of the marginalised group representatives. Based on the conventional method of evaluation, performance of the Gram Panchayat leaders belonging to Dalit community and women have been evaluated and brought to light the major breakthroughs and the barriers they faced to make achievements.

"Networking of Elected Women Representatives at the Grassroots" (G. Palanithurai, G. Uma and J. Vanishree, 2010) is a record of the activities carried out by the Federation of Elected Women Representatives of Tamil Nadu. Series of activities have been carried out by the Federation of Elected Women Representatives. The authors have documented the events conducted by the Elected Women Representatives and analysed the process of functioning of the federation. Its impact has also been analysed.

"Elected Women Representatives and Empowerment of Women" (G. Palanithurai, 2012) is a compilation of articles written by different scholars from four South Indian states on the activities of the Elected Women Representatives on the issues of women empowerment. Achievements and barriers the Elected Women Representatives faced have been covered in all those articles.

"Buildings Alliance and Capabilities among the Elected Women Representatives of Grassroots" (G. Palanithurai, 2003) is also a document prepared based on the training programme conducted for them on leadership and the networking process initiated to link with other states. How Elected Women Representatives have established their connections and how increased their capacity have been analysed in this work.

"Dalits and Dalit Representatives in Rural Governance voices from the field" (G. Palanithurai, 2013) is the result of a large survey conducted among the Dalits and Dalit representatives in Tamil Nadu. The deplorable conditions of Dalit and the precarious positions of the Dalit representatives have been focused in this study.

The study conducted in Tamil Nadu entitled "Communities, Panchayats and Governance at Grassroots" (G. Palanithurai and V. Ragupathy, 2007) gives a detailed account of the functioning of community Panchayats and the rule played in formal Panchayats. It analyses how they added strength to formal Panchayats and how they have weakened the constitutional Panchayats have been analysed.

"Panchayats, Communities and Social Development" (G. Palanithurai, 2003) is a study conducted on the project of population foundation of India. It has analysed the impact of Panchayats and communities on social development issues in the project area to demonstrate the potentials of the grassroots institutions.

Through yet another study "Synergisation of Traditional Panchayat with Formal Panchayati Raj System in Managing Community Affairs" (G. Palanithurai, 2003) focuses its attention through a case analysis on the vital role played by both jointly in managing commons and community affairs for the benefit of the poor women and other marginalised.

All the studies have focused their attention on performance by adopting different approaches. Most of the studies have adopted case study method. No study has analysed the empowerment and development process of the Elected Women Representatives from the empowerment perspective. So a state specific empirical analysis is needed. Further, such study should concentrate on the conditions and positions of the elected Women Representatives and the implications of their performance in the institutions and the larger society. This is a gap to be filled through the present study.

Analytical Framework to Measure Empowerment

Empowerment of women is gaining currency among academics and policy-makers now. Empowerment has been defined differently by different scholars contextually (Srilatha Batliwala, 1995). But many scholars have given a broader interpretation to the concept – empowerment (Gita Sen and Caren Grown, 1987). It is a method of tackling powerlessness in encountering and combating personal and social problems. It enhances individual's or group's capacity to make choices and transform those choices into desired actions and outcomes. Degree of empowerment can be assessed by measuring the extent to which some categories of people are able to control their own destinies even when their interests are opposed by others with whom they interact. Empowerment is distinguished by its focus on developing critical awareness, increasing the feeling of collective and self efficacy and developing skills for personal, interpersonal or social change. This empowerment can be defined as control over material assets, intellectual resources and ideology. It is process of creating awareness, building capacity, and leading to greater participation, greater decision-making power and control and to transformative action.

To study the empowerment of women in India Second National Family Health Survey (NFHS-2) was conducted throughout India in 1998-99. This survey was comprehensive one covering several aspects of the empowerment of women. Defining empowerment is not a difficult job but operationalising the definition is the problematic one. Because it has got both qualitative and quantitative aspects. Kishor has developed a framework (Kishor, 2000) and subsequently Kabeer (Kabeer, 2001) has evolved yet another conceptual framework for measuring empowerment. Both frameworks are having more similarities. Yet, Kishor framework will be of much more operationable one than Kabeers.

To study the empowerment process for women and the elected women representatives, the framework for understanding and measuring empowerment developed by Ruth Alsop and Nina Heinsoln is selected (Ruth Alsop and Nina Heinsohn, 2005). This framework has been selected for this study due to comparative advantage of its utility compared to other frameworks. The basic principle underlines the fact that if a group or an individual is empowered, they possess the capacity to make effective choices.

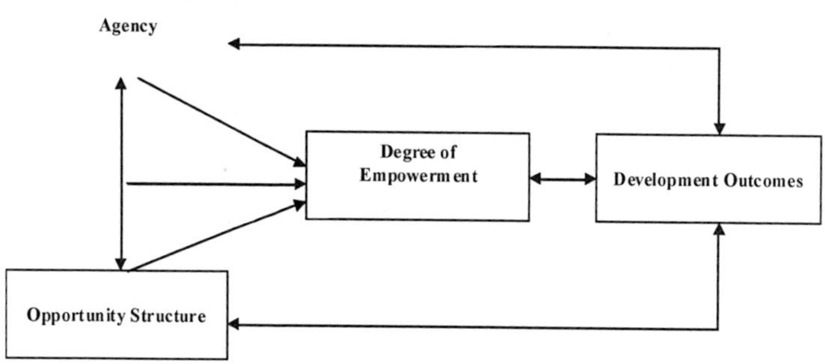

Figure – 1

Analytical Framework to Study Critical Mass's Critical Function

The choices will be translated into desired actions and outcomes. As per this framework, empowerment is the result of two sets of factors. They are agency factors and opportunity structure factors. Agency is defined as an actor's ability to make meaningful choices. The actor is able to envisage options and make a choice. Opportunity structure is defined as the formal and informal contexts in which actors operate. By working together these factors give rise to different degree of empowerment.

The degree of empowerment can be measured by assessing (1) whether a person has the opportunity to make a choice; (2) whether a person actually uses the opportunity to choose; and (3) once the choice is made, whether it brings the desired outcome. How can the agency – the capacity to make meaningful choice be measured? Agency comprises of asset endowments which are used as indicators of the ability to choose. These assets are psychological, informative, organisational, material, financial and human. Opportunity structure is shaped by the presence and operation of formal and informal institutions or rules of the game. These include the laws, regulatory frameworks and norms governing people's behaviour.

Measurement of assets and institutions provides intermediary indicators of empowerment. Empowerment can be measured by assessing: (a) Whether an opportunity to make a choice exists (Existence of choice); (b) whether a person actually uses the opportunity to choose (Use of choice); and (c) Whether the choice results in the desired results (Achievements of choice). The above framework is operationalised and used to analyse the empowerment process of Elected Women Representatives and through which empowerment process of the women and marginalised could be traced.

Operationalisation of the Framework

Agency and opportunity structure are the determinant factors of empowerment. The level of empowerment is determined by the agency and the opportunity structure. To measure the agency, first indicators have to be fixed. All asset endowments of an individual are used as indicators of agency. They are the skills, capacity, vision, social background, economic background, level of confidence, personal initiatives, educational background, support structure, training undergone, political affiliation, and mobility. In the same way, opportunity structure is to be measured. Opportunity structure consists of the available institutional arrangements. They are the Panchayat council, committees, Gram Sabha, deliberative process, resources available to perform, budgetary and planning process. Empowerment of the women is measured in terms of the functioning of the institution under the guidance of the Elected Women Representatives. Development outcome is measured in terms of the activities carried out by the Panchayats in favour of women, Dalits, children and others.

Questions have been formulated to assess the agency indicators namely, material assets, financial assets, informational assets, organisational assets, capability assets. Sixty seven questions have been framed to elicit response to measure the level of agency indicators. In order to measure the opportunity structure questions have been framed. Forty five questions have been formulated to cover the existing political, governance and administrative legal arrangement to perform the role, responsibilities and tasks of the Elected Women Representatives. Finally to study the outcome of the empowerment, service delivery aspects have been incorporated. Questions have been framed to elicit the response from the Elected Women Representatives on the performance or activities carried out in the respective Panchayats. Forty questions have been set in this section. Along with the achievements, the problems and challenges faced by the Elected Women Representatives have also been analysed. For that seven questions have been arranged in the interview schedule. From the response of the Elected Women representatives simple tables have been constructed and explained and they are related to each other to assess the extent of association each one on the other by using statistical tool. Finally they are tested.

Objectives of the Study

Following objectives are drawn from the analytical framework:

(a) To study the recruitment process of the Elected Women Representatives to the Local Bodies;

(b) To study the empowerment process of the Elected Women Representatives;

(c) To study the empowerment process of the women in the areas where Gram Panchayat presidents are women;

(d) To study the problems faced by the Elected Women Representatives in handling the opportunities in Local Bodies;

(e) To study and analyse the support structure created for Elected Women Representatives; and

(f) To study the performance of the Elected Women Representatives on the issues of women, children and other marginalised groups.

Hypotheses

- The functional outcome of the Elected Women Representatives depends on the utilisation of agency and opportunity structures.
- The higher the level of skill, capacity, support structure and higher will be the possibility of tackling the issue of the marginalised and more particularly women and children.
- The higher the degree of devolution and freedom, the higher the level of performance of the elected women representatives.

Research Methodology

To test the hypotheses data have been generated basically from the Gram Panchayats which are under the leadership of the women. The whole of Tamil Nadu has been divided into five geographical zones and samples are drawn from all the five zones. Three per cent of total Elected Women Representatives have been selected for interaction and data have been generated from them. Within three per cent of the sample, one-fourth Dalit Elected Women Representatives have been interviewed. A well structured interview schedule has been prepared through which data have been elicited from the Elected Women Representatives. Questions pertinent to the existence of choice, use of choice and achievements of choice have been incorporated in the interview schedule. Scores are given for each segment and they are calculated cumulatively to measure the empowerment level. Further another set of data have been collected from the Panchayat records. Apart from the above the entire Panchayat areas have been visited by the investigators to find out the available infrastructure and their conditions. The secondary data have been drawn from the published records, books and articles. This study included some of the best cases of success stories of women representatives and equally the struggle of the elected women representatives by adopting a case study method. It will be full length narrative to bring out the intricacies of the struggle and success. Though cases may not help for generalisation, it will bring to light the subtle issues involved in the process of empowerment. The collected primary data have been analysed by using appropriate statistical tools. Results are explained and interpreted in the backdrop of the framework on empowerment.

Drawbacks in Research

Contacting elected women representatives for interaction is not an easy job as they are by and large under the protection of the male members of their family. Even after getting the concurrence of the male members, the Elected Women Representatives are not allowed to give details to the researchers. The respondents were allowed to interact with researchers and yet most of the answers were given by the male family members and they were endorsed by the Elected Women Representatives. To collect data from the Panchayat, Panchayat clerks have to cooperate with us. In fact, the Panchayat clerks get permission from the higher officials to share data with us. Cross-verification will bring truth in the process of data collection and in this case the officials and Elected Women Representatives made this research very difficult. After visiting the entire Panchayat areas for reconfirmation of data, the investigator has contacted the respondents and they informed intricate details about the whole functioning of the Panchayati Raj system. While giving such details they informed the investigator that the information provided by them should not be quoted. Since the respondents have given information about the role of traditional Panchayats, officials, family members, community leaders, they developed fear over reaction on that information. Because in Tamil Nadu environment is not conducive for decentralisation. Further for this project we collected data from two periods. When we were in data collection, election held for local bodies. Our work continued with newly Elected Women Representatives. Hence both sets of data have been analysed. At every stage we face problems. The respondents were from both regimes.

Chapterisation

This report consists of eight chapters. First chapter discusses the problem and need of the study with the methodological nuances adopted in generating data and analysis of the same. Further, the theoretical framework for studying the empowerment process of elected women representatives and its implication has been incorporated in the same chapter. Second chapter gives the background of the Tamil Nadu Panchayati Raj system and in which a thorough analysis has been made on the devolution process along with the structural arrangement. Detailed analysis has been made on the powers and resources conferred on the three tiers Panchayati Raj system in Tamil Nadu. Third chapter focuses its attention on the agency. This chapter brings to light socio-economic background of the respondents, informational assets the respondents have gained, organisational support they have acquired and skill, capacity and capability they have gained in the process. Fourth chapter gives the details of the opportunity structure namely, Panchayati Council, Gram Sabha, committees of the Panchayats and other institutional arrangements in which they operate. Fifth chapter focuses on the development outcome of the above. It is primarily service delivery. Sixth chapter makes an integrated analysis and seventh chapter forms conclusion.

Limitations

This study uses data generated from the Elected Women Representatives who held position in the previous period and the Elected Women Representatives holding position now. When the data generation process was on, election to local bodies had been conducted. Hence rest of the data has been generated from the newly recruited women representatives. One set of Elected Women Representatives with five years of governance and development experience responded to our questions and another set of Elected Women Representatives are fresh and new to the job. Without much experience they have responded to our questions. Results are the reflections of both experienced and the fresh representatives. Since Rajiv Gandhi Chair for Panchayati Raj Studies have been carrying out a variety of studies for different agencies, data generated for other projects have been used.

Notes and References

1. Batliwala, Srilatha, "The Meaning of Women's Empowerment" Women's World, 23-34.
2. Buch, Nirmala, From Oppression to Assertion: A Study of Panchayats and Women in Madhya Pradesh, Rajasthan and Uttar Pradesh (Mimo) New Delhi, CWDS, 1999.
3. Caroline, Moser, "Gender Planning in Third World: Meeting practical and strategic gender needs" World Development, Vol. 17, No.11 (1989).
4. Rani, Celine A, Women Leadership at Grassroots, New Delhi: Gyan Publishing House, 2004.
5. Chaney, Paul, "Critical Mass, Deliberation and the Substantative Representation of Women: Evidence from the UK's Devolution Programme" Political Studies (2006) Vol. 54, pp. 691-714.
6. Chathukulam, Jos and John MS, "Empowerment of Women Panchayat Members: Learning from Kerala" Asian Journal of Women Studies, Vol. 6, No. 4 (1985).
7. Damyanty Sridharan and Vesna Rodic (eds), Breaking the Political Class Ceiling: Women and Local Governance in South Asia, New Delhi: Fredrich Ebert Stiftung, 2004.
8. Gargarella, R, "Full Representation, Deliberation and Impartiality" in J. Elster (ed) Deliberative Democracy Cambridge: Cambridge University Press, 1998, pp.142-163.

9. Government of India, Towards Equality: Report of the Committee on the status of women in India, New Delhi: Government of India, 1975.
10. Ministry of Panchayati Raj, Study on Elected Women Representatives in Panchayati Raj Institutions, New Delhi: Ministry of Panchayati Raj, 2008.
11. Narashimhan, Sakuntala, Empowering Women: An Alternative Strategy from Rural India, New Delhi, Sage Publications, 1999.
12. Norris, P. Lovenduski, J Blair's Babes: Critical Mass Theory, Gender and Legislative Life (Working paper series) John F. Kennedy School of Government, Harvard University, 2001.
13. Palanithurai, G, Governance from the Perspective of Elected Women Representatives (Monograph) Gandhigram: Rajiv Gandhi Chair for Panchayati Raj Studies, 2004.
14. Palanithurai, G, Change Makers at Grassroots: Leadership Matters Much, New Delhi: Concept Publishing Company, 2008.
15. Palanithurai, G, Process and Performance of Gram Panchayat Women and Dalit Presidents, New Delhi: Concept Publishing Company, 2005.
16. Palanithurai, G, Dalits and Dalit Representatives in Rural Local Governance: Voices from the Filed, New Delhi, Concept Publishing Company, 2013.
17. Palanithurai, G and Ragupathy, V, Communities, Panchayats and Governance at Grassroots, New Delhi, Concept Publishing Company, 2007.
18. Palanithurai, G, Panchayats, Communities and Social Development (Monograph) Gandhigram, Rajiv Gandhi Chair for Panchayati Raj Studies, 2003.
19. Palanithurai, G, Synergisation of Traditional Panchayat with Formal Panchayati Raj System in Managing Community Affairs (Monograph) Gandhigram, Rajiv Gandhi Chair for Panchayati Raj Studies, 2003.
20. Phillips, A, "Representing Difference: Why it matters if women get elected: in A Coote (ed) New Gender Agenda London:!! PR, 2000.
21. Alsop Ruth and Nina Heinsohn, Measuring Empowerment in Pratice: Structuring Analysis and Framing Indicators, Working Paper 3510, Washington DC: World Bank, 2005.
22. Gupta, Sen, "Poverty, Economic Growth and Gender Equity: The Asian and Pacific Experience" in Gender Economic Growth and Poverty, Nocleen Heyzer and Gita Sen, New Delhi: Kali For women, 1994.
23. Gupta, Sen and Grown Caren, Development Crises and Alternative Visions: Third World Perspectives, New York: Monthly Review Press, 1987.
24. The Hunger Project, Thus Spoke the Press: Select Articles on Elected Women Leaders in Village Panchayats, New Delhi: The Hunger Project, 2006, 2007 and 2008.
25. Sekhon, Joti, "Engendering Grassroots Democracy: Research, Training and Networking for Women in Local Self Governance in India" NWSA Journal Vol. 18, No. 2 (Summer, 2006).

26. Kishor, Sunita, "Empowerment of Women in Egypt and Links to the Survival and Health of their Infants" in Harriet B. Presger and Gita Sen (eds) Women's Empowerment and Demographic Process, New York: Oxford University Press, 2000.
27. Kabeer Naila, "Reflections on the Measurement of Women's Empowerment" in Discussing Women's Empowerment: Theory and Practice, Sida studies No. 3 Stockholm: Novum Grafiska AB, 2001.
28. Palanithurai, G, Building Alliance and Capabilities among the Elected Women Representatives of Grassroots, Gandhigram: Rajiv Gandhi Chair for Panchayati Raj Studies, 2003.
29. Palanithurai, G, Governance: From the Perspective of Elected Women Representatives, Gandhigram: Rajiv Gandhi Chair for Panchayati Raj Studies, 2004.
30. Palanithurai, G, Elected Women Representatives and Emerging Alternative Governance, Gandhigram: Rajiv Gandhi Chair for Panchayati Raj Studies, 2005.
31. Palanithurai, G, Elected Women Representatives and Empowerment, New Delhi: Concept Publishing Company, 2012.
32. Palanithurai, G, Experience of the Elected Women Representatives in Grassroots Institutions Gandhigram: Rajiv Gandhi Chair for Panchayati Raj Studies, 2004.
33. Palanithurai, G, Evaluation of the Process and Performance of Women and Dalit Leaders in Gram Panchayats, New Delhi: Concept Publishing Company, 2005.
34. Palanithurai, G, Uma. G and Vanishree, J, Networking of Elected Women Representaives New Delhi: Concept Publishing Company, 2012.
35. Mangubhai Jayshree, Irudayam SJ Aloysius and Sydenham Emma, Dalit Women's Right to Political Participation in Rural Panchayati Raj, The Netherlands: Justiatia et pax, 2009.

Chapter - II

New Panchayati Raj System in Tamil Nadu

Introduction

Tamil Nadu had an experience of a century in local governance in the pre-independence period which, in fact, forms the basis of the new local governance in the post-independence era. Though it was intended to create Panchayats as institutions of self governance, in practice, they were made institutions to implement the schemes and programmes of the centre and state governments. Till the enactment of the 73rd Amendment, the structure of the Panchayat system in Tamil Nadu was of three tiers and two tiers in two different periods. In the three tier Panchayat system, District Boards, Taluk Boards and Village Panchayats constituted the structural arrangement in the pre-independence period. Even after the enactment of the 73rd Amendment to the Constitution of India, discussion was on about the two tier system. But to confirm the 73rd Amendment in 1994, the Tamil Nadu government enacted a conformity legislation in which the three tier Panchayat system was created. Originally, in the pre-independence period, from 1884 to 1934, it was a three tier structure and, when the Taluk Boards were abolished by the government, the two tier system came into vogue. In post-independence India, as per the 1950 decision, there were two tiers, namely, District Board and Village Panchayat, through two different

Acts. With regard to powers, service functions were entrusted to local bodies during the pre-independence period and development functions were entrusted to local bodies along with service functions in the post-independence period.

It is an irony that at present the two ethnic political parties in Tamil Nadu, namely, the Dravida Munnetra Kazhagam (DMK) and the All India Anna Dravida Munnetra Kazhagam (AIADMK), never concurred on any issue but both agreed on one issue, namely, opposing the three tier Panchayat structure at the grassroots for governance. The two political parties are ardent advocates of devolution of powers from the Centre to the State and they call it as 'state autonomy'. Now they do not talk about state autonomy as they are partners in the coalition government at the Centre. But they are the ardent opponents of creating a vibrant three tier democratic governance structure at the district level and hence they opposed the 64th Amendment Bill and the 72nd Amendment Bill to the Constitution of India. It is only during the DMK and the AIADMK periods that the powers of the Panchayats were eroded. Panchayats came to a standstill only during the 1980s. It is only during the regimes of these parties that the bureaucratic raj was well established under the tight control of the District Collector. A well built bureaucratic culture has been growing in the past three decades.

The bureaucracy has been empowered only during this era. When the Congress Party was in power, if the State Government arranged a meeting and ministers participated, it happened under the Chairmanship of the MLA of the constituency. It has been changed and the District Collector has been made to preside over the meetings during the era of the Dravidian parties. Officials have been empowered in an unfathomable measure. Their opposition to District Panchayats and District Planning Committee is obvious as they don't want to see any parallel power at the district level equal to MLAs, and MLAs are made subservient to the District Collector. The State Government can do and undo things with the help of the District Collector. But when Panchayats are in position at the district level it will be a hindrance to the power of the State Government. This has been the considered opinion of the two Dravidian political parties in Tamil Nadu. This was the belief of the State Congress Party also when it abolished the District Boards. It considered the District Board a threat to State Government. The ethnic political parties (both the DMK and the AIADMK) have looked at the decentralisation process from the ideological perspective. It is to be noted here that powers of states are slowly being eroded and centralised through various means and strategies adopted by the central government. At this juncture, they do not want to strengthen the Panchayati Raj System as a whole. By strengthening Panchayati Raj, they feel that they are weakening the state government. The two political parties could have raised their voice against centralisation. But they are not doing so because of the political compulsions. Instead of strengthening the entire Panchayati Raj System, they strengthen the Gram Panchayat with a view to deliver the services effectively and carryout the programmes of the centre and state governments more effectively. It is the considered opinion of the two political parties that the Panchayati Raj System is only the implementing agency rather than a unit of self governance.

Whether they accept or reject, the new system of governance at the grassroots ideologically they have to comply with the mandate of the Constitutional requirement and hence the State Government enacted conformity legislation in the year 1994 after sleeping over the mandate for one year. A historic legislation was passed in the Tamil Nadu Legislative Assembly without any discussion and thereby one can easily judge to what extent the state government attached importance to the new Panchayati Raj System. After enacting the legislation, the government was again looking for reasons to delay the conduct of election. Tamil Nadu is known for giving reasons for postponing the Panchayat elections. After passing the legislation there was no public pressure or political pressure on the State Government to conduct the elections. There were only a few civil society organisations which took the initiative to create awareness among the public about the new dispensation. When the political climate prepared for general elections in 1996, Panchayati Raj drew the attention of the political parties and it was incorporated in the manifesto of the political parties of which the Dravida Munnetra

Kazhagam (DMK) gave prominence to the conduct of Panchayati Raj elections in its manifesto. The DMK gave promises during the elections that the DMK would conduct the elections to Panchayats and accused the AIADMK of not conducting the Panchayat elections. Thus, it was the expectation at every level that 1996 would be a turning point for the Panchayats. In the general elections, the AIADMK was defeated and the DMK won the election and to fulfill the poll promise it conducted the Panchayat elections at one stroke. The DMK gave life to the Panchayat in Tamil Nadu.

Even before the conduct of the Panchayat elections, the Government of Tamil Nadu constituted the First State Finance Commission. After the elections a high level committee was constituted to devolve powers to three tiers Panchayati Raj System in Tamil Nadu in the year 1996 in the State Planning Commission under the leadership of L.C. Jain. Since elections were conducted for Panchayati Raj System, activities and responsibilities have to be given to them. In the meanwhile steps were taken to give assignments to all the three tiers of the new Panchayati Raj System. As a result, the rural development schemes were distributed among the three tiers. In the meanwhile the First State Finance Commission submitted its report. Before finalising the decision on functions and responsibilities among the three tiers, the State Finance Commission had made recommendations. Subsequently, L.C. Jain submitted his Committee's report to the state government in the year 1997. The government did not accept the report fully. But based on the recommendations, some orders were issued with regard to entrustment of responsibilities to the three tier Panchayats. Arguments and criticism were levelled against the government for poor devolution of powers. As a result, under the Chairmanship of the then Local Administration Minister Ko.Si.Mani, a high power committee was constituted with representatives of the political parties in the year 1997. The above committee also submitted its report. Following the submission, Executive orders were issued. Even then criticisms were levelled against the state government for poor devolution of powers, functionaries and finance to panchayats. As a result, yet another high level committee was constituted in the year 2007 under the chairmanship of the Minister for Local Bodies M.K. Stalin to devolve further powers. The above committee has submitted its report in the same year. It is to be noted here that the Government of Tamil Nadu expressed its position on the 73rd Amendment on the Constitution of India. In this regard it passed a resolution in 2006 in Tamil Nadu Legislative Assembly that the Tamil Nadu would press for the amendment of the Constitution seeking a two tier system of panchayats and the abolition of District Panchayats. Further it stresses that the Government of Tamil Nadu believes in direct election. In the same way the Government of Tamil Nadu expressed its views on the status of District Rural Development Agency (DRDA). It strongly argues that DRDA is an instrument delivering development programmes and services very effectively and hence it need not be merged with District Panchayat as District Panchayat is a political institution. This is the policy position of the Government of Tamil Nadu.

Some Vital Statistics on Panchayats in Tamil Nadu

Table 1: 2011 Rural Population in Tamil Nadu

1.	Total Population	72,147,030
2.	Male Population	36,137,975
3.	Female Population	36,009,055

Table 2: Village Panchayats Based on Population in Tamil Nadu

1.	Less than 3,000 population	8,484
2.	Above 3,000 population	4,136

Table 3: Elected Panchayat Representatives in Tamil Nadu

1.	Village Panchayat Members	99,333
2.	Village Panchayat Women Members	33,121
3.	Village Panchayat Presidents	12,620
4.	Village Panchayat Women Presidents	4,289
5.	Panchayat Union Members	6,471
6.	Presidents of Panchayat Union	385
7.	District Panchayat Members	655
8.	District Panchayat Presidents	31

The position regarding reservations in Tamil Nadu as per the provisions in the Tamil Nadu Panchayats Act 1994 and the Tamil Nadu Panchayats (Reservation of seats and Rotation of Reserved seats) Rules 1995 is given below:

Table 4: Reservation of Seats in Panchayats

Category determining the proportion	*Unit of Population used for notify the reservations*	*Authority Competent to of seats to be reserved*
Village Panchayats Ward Member	Village Panchayat Population	Inspector of Panchayats (Collector)
Village Panchayat President	Panchayat Union Population	Government
Village Panchayat President	Panchayat Union Population	Government
Village Panchayat President	Panchayat Union Population	Government
Panchayat Union Ward Member	Panchayat Union Population	Government
Panchayat Union Chairperson	District Rural Population	Government
District Panchayat Ward Member	District Rural Population	Government
District Chairperson	State Rural Population	Government

Source: Rural Development and Panchayati Raj Development. Policy Note 2010 -2011.

Table 5: Reservation of Offices and Seats for Women, SCs and ST

Sl. No.	Category of Reservation	Total no. of offices / seats	Reserved for Women		Reserved for SCs		Reserved for STs	
			No	Per cent	No	Per cent	No	Per cent
1.	District Panchayat Chairpersons	29	10	34	7	24	0	0
2.	Panchayat Union Council Chairpersons	385	140	36	87	23	4	1
3.	Village Panchayat Presidents	12,618	4,275	34	3,143	25	156	1
4.	District Panchayat Ward Members	656	226	34	154	23	8	1
5.	Panchayat Union Ward Members	6,570	2,302	35	1,534	23	64	1
6.	Village Panchayat Ward Members	97,458	32,638	33	24,630	25	983	1

Source: Rural Development and Panchayati Raj Development. Policy Note 2010-2011.

Village Panchayat

There are 12,618 Village Panchayats in the State spread across the 29 Districts and the 385 Blocks. The average number of Village Panchayats per district is 435 and per Block is 32. The Nilgiris District (35), Kanniyakumari (99), Theni (130) and Karur (158) are some of the districts with fewer Village Panchayats while Villupuram (1104), Tiruvannamalai (860), Vellore (753), Cuddalore (681) and Kancheepuram (648) are some of the districts with a large number of Village Panchayats. As can be seen from Table below, the populations even below 500 while others have populations exceeding 25,000.

Table 6: Classification of Village Panchayats on the basis of Population (2001 census)

Sl. No.	*Population*	*Number of Village Panchayats*
1.	Below 500	66
2.	501 – 3,000	8,418
3.	3,001 – 10,000	3,950
4.	Above 10,000	186
	Total	**12,620**

Source: Rural Development and Panchayati Raj Development. Policy Note 2010-2011.

Similarly, wide variations are also noticed in the income levels of the various Village Panchayats as can be seen from Table given below.

Table 7: Income-wise Classification of Village Panchayats

Sl. No.	*Income Range*	*Number of Village Panchayats during 2005 - 2006*	*No. of Villages Panchayats 2009-2010*
1.	Upto Rs 50,000	16	0
2.	Rs 50,000 to Rs 1 lakh	142	0
3.	Rs 1 lakh to Rs 5 lakhs	7,028	1021
4.	Rs 5 lakhs to Rs 10 lakhs	3,718	7146
5.	Rs 10 lakhs to Rs 25 lakhs	1,444	3902
6.	Rs 25 lakhs to Rs 50 lakhs	195	393
7.	Rs 50 lakhs to Rs 1 crore	45	121
8.	Rs 1 crore to Rs 3 crores	29	32
9.	Above Rs 3 crores	1	3
	Total	**12,618**	**12,618**

Source: Rural Development and Panchayati Raj Development. Policy Note 2010-2011.

Gram Sabha

The Gram Sabha is the nucleus of the New Panchayati Raj System. All the registered voters are members of the Gram Sabha of that Village Panchayat. As per the Act it has to meet thrice a year and at least once in six months. The President of Gram Panchayat is the presiding officer of the meetings of the Gram Sabha. The Gram Sabha has to give approval to the budget proposal and annual plan of the Village Panchayat. Further it has to give approval to the annual audited statement of the expenditure of the Village Panchayat. One-third forms the quorum to transact the business of the Gram Sabha as per the Act. In Tamil Nadu, the Gram Sabha is a neglected subject and unit in the local body arrangement as both elected leaders and officials have not shown any interest in it due to many reasons. As per the government orders, even beneficiaries for many government schemes are to be selected only in the Gram Sabha. But in reality it does not happen. Beneficiaries are selected not in the Gram Sabha but in the Panchayat Council, which is violative of the provisions of the Local Body Act of Tamil Nadu. It is a government approved unconstitutional activity. The Government of Tamil Nadu emphasises transparent activities in all government programmes and schemes but there is no way to execute it as the Gram Sabha is made defunct. It is a nightmare to many who have been enjoying power and resources all along. In order to strengthen the Gram Sabha, recently, the government passed an order that all Gram Panchayats have to convene the Gram Sabha meeting four times in a year on 15th August, 2nd October, 26th January and 1st May and transact the activities as per the provisions available in the Act. Further the quorum for the Gram Sabha has been reduced from one-third to one-tenth. Further it is reduced as shown in the below table:

Table 8: Revised Quorum for Gram Sabha

Sl. No.	*Population of a Village Panchayat*	*Quorum for the Meeting*
1.	Up to 500	50
2.	501 – 3000	100
3.	3001 – 10,000	200
4.	Above 10,000	300

Source: Rural Development and Panchayati Raj Development. Policy Note 2010-2011.

Officials from all the government offices related to development will also participate in the Gram Sabha meeting as observers of the meeting and will report the proceedings of the Gram Sabha to the Inspector of Panchayats. The responsibility of the observer is to provide the details of the government schemes and programmes to the people in the Gram Sabha. Recently, in the State Legislative Assembly a policy note was placed and the same was approved and in the policy note it is mentioned that participation of women and Dalit Gram Sabha members is a must and for which a quorum has to be fixed. It is to be noted here that with the quorum specified one-third shall be women and the number of SC/ST participants shall bear the same proportion to the quorum as the population of SC/STs bears to the total population of the village Panchayats. Recording of Gram Sabha attendance and proceedings through proper registers and keeping photographic record have been made mandatory for the conduct of Gram Sabha. For conducting Gram Sabha expenditure limit has been increased from Rs 500 to Rs 1000.

Village Panchayat

A Village Panchayat or Gram Panchayat is constituted for a minimum of five hundred populations. But there are 60 Panchayats do not have even 500 populations. In the Village Panchayat the Ward Members and the President, are to be elected directly by the voters. The Vice-President of the Village Panchayat is elected indirectly from among the elected Ward Members of the Village Panchayat. The Village Panchayat has to look after the following subjects:

(a) Construction, repair and maintenance of Village Panchayat roads;

(b) Lighting of public roads and public places;

(c) Providing drainage facilities;

(d) Extension of village sites and the regulation of buildings;

(e) Sinking and repairing of wells, the excavation repair and maintenance of ponds or tanks and the construction and maintenance of water works for the supply of water;

(f) Maintenance of parks and reading rooms;

(g) Implementation of schemes such as Indira Awaas Yojaja (IAY) and National Rural Employment Guarantee Scheme (NREGS);

(h) Cleaning of streets;

(i) Providing public latrines;

(j) Providing burial and burning grounds;

(k) Providing water for washing and bathing purposes; and

(l) Such other duties notified by the government then and there.

Resources

Village Panchayat has got the following sources of revenue:

(a) *Tax Revenue:* Of the three tier Panchayats village Panchayat alone has got power to levy taxes. House tax, profession tax and Advertisement tax are the commonly levied taxes.

(b) *Non Tax Revenue:* Licensing fees for building plan and layout approval, fees charges on dangerous and offensive trades, water charges, fees on cart stands, fishery rentals, 2c pattas fees, income from markets and fairs, ferries, fines and penalties and so on.

(c) *Assigned and Shared Revenue:* It includes the in terms pooled at the state level (surcharge on stamp duty and entertainment tax) which are released by the Director of Rural Development and Panchayati Raj to all the three tiers of the Panchayats including the village Panchayats. Other items of assigned and shared revenues for the village Panchayats include the seigiorage fees (100 per cent) and lease amount 50 per cent share on minor minerals and social forestry auctions amount.

(d) *Grants:* Central Finance Commission Grants, State Finance Commission Grants, Development Grants under centrally sponsored and state schemes.

Administrative Powers

Gram Panchayat have been empowered to give administrative sanction and executive individual works upto Rs 2 lakh from their general funds. It has been given powers to execute urgent works upto Rs 2000 at a time and upto Rs 5000 for a year without anybody's. The President can draw self cheque upto Rs 500 to meet contingent expenditure. It can attend to repairs and maintenance of hand pumps, power pumps and Rs 7500 per power pump per year without reference to engineer for preparation of estimates or passing of bills. In order to encourage the Village Panchayats to carryout innovative works in the villages Uthamar Gandhi village Panchayat awards are being given to the best adjusted Panchayats based on their performance. A citation with Rs 5 lakh cash award is being given to each best adjusted best Gram Panchayats.

Panchayati Union

For each development block a Panchayat Union is formed. Each Panchayati Union has a Chairperson and a Vice-Chairperson elected indirectly by the members of the Panchayat Council. Union Council Members are elected directly by the people. For every 5,000 population, one Union Council Member will be elected by the people. Members of Parliament and Legislative Assembly elected from that area are ex-officio members of the Panchayat Union Council.

The Panchayati Union has the following duties and responsibilities:

(a) Construction, repair and maintenance of Public roads;

Construction of water works for the supply of water for drinking, washing and bathing purposes;

(b) Establishment and maintenance of dispensaries;

(c) Construction and maintenance of elementary schools;

(d) Preventive and remedial measures connected with any epidemic;

(e) Conduct of fairs and festivals;

(f) Vetenary relief;

(g) Opening and maintenance of Panchayat Union markets;

(h) Extension of village sites and regulation of buildings;

(i) Maintenance of statistics related to births and deaths;

(j) Improvement of agriculture and agriculture stock;

Implementing various centrally sponsored and state schemes;

(k) Promotion and encouragement of cottage industries;

Preventive and remedial measures connected with any epidemic or with malaria;

(i) Other duties and responsibilities entrusted to Panchayati Union by the government through government notification.

To enable the Panchayat Union to perform its duties the Government of Tamil Nadu has issued a notification to take up the following activities:

(a) Construction and maintaining Panchayat Union roads, irrigation tanks, and lakes, initiating family welfare activities, executing noon meal schemes and implementing schemes for Adi Dravidas;

(b) Works have to be identified from Employment Assurance schemes and they are to be executed;

(c) Draught relief works have to be identified and executed;

(d) M.P. and M.L.A. area development schemes akin to union have to be executed;

(e) Panchayat Union buildings have to be maintained by the union itself;

(f) Panchayat Union can supervise the activities in the domain of public health, primary education, drinking water supply, roads, small culverts, khadi and village industries works, technical training education, libraries, rural electricity and non-conventional energy.

The Panchayat Union administrative arrangement has been modified by which works have been classified into two divisions and entrusted to Block Development Officer and Assistant Block Development Officer. The two sections work independently with their supporting staff. Infrastructural facilities have also been divided and attached to the two divisions.

Resource

Panchayat unions cannot levy any tax. The revenue of a Panchayat union consists of the following:

(a) *Non Tax Revenue:* License fees, market fees, receipt from rentals and properties, fines and penalties.

(b) *Assigned and Shared Revenues:* Local access surcharge and entertainment tax (30 per cent share).

(c) *Grants:* Central Finance Commission Grants, State Finance Commission Grants, Development Grants under centrally sponsored schemes and state schemes, grants for maternity centers and rural dispensaries. The Panchayat unions can sanction and execute works upto Rs 10 lakh from their general funds without any external approvals. However, for centrally sponsored and state schemes prior administrative sanction of the District Collector is necessary.

District Panchayat

The District Panchayat is constituted with directly elected members for every 50,000 population and indirectly elected Chairperson and Vice-Chairperson from among the Council Members. The District Panchayat will have to perform the following functions:

(a) Preparation of development plan for the district;

(b) Compilation of administrative reports of village Panchayats and Panchayat union councils of the district and preparation of Annual Report for the District;

(c) Planning and review of Agriculture, Land Development, Animal Husbandry, Dairy, Poultry, Fisheries and Rural Industries;

(d) Planning and review of Rural Housing Programmes particularly housing for SC/STs;

(e) Identification of major water supply schemes.

To enable the District Panchayat to perform the earmarked functions, an administrative change has been effected by which the Divisional Development Office which is nearer to the district headquarters will supervise the District Panchayat activities. Yet another office which is away from the headquarters will look after auditing of the District Panchayat activities and the third one will be attached to the District Panchayat.

Resources

The District Panchayat has no taxation powers. Its only source of revenue is from statutory grants like State Finance Commission Grants and development grants under centrally sponsored schemes.

District Panchayats can sanction and execute works up to Rs 20 lakhs from their general funds without any external approvals. However, in the case of centrally sponsored schemes, prior administrative sanction of the District Collector is necessary.

State Finance Commission Grant

To augment the resources of the local bodies, financial devolution to the local bodies is made on the basis of recommendations of the State Finance Commission (SFC). In the beginning eight per cent of the State's total own net tax revenues (other than entertainment tax) was devolved to the rural and urban local bodies in the ratio of 58.42 respectively. Eighty seven per cent of the allocation for rural local bodies is being shared among the three tiers in the ratio of 47:45:8 among Village Panchayats, Panchayat Union Councils and District Panchayats respectively. This grant was being released every month to the local bodies. The balance 13 per cent consists of Equalisation Fund (six per cent), Incentive Fund (five per cent), and Reserve Fund (two per cent).

The SFC grant is generally utilised for the following purposes:

(a) Salaries, pensions, office maintenance, etc.;

(b) Maintenance of drinking water facilities;

(c) Maintenance of street lights; payment of electricity charges;

(d) Maintenance of Village Panchayat and Panchayat Union roads;
(e) Maintenance of minor irrigation tanks; and
(f) Public health, sanitation, sewerage, etc.

The first Finance Commission recommended devolution of state owned tax resources from eight per cent to 12 per cent by increasing one per cent annually from 1996-1997. But the state government decided to freeze it at eight per cent of its resources for the first five years. The second Finance Commission recommended devolution of eight per cent from state owned tax resources for the first two years and nine per cent for the next two years and 10 per cent for last one year. But the government issued orders freezing the devolution of funds to eight per cent for each year. The third State Finance Commission recommended financial devolution of ten per cent to the local bodies for the entire award period. But the government ordered devolution of funds from nine per cent to ten per cent from 2007-08 to 2011-2012 in the following order: nine per cent, nine per cent, 9.5 per cent, 10 per cent, and 10 per cent. The State Government consistently violated and contradicted with the recommendations of all three State Finance Commissions in terms of devolution of financial resources due to Panchayats. Further, Panchayats are facing more and more pressure and burden to meet the basic requirements of the people have continuously weakened the financial position of the Panchayati Raj. Further, they are made as subservient to the State Government.

District Planning Committee

The Government of Tamil Nadu shall constitute in every district a District Planning Committee to consolidate the plans prepared by the District Panchayat, Panchayat Union Councils, Village Panchayats, Municipal Councils, and Municipal Corporations in the district and to prepare a draft development plan for the district as a whole. The Committee shall consist of the Collector of the district, members of the House of People who represent whole or part of the district, members of the Council of States, Members of Legislative Assembly whose constituencies lie within the district, the Mayor of the City Municipal Corporation and all Chairpersons of the Municipalities of the district, Chairpersons of the District Panchayats, one-fifth of the total number of chairpersons of the Town Panchayats and Panchayat Union notified by the government every year by rotation, and such number of persons not less than four-fifth of the total number of the committee as specified by the government elected from among the members of the District Panchayat, Town Panchayats, Municipal Councils and Corporations in the district in proportion to the ratio between the population of the rural areas and the urban areas. The Committee shall allocate funds to various schemes in the Panchayats and Panchayat Unions and shall monitor the implementation of the schemes. Now the government has changed the chairmanship of the District Planning Committee from the Collector to the President of the District Panchayat. It is an irony that the District Planning Committees of the districts have convened their meetings and reviewed the activities of the sectoral departments but never took any step to prepare the District Plan. Further, it is to be noted that even in the review meeting, district level officials do not participate. They send their officials to these meetings. It is a routine meeting without much of importance.

Reservation

One-third of positions at all levels of the bodies are reserved for women. SC and ST get reservation of positions at all levels of the bodies in proportion to their population. In Tamil Nadu, the rotation of positions, especially for women and Dalits, is for once in ten years. It is unique in the whole of the country. This change was due to the pressure given by the women Panchayat leaders through their federation.

Election and Finance Commissions

An Election Commission headed by the State Election Commissioner appointed by the Governor to conduct the local body elections is mandatory. The Election Commissioner enjoys the powers and privileges and status of a judge of the High Court. The tenure of office of the Election Commissioner is two years. However, the

Commissioner can be given extension for four more years. In Tamil Nadu, elections are conducted on party lines for District Panchayats and Panchayat Unions. Elections to Village Panchayats are not on party lines. In Tamil Nadu, elections to Local Bodies, both urban and rural, will be conducted at one stroke. When the election was conducted in few places auctions were conducted, bidding was made, and nominations were made by the traditional Panchayat leaders for Gram Panchayat Presidents' posts. After the enactment of the 73rd Amendment, elections were conducted periodically without any lapse or gap. Elections were conducted at one stroke for rural and urban local bodies.

There will be a Finance Commission constituted every five years to review the financial position of the Panchayats and to make recommendations to the Governor to fix the principles to govern the distribution between the state and Panchayats of the net proceeds of the taxes, duties, tolls and fees leviable by the government and to identify the logistics for making grants in aid to the Panchayats from the consolidated fund of the state and the measures needed to improve the financial position of the Panchayats. The Finance Commission shall consist of a chairman and four other members. In Tamil Nadu, the Finance Commission was constituted periodically within the stipulated time and so far three State Finance Commissions were constituted. They made recommendations and some of the recommendations were also implemented. Further State Finance Commission was also constituted. Despite all the efforts Panchayats are not strengthened. Panchayats in Tamil Nadu are in form not is spirit.

Critical Evaluation of Decentralisation

The present Tamil Nadu Panchayat Act does not provide much scope for giving life to the spirit of the 73rd Constitutional Amendment Act in Tamil Nadu. Subjects in the 11th Schedule do not find a place in the body of the Act, especially in the chapter on "Functions of Panchayat Bodies." Development officials who work in the Panchayat bodies are declared government officials and they do not come under the purview of local bodies. As a result, the local bodies cannot supervise the activities of the officials of local bodies. While comparing the old Act of Panchayati Raj of 1958 with the new one, one finds adequate powers to local bodies in the old act to supervise regulate and control the officials working in the local bodies. In the new Act the District Collector is vested with the power of controlling the functioning of Village Panchayats. The District Collector's power to suspend and dissolve the Gram Panchayats is against the spirit of decentralisation of powers. The DRDA (District Rural Development Agency) is a registered society, which is under the control of the Project Officer and the District Collector.

The Gram Sabha has not been activated to develop democratic culture in decision-making, to bring about transparency in the activities of the government and to involve the people in the development process of the community. Enactment of legislation and conduct of elections alone will not bring about any change in the functioning of the local bodies. Proper enhancement of the capacity of the leaders, enabling suitable government orders and provision of adequate resources can alone bring about needed change in the functioning of the local bodies.

Steps have been taken to train the Panchayat leaders for which training modules have been prepared. In the meanwhile training programmes have been conducted by a few institutions. Panchayat leaders have formed their associations to exert pressure on the government for more devolution of powers. Gram Panchayat Presidents have formed an association. Likewise the elected women representatives of Gram Panchayats have formed their own association. Dalit men and women elected to Gram Panchayats have formed their association. District Panchayat Presidents have formed their forum. Likewise the Block Panchayat Presidents have formed their association. Even among the Block Panchayat Presidents Dalit Women Presidents have formed their association. All these above associations prepare a charter of demands and sent it to the government periodically. Of the associations the Gram Panchayat Women Presidents Association is vibrant and active. It is always visible and highly articulate. As a result of the elected women representatives' continuous demand, the Government of Tamil Nadu has made an amendment in the existing arrangements for reservation in Tamil Nadu to reserve the constituencies in all the three tiers for two continuous terms to the women and Dalits by which whether it be a Ward of the Gram Panchayat or Gram Panchayat or a Ward of the Block Panchayat or Ward of the District Panchayat once reserved for women and Dalits will be reserved for two terms. The concept of rotation of reservation of position in Tamil Nadu is for ten years not for every five year term. The government issued a directive to all the District Collectors that whenever the elected women representatives' organisation demanded a meeting with officials to sort out their problems, the District Collector has to organise such interface and sort out the problems faced by the women leaders. It is for women leaders alone.

In terms of resources, the Panchayat has to face a financial crisis due to the changes made in the formula for matching grant. Further diversion of funds, and not facilitating Panchayats to get their dues from assigned revenue made Panchayat institutions to weaken their base and autonomy. Sizeable reduction of resources from the State Government has reduced the activities of the Panchayats. Further revenue from minor minerals and sand quarrying from the Panchayat area has been totally stopped as the activity of sand quarrying has been taken over by the State Government. Dues from Social Forestry are not being given as the money has yet to come from the Social Forestry Department.

The next important issue is that the tariff of the Electricity Board for the electricity consumption of Panchayats. Panchayats have to pay commercial rates for the consumption of electricity. It has been raised from Rs 1.20 to Rs 3.40 per unit for public consumption by the Panchayats. This has increased the expenditure of the Panchayats. The entire electricity charge has been excluded from the State Finance Commission grant which is due to the Panchayats. The Block Panchayat Councilor is operating schemes which are meant for the village independently without consulting the Gram Panchayats. District Panchayat Councilors are also operating their schemes without consulting the Gram Panchayats. MLAs are operating their constituency development fund without consulting the Gram Panchayats. In the same way MPs are also spending their money without consulting the Gram Panchayats. Apart from the above the sectoral departments have their own funds. They carry out their activities without consulting the Gram Panchayats. Money is being spent in huge quantities but not on the demands of the people. They spend the money as they prioritise the works. In all the four Gram Sabha meetings people project their felt needs but to meet the felt needs of the people there is no untied fund available at the disposal of the Gram Panchayat. Even the small quantum they get from the State Finance Commission is to be spent for electricity charge remittance. Virtually funds are operated by different agencies on their own priorities and not on the priorities of the people finalised in the Gram Sabha. As a result, the Gram Sabha has been weakened. It is being made a ritual. The District Planning Committee has been constituted and they meet periodically and review the works of the departments. There is no concerted effort on the part of the District Planning Committee to prepare a plan. Neither the District Planning Committee nor the officials show any interest in planning exercise at the grassroots level. The State Planning Commission has developed a module for training in multi level planning and conducted a training programme also. They have prepared guidelines for the preparation of perspective development plan for the whole of a district. Nothing moves in the absence of political will. Finally, the State Planning Commission has given instructions to all District Planning Cells to prepare Village Development Reports (VDR) in select Panchayats. It is a mere compilation of data. In select districts, the Village Development Plan was prepared in select Panchayats with the assistance of the development organisations for which the respective Collectors helped and in turn the District Collectors passed orders to all the sectoral departments to work on the prioritised activities of the plan prepared by the people.

In the context of the non-functioning of the District Planning Committee, the recent notification of the Government Order, G.O.(Ms.) No.140 dated 10.09.2004, is a path breaking event as it envisages a holistic development plan for each and every Gram Panchayat with the participation of the people. The new proposal envisions the participation of the people in the sustainable development of villages and the improvement of the quality of life through good governance and convergence of schemes and programmes. It focuses on resource mapping and community mobilisation for village development, micro planning and prioritisation of needs among village communities, convergence of funds and functionaries of all schemes at the village level, and community led improvement in the overall quality of life.

It is a path breaking exercise in decentralised governance in Tamil Nadu, which is known for its centralised culture in carrying out development activities. It is a demand driven exercise and not a supply driven one. It envisages the participation of the people. It aims at improvement of the quality of life. It strengthens the physical resources for the improvement of the quality of life. It works for the convergence of the schemes and programmes of the government towards the needs of the community as identified by the people. It ensures the participation of sectoral departments in the implementation of the plan prepared by the Gram Panchayats with the participation of the people. It creates a synergy between the schemes and programmes of the governments (both the Centre and the State) and the needs prioritised by the people. It specifically focuses on such sectors as water, sanitation, environment, ecology, education, health, social security and on social issues (elimination of sex selective abortions, prevention of child abuse, age at marriage of women to be not less than 21, prevention of crimes against woman and immoral trafficking, prevention of untouchability and promotion of communal harmony).

The whole exercise is expected to be in a movement mode by carrying out specific campaigns by involving all the stakeholders in the field of rural development. Awareness creation, building and enhancing the skills and capacity of all stakeholders are continuous activities. Each and every Gram Panchayat will have a legal plan document ready for implementation.

Relevance

Panchayati institutions have brought people's representatives closer to the people. For the past several years below the state government there was no representative democratic institution close to the people. Below the state government level it was the rule of the bureaucracy. It is a well known fact that the expansion of the bureaucracy will alienate the people. Middlemen establish links between the people and the bureaucracy and thereby brokerage becomes the accepted formula for all development activities. Now elected representatives are placed in all the areas and people can approach them easily. People will raise questions in the Gram Sabha. If water is not sufficiently available, people can raise the question face to face in the Gram Sabha. If the medical staff from the Primary Health Centre is not visiting villages periodically people will question the Panchayati leader. Likewise if the primary school teacher is not regular in reaching the school, it can be raised in the Panchayat. When they raise questions, the leaders cannot shirk the responsibility by saying that they have no power or resources. They have to seek power and finance for which they have to work hard and purposefully.

In the whole process, people have developed the attitude that these are the works to be attended to by the Panchayats for which the elected Panchayat leaders have to work. Panchayat leaders have developed the attitude that in the absence of required power and finance to fulfill the needs and demands of the people, people have to be mobilised to exert pressure on the government to get things done for the people. In the whole process, people are being mobilised by the Panchayats. Mobilisation is being done in many ways of which the Gram Sabha is one and an important one. No doubt in India people are mobilised for cultural activities, religious activities and political activities periodically by various groups and the political parties. But they are not mobilised for development work. But now Panchayats are mobilising the people for development activities. It is true that the Panchayat leaders are drawn from the place wherefrom MLAs and MPs are drawn. But MLAs and MPs can keep themselves aloof from the community. Panchayat leaders have to live with the people and in the community and hence they have to be responsible and responsive to the communities. Provision has been made in the structure so that the marginalised and women can find a place legitimately in the institution for governance. Women and Dalits, who never had any experience in governance, have come to power. A large number of them want to be transparent because the community has a hold over them. In many places a conducive atmosphere for transparent governance by women and Dalits which can serve as a model for others. Women have started attending the Gram Sabha meeting. A large number of SHG members attend the Gram Sabha meetings and they raise a lot of developmental issues in the meeting as they are oriented in social development activities by the NGOs. As a result, even the process of governance at the grassroots will be changed.

Electing a good leader is in the hands of the electorate. Shaping a leader and making him good lies in the hands of everyone. The leaders at the grassroots have to be conscientised on development and their skill and capacity have to be enhanced for proper management of institutions to achieve development and social justice. Once the leaders are properly trained, they will deliver the goods to the level of the expectations of the masses.

Conclusion

It is true that there are very many weaknesses in the Tamil Nadu Panchayat Act itself and a variety of existing Acts of different departments do not permit the state to devolve powers. The capacity of the leaders is not so high as to handle all the subjects earmarked for Panchayati Raj and yet leaders are alert and optimistic at present that the Panchayat Raj System is the only solution to solve most of the problems in the rural areas. Steps are on to rectify the defects. Local body leaders are putting out a one point demand to the state government to devolve adequate powers and resources to the local bodies. Expected pressure has come from the people for devolution of powers and the leaders of local bodies have come to a stage to take powers from the state government on their own in the event of denial of powers to the local bodies.

Thus, the Panchayat Raj System in Tamil Nadu is being kept in operation not because of the devolved powers and resources but because of the leadership at the Village Panchayat level. No doubt Panchayats are fulfilling the obligatory functions. A lot of innovations have happened in Panchayats due to the exceptional leadership qualities of the Panchayat leaders. Wherever Panchayat leaders are strong, vibrant, capacitated, and committed they perform very well. Whenever the District Collector and Project Officer, DRDA, is pro-Panchayat, the Panchayats perform very well despite several problems and constraints. District Collectors and Project Officers see this dispensation as very positive as they can achieve the targets in out rural development schemes through the Panchayats. Thus, it becomes a partnership between the district administration and the Panchayats. In Tamil Nadu, Panchayats are evolving on their own. Devolution becomes evolution in Tamil Nadu.

Panchayats are instruments of the people created for governance with the participation of the people to achieve development. Though Panchayat leaders are drawn from the place wherefrom MLAs and MPs are drawn they cannot adopt the attitude and behaviour of the MPs and MLAs as they have to work with the community closely. By increasing their capacity and sensitising them on developmental issues, Panchayats can be prepared to achieve development and social justice. Capacity building, continuous support extended by the support structure, forming network with the media and NGOs and providing needed information could make them achievers and path finder's. If state governments really want to achieve social development, it can be achieved through the Panchayats. People should be mobilised to participate in the development process. In the long run people will assert and claim their rights and entitlements through the Panchayats.

Notes and References

1. Athreya, V.B. and Rajeswari K.S., Women's Participation in Panchayati Raj: A Case Study from Tamil Nadu, Chennai: M.S. Swaminathan Research Foundation, 1999.
2. Dharampal, The Madras Panchayat System Vol. II A General Assessment, New Delhi: Impex India, 1972.

3. Government of India, Powers and Functions of Panchayati Raj Institutions A Framework, New Delhi: Ministry of Rural Development, 1994.
4. Government of India, Renewing Local Self Government in Rural India, New Delhi: Ministry of Rural Development, 1994.
5. Government of Tamil Nadu, Democratic Decentralisation: Powers entrusted to Panchayati Raj Institutions, Chennai: Rural Development Department, 1999.
6. Government of Tamil Nadu, High Power Committee Report on Entrustment of Powers to three tier Local Bodies in Tamil Nadu, Chennai: State Planning Commission, 1998.
7. Jennie Litvack, Junaid Ahmed, Rethinking Decentralisation in Developing and Richard Bird Countries, Washington D.C.: The World Bank, 1998.
8. Palanithurai, G., "Building Alliances and Capabilities among the elected women representatives of Grassroots institutions", Womens Link, Vol.10, No.1 (Jan-Mar 2004) pp.18-25.
9. Palanithurai, G., "Towards Participatory Governance at Grassroots: Synergisation of Rural Communities and Institutions" South Asian Journal of Socio Political Studies, Vol. 4, No.1 (Dec, 2003).
10. Palanithurai, G., Capacity Building for Local Body Leaders, New Delhi: Concept Publishing Company, 2001.
11. Palanithurai, G., Development Role Reversed: From Government to People, Gandhigram: Rajiv Gandhi Chair for Panchayati Raj Studies, 2003.
12. Palanithurai, G., Dwaraki B.R. and Narayanasamy S., (Eds), Major Issues in New Panchayati Raj System (Eds) New Delhi: Kanishka Publications, 1997.
13. Palanithurai, G., Empowering People for prosperity: A study in New Panchayati Raj System, New Delhi: Kanishka Publications, 1994.
14. Palanithurai, G., Evaluation of Process and Performance of Gram Panchayat Women and Dalit Presidents in Tamil Nadu, Gandhigram: Rajiv Gandhi Chair, 2003.
15. Palanithurai, G., Grassroots Democracy in Indian Society, New Delhi: Concept Publications, 1997.
16. Palanithurai, G., New Panchayati Raj System at Work: An Evaluation, New Delhi: Concept Publishing Company, 2000.
17. Palanithurai, G., New Panchayati Raj System at Work: An Evaluation, New Delhi: Concept Publications, 1999.
18. Palanithurai, G., New Panchayati Raj System: Status and Prospects, New Delhi: Kaniska Publications, 1996, pp. 57-64.
19. Palanithurai, G., Panchayats, Communities and Social Development, Gandhigram: Rajiv Gandhi Chair for Panchayati Raj Studies, 2003.

20. Palanithurai, G.,(Ed), Empowering People: Issues and Solutions, New Delhi: Kanishka Publications, 1996.
21. Palanithurai, G.,(Ed), New Panchayati Raj System Status and Prospects, New Delhi: Kanishka Publications, 1996.
22. Population Foundation of India, Empowerment of Panchayati Raj Institutions on Issues Related to Population, Health and Social Development, A Final Report, New Delhi: Population Foundation of India, 2001.
23. Rajiv Gandhi Chair, Functional Efficiency of Gram Sabha: A Report submitted to II State Finance Commission, Gandhigram: Rajiv Gandhi Chair for Panchayati Raj Studies, 2000.
24. Rajiv Gandhi Chair, Problems faced by the Gram Panchayati Leaders, Gandhigram: Rajiv Gandhi Chair for Panchayati Raj Studies, 2000.
25. Rajiv Gandhi Foundation, Dialogue on Panchayat: Summary proceedings of four Regional Tripartile Interface Interactive workshops, New Delhi: Rajiv Gandhi Foundation, 1999.
26. Rajiv Gandhi Foundation, Panchayati Raj in India: Status Report, New Delhi: Rajiv Gandhi Foundation, 2000.
27. Rajiv Gandhi Foundation, Proceedings of the National Seminar on Panchayats, New Delhi: Rajiv Gandhi Foundation, 1997.
28. Rajiv Gandhi Foundation, Proceedings of the National Seminar on Panchayats, New Delhi: Rajiv Gandhi Foundation, 1993.
29. Rajiv Gandhi Foundation, Revitalisation of Panchayati Raj in India, New Delhi: Rajiv Gandhi Foundation, 1999.
30. Rajiv Gandhi Foundation, Voices from Below: Summary proceedings of Sub-Regional workshops on Panchayats: Issues and Recommendations, New Delhi: Rajiv Gandhi Foundation, 2001.
31. Rukmani, R., Panchayati Raj Institutions in Tamil Nadu: A Historical Review, Chennai: Madras Institute of Development Studies, 1996.
32. Rural Development Department, Democratic Decentralisation: Panchayati Raj System in Tamil Nadu, Chennai: Rural Development Department, 1999.
33. Sarasvathi, The Madras Panchayat System Vol. I A Historical Survey, Delhi: Impex India, 1973.
34. Siddartha, Sivaramakrishnan, Panchayati Raj Institutions in India - A Society Study for the World Bank, Washington DC: World Bank, 1999.
35. Siddartha, Sivaramakrishnan, Discussion: Challenges and Opportunities for Panchayati Raj, New Delhi: World Bank, 1999.
36. State Finance Commission, Summary of Recommendations of the State Finance Commission for Local Bodies, Chennai: State Finance Commission, 1966.
37. State Planning Commission, Report of the working group on Decentralised Planning and Panchayati Raj, Chennai: State Planning Commission, 1997.

38. State Planning Commission, Report on the Entrustment of Powers to Panchayats, Chennai: State Planning Commission, 1997.

39. The Hunger Project, Report on the workshop on Panchayati Raj: Trials and Triumphs, Gandhigram: Rajiv Gandhi Chair for Panchayati Raj Studies, 2003.

40. The Hunger Project, Women and Panchayati Raj: The Pathway to Social Transformation and a New Future for India, Bombay: The Hunger Project, 1999.

Chapter – III

Agency

As per the framework of analysis for empowerment, agency comprises certain assets. These assets make them to be effective in discharging responsibilities. Asset endowments are used as indicators of agency. They are psychological, informative, organisational, material financial and human. To study the above assets, it is necessary to elicit response from the respondents on the following aspects: their psychological conditions; information they have acquired on governance, administration and development; support they gain from organisations and institutions, material support in terms of their family economic background; financial and human power they enjoy in the system where they occupy position. In order to get the above details for analysis and discussion battery of questions have been arranged in the interview schedule and for which we elicited answers through our interaction with them. All the above aspects have been discussed in this section. It is to be noted here that all assets cannot be measured quantitatively.

Socio-economic Profile of the Respondents

Women participation in elected politics remains low in the world (Burn, 2001, 187-191). Yet women representation has increased in many parts of the world and it is highest in Scandinavian countries. One cannot find evenness in representation of women throughout the world. In India, the percentage of women in the Lok Sabha has ranged between 2.8 per cent to 3.5 per cent from 1952 to 1977 (Santha, 1999, 15). Women participation in state and local bodies is also low. The reservation of seats for women in Local Bodies assumes significance in engendering local democracy, local government and local development. It is to be noted here that the patriarchical structure translates into unequal position of men and women in public life (Sekhon, 2001, 884). While looking at several studies conducted in North India, reveal that majority hails from dominant castes (Mohanty, 1999 and Rai *et al,* 2001).

The opportunity created through reservation of seats for women enabled a major segment from the poor and underprivileged to move into the corridors of power. They never had such an opportunity to get such social recognition and equally challenges from the dominant communities and men folk. This new opportunity brought women to the centres of power but how they make use of power depends on the preparation of the women leaders to equip themselves to face the challenges. For any analysis social and economic conditions are the basic and fundamental. To study any group behaviour analysis of socio-economic characteristic is sin quo non. It is the earliest approach in social science (Sidney Verba, Norman H. Nie, Jac on Kim, 1978, 2-3). It is to be understood that without any discrepancy and difference between the developed society and the developing society the socio-economic conditions do play an important role in the political process. Generally while considering the political activities of an individual is a group and the group in the political process one has to consider two options namely: (a) the impact of socio-demographic characteristics of the individuals in the political activities outside and (b) the cumulative effect of the socio-demographic characteristics of the individuals and their impact on the functioning of the political institutions (G. Palanithurai, 1995, p. 27). That too in India, it plays a predominant role in influencing the dependant variable. Hence in this section the socio-economic profiles of the respondents are being explained in the following pages. Around 80 per cent of the respondents are below the age of 50 and 41 per cent are from Backward Community, 23 per cent are from Most Background Community and 35 per cent are from the SC and

ST communities. Caste and age both have their own impact in the political process in India (Ghanshyam Shah, 1975). Primarily 10 per cent of the respondents are illiterates, eight per cent are graduates and the rest had only schooling. It is to be noted that people from the marginalised section and backward class got opportunity to come to power. They are in power and they have opportunity to serve the marginalised by responding to all the challenges before them. No doubt, there is a marked difference between north and south and more particularly in Tamil Nadu in terms of women empowerment. From the days of freedom struggle women participation in public activities had been very high and for which the role of E.V. Ramasamy Periyar and his movement played a critical role. Subsequently, both the Dravidian political parties continuously played their role in mobilising women for political activities. Apart from the above the self help groups had been formed and through which women have been mobilised for economic activities collectively. Six decades political mobilisation of women by Dravidian movement and two decades of women mobilisation for livelihood activities have greatly influenced the thought and action process of the poor women in Tamil Nadu. As it has been witnessed in North India, there is no resistance to women coming to public space in Tamil Nadu. Hence coming to public space and public office is not a difficult process but in the office how they played their roles and discharged their responsibilities is a crucial question.

Education is the basic instrument through which individuals and collectivities acquire information and knowledge. Hence access to education is considered as key for development. In order to enable the people to be informed, active and decisive, education has been made as right. First people have to use the opportunity of using the instrument education to empower themselves and to use the advantage they have gained through education to others. Education is powerful instrument in transforming the individuals, groups, communities and societies. There is always a correlation between the level of education and the level of development. It will empower individuals and groups. It increases the capacity and capability of the individuals. For any impact analysis, educational background has to be studied.

Tamil Nadu is known for its social development activities. Literacy rate is very high nearer to Kerala. Women literacy is also high compared to other developed states. Against this background details have been elicited from the respondents. Education is a potential source of women empowerment. It is one of the most important mediums through which knowledge and information is acquired. The empowering role of education is not only affecting the every aspect of women's life but also the entire household lives. It has multidimensional potential and hence it is to be used strategically (Sunita Kishor and Kamla Gupta, 2004).

Education will play an important role in increasing the level of skill and understanding of respondent about the management nuances of the governing institutions. Table 12 gives the educational background of the Elected Women Representatives. Of them 9.9 per cent are illiterate and 24.8 per cent have got only school education, 51 per cent of the respondents had schooling up to higher secondary from upper primary. Eight per cent of the respondents are graduates. While seeing the family profile one would see the poor economic conditions of the elected women representatives. Seventy three per cent of the respondents are owning their houses in the respective places and others are in rented houses. 81.82 per cent of the leaders are married and 16.52 per cent are unmarried. Of the respondents 83.48 per cent are the Hindus and 16.52 are Christians and Muslims. Ninety per cent of the respondents' expenditure fell below Rs 12000 per month. Only 48 per cent of the respondents' income lies between Rs 4000 and above. Fifty two per cent of the respondent's monthly income is less than Rs 4000. It is interesting to look at the occupational profile of the Panchayat leaders. 65.29 per cent of the respondents are the farmers. 13.22 per cent of them are coolies. 9.92 per cent are working in private agencies. Their economic conditions are not so high. The respondents are having sanitation service for their families. Of the respondents only 21.49 per cent of them are not having any such sanitation facilities in their houses. Likewise 61.99 per cent of them are using public tape water for drinking purposes. Twenty eight per cent of them still relying on private wells for drinking water supply. 30.5 per cent of the respondents are living in tiled houses. The rest are in small hut type houses. 27.27 per cent of the respondents do not have any land. 36.37 per cent of the respondents are having lands upto two acres. From the above description one can easily infer the poor socio-economic conditions of the majority of the respondents. This background has its own impact on the perception and performance of the respondents. While considering the socio-economic conditions of the respondents it is always argued that sound economic background and higher social status would help and enable them to perform better. The respondents need not bother about their livelihood and they can devote their whole time for the role assigned to them. Their high social status will unremittingly help them to manage with confidence and self respect. There is yet another argument projected against the above argument. When the respondents are belonging to marginalised segment, they tend to project problems of marginalised when they get opportunity in the decision-making process. When they come in large number to decision-making bodies, they will highlight their problems which had been so far not represented. Against this background backgrounds of respondents are booked at end visualised.

Information Assets

It is necessary that the elected women representatives have to perform critical functions and for which they should have adequate information relating to the conditions of the women and children and other marginalised segments. They should have adequate knowledge and information about the potentials of the Panchayati Raj Institutions to address the issues of women. Information relating to governance, administration, government welfare schemes and problems of the people more particularly the women and children are very essential for successful management of the Panchayats. They are really the assets for the Panchayati leaders. In all those aspects questions have been asked to the respondents. They have responded to all the above questions. Three-fourth of the respondents are aware the potentials of the Panchayats in making the Panchayat women friendly and Panchayats has got scope for achieving gender equity and equality. Further, Panchayat can prevent violence against women.

Nearly 75 per cent of the respondents are aware of the health problems of the women in the rural areas. Equally they are aware of the health conditions of the children. The respondents get to know all the details from newspaper, television and other mass media.

Majority of the respondents have learnt the art of governance through the mass media. Media both print and electronic have exposed the elected women representatives to the issues of governance and development. Majority of the respondents have got access to media. They regularly watch Television, hear news in All India Radio and read newspapers. Budget preparation, data collection, micro planning, Gram Sabha and Gram Panchayat Council meeting details have been learnt over a period of time through formal training done by the officials and informal training they gain from day-to-day administration.

Major segment of the Elected Women Representatives have acquired information and thereby they are aware of the potentials of the Panchayati Raj system. They know how women and children are affected and more particularly the poor women and children due to poverty. Their health conditions are poor because of anemia and malnutrition. They could be effectively tackled through the governance of the Panchayats as government has got series of programmes and schemes. They have aspiration to achieve the same. Majority of the respondents expressed that they know how to address gender equality and equity issues. When the representatives were asked about the details of the training, they informed that they got training in Block Development office for a period of two days. Further, they informed that they were informed about dos and don'ts do's. Beyond that they have not learnt anything. In this context that capacity building exercise for local body leaders is a very serious exercise. It requires skilled trainers to conduct capacity building programme. Series of exercises are needed before training the local body leaders from preparation of training module, training manual and master trainers to selecting appropriate training ambience. (For more details see Appendix-II- Capacity Building Exercise in Rajiv Gandhi Chair for Panchayati Raj Studies)

For empowerment of women media and mobility are essential need. Elected Women Representatives have come out from their houses for public space for common action. To orient themselves to discharge their responsibilities, they have to visit different offices and meet officials. Apart from the above they have to connect themselves with other support organisations. Further to equip themselves vital information are necessary. To get what all they needed what they have to do is connect themselves with print media and electronic media. There are programmes meant for local governance in TV channels and print media also. If they are followed, the elected Women Representatives will gain adequate information needed to discharge their responsibilities. Majority of the respondents have access to television print media, Radio and they listen to those media. They develop a habit of listening news in TV and Radio and read newspapers regularly. They gain development information only from the media.

Gram Sabha is the space created constitutionally for people's participation in the process of development and governance. It is yet another instrument to empower ordinary citizens of India. Gram Sabha is transforming the character of our democracy from representative to representative and participatory. It is a training ground for citizens in deliberative democracy. Every Panchayat president has to take initiative for fixing agenda for Gram Sabha in Panchayat Council meeting. Only 11.58 per cent of the respondents had clear understanding of the functioning of Gram Sabha. Majority are not clear about the procedures to be followed in convening Gram Sabha meeting. Regarding the quorum for Gram Sabha meeting, they are not able to express the exact details of number for quorum. For many of they are being guided by the Panchayat clerks. They do not have any idea about the importance of Gram Sabha. They are not comfortable with crowd. They are able to manage the crowd because of the presence of self help group members. Ninety per cent of the respondents informed that they know the procedures of implementing the resolutions passed. But in the discussion they informed that they used to send the resolutions to district collector. The resolutions have to be classified and they are to be identified in terms of the department which will find solutions to the problem of Panchayat administration. Most of the presidents are sending the resolution passed in the Gram Sabha and they are to be sent to the appropriate government department for speedy redressal same way when they are asked about the procedures for council meeting, 90 per cent said that they know the procedure. When they are asked to spell out, they could not explain to a small question how to allot time to members and how to deliberate on subject in the council. They are all the subjects to be taught in the training programme. For vital questions on decision-making, planning for Village Integrated Development, budget preparation and tracking Panchayat finance more than 80 per cent of the Elected Women Representatives informed us that they are aware of the procedures. No respondent was able to show the plan document of the village. No Elected Women Representatives have explained to us the fund flow through other departments of government to Gram Panchayat. Whatever money comes through DRDA, to Gram Panchayat, they operate and beyond that they are not able to trace it.

From the above one can easily infer the agency assets of the respondents. Majority of them hailing from a humble background. Their economic conditions are not so sound. They have to struggle for their livelihood. Their social status is also not so high as they belong to most background class and scheduled caste. At one level it is positive. Since they are struggling for their livelihood and development, they will be able to address those issues when they are discharging their responsibilities as presidents of Gram Panchayat. In yet another level it is considered as barrier as the respondents have to overcome the difficulties arising out the poor socio-economic conditions.

Table 9: Age Profile of the Respondents

Sl. No.	*Respondents Age Profile*	*No. of Respondents*	*Percentage*
1.	21-30	16	13.22
2.	31-40	44	36.37
3.	41-50	36	29.75
4.	51 and above	25	20.66
	Total	**121**	**100.00**

Source: Computed.

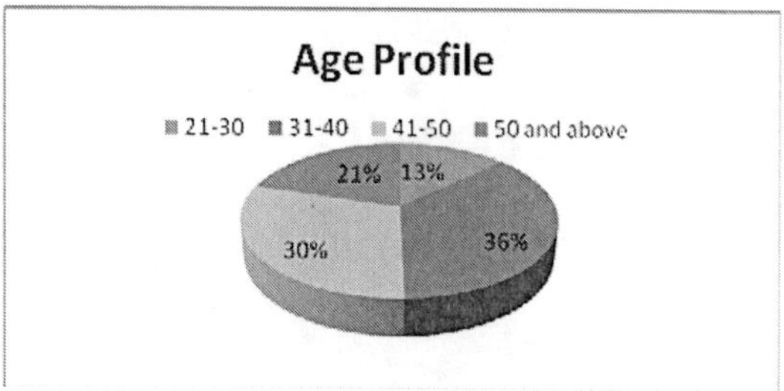

Table 10: Community Profile of the Respondents

Sl. No.	*Communities Profile*	*No. of Respondents*	*Percentage*
1.	BC	50	41.32
2.	MBC	28	23.14
3.	SC/ST	43	35.54
	Total	**121**	**100.00**

Source: Computed.

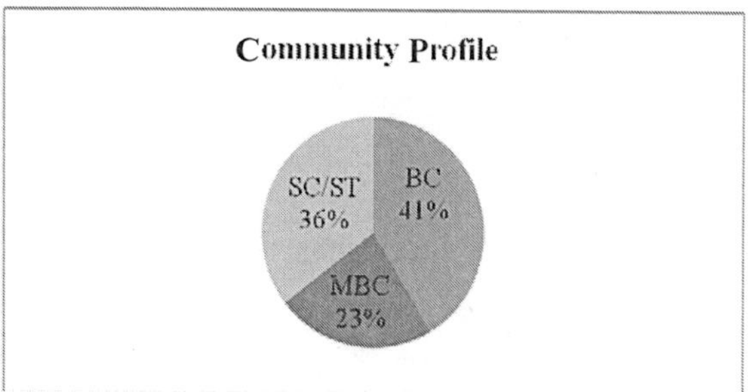

Table 11: Education Profile of the Respondents

Sl. No.	*Education*	*No. of Respondents*	*Percentage*
1.	Illiterate	12	9.91
2.	Upto V	30	24.80
3.	VI to VIII	15	12.40
4.	IX to X	45	37.20
5.	X to XII	9	7.43
6.	Graduate	10	8.26
	Total	**121**	**100.00**

Source: Computed.

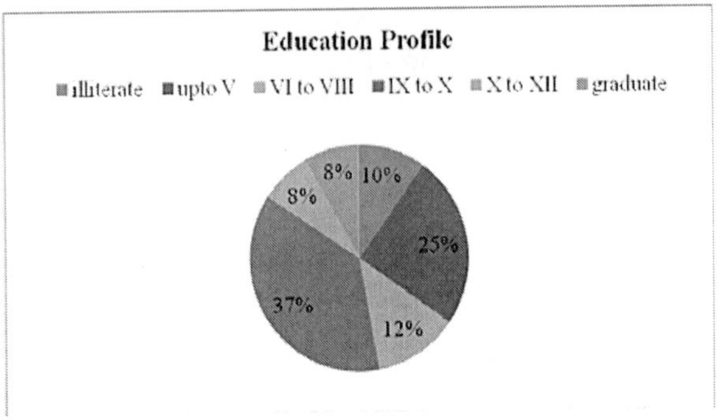

Table 12: Housing Details of the Respondents

Sl. No.	*House Details*	*No. of Respondents*	*Percentage*
1.	Own house	89	73.56
2.	Rented house	32	26.44
	Total	**121**	**100.00**

Source: Computed.

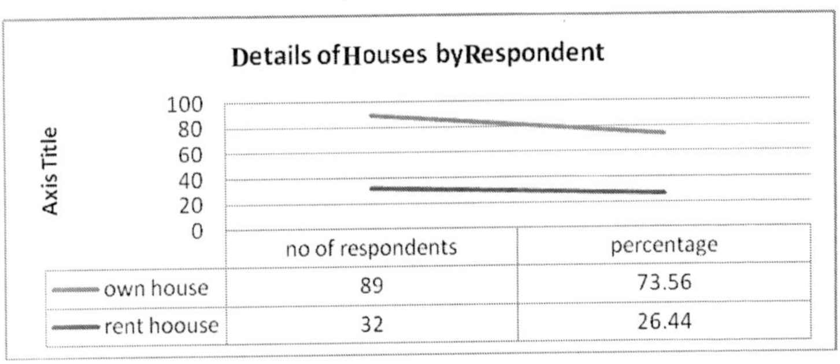

Table 13: Marital Status of the Respondents

Sl. No.	*Marital status*	*No. of Respondents*	*Percentage*
1.	Married	99	81.82
2.	Unmarried	20	16.52
3.	Widowed	2	1.66
	Total	**121**	**100.00**

Source: Computed.

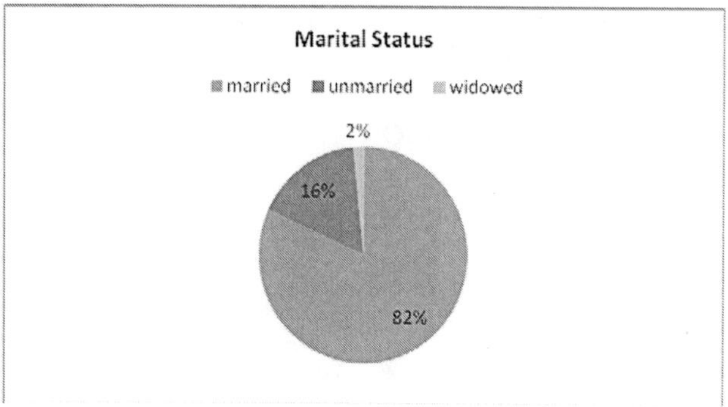

Table 14: Religious Background of the Respondents

Sl. No.	*Types of Religion*	*No. of Respondents*	*Percentage*
1.	Hindu	101	83.48
2.	Others	20	16.52
	Total	**121**	**100.00**

Source: Computed.

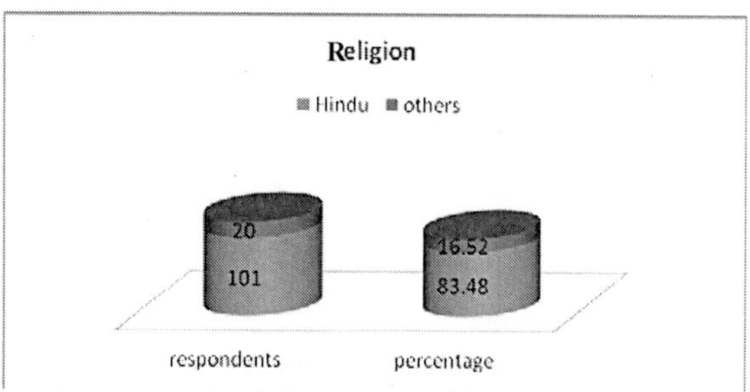

Table 15: Details of Monthly Expenditure of the Respondents

Sl. No.	*Monthly Expenditure*	*No. of Respondents*	*Percentage*
1.	5000 - 8000	57	47.10
2.	9000 - 12000	52	42.98
3.	12000 - 14000	6	4.96
4.	15000 and above	6	4.96
	Total	**121**	**100.00**

Source: Computed.

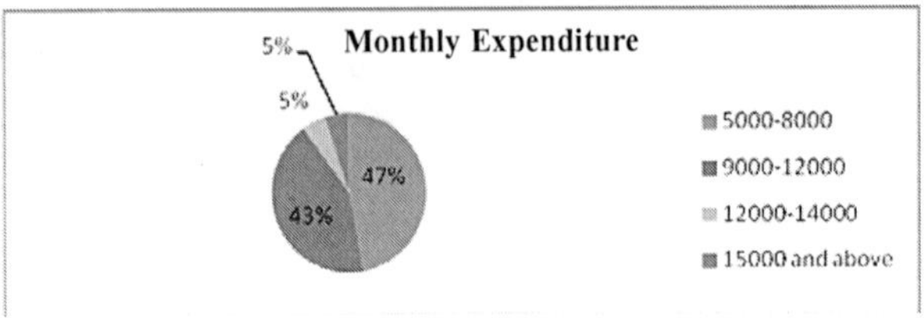

Table 16: Details of Monthly Income of the Respondents

Sl. No.	Monthly Income	No. of Respondents	Percentage
1.	1000-1500	7	5.79
2.	1500-2000	7	5.79
3.	2000-3000	16	13.22
4.	3000-4000	32	26.44
5.	4000 and above	59	48.76
	Total	**121**	**100.00**

Source: Computed.

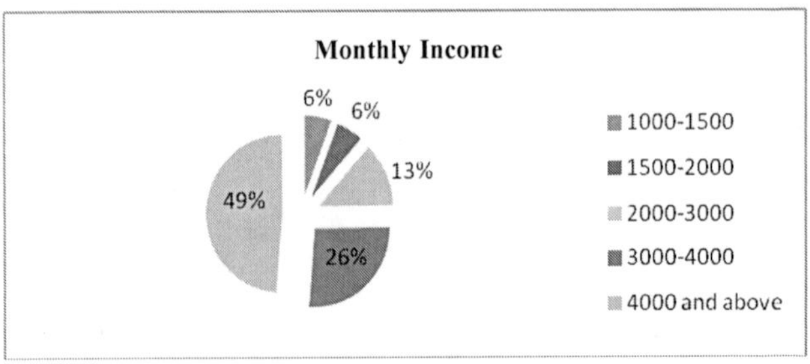

Table 17: Occupational Details of the Respondents

Sl. No.	Occupation	No. of Respondents	Percentage
1.	Farmer	79	65.29
2.	Coolie	16	13.22
3.	Private Employee	12	9.92
4.	Small Business	13	10.75
5.	Business	1	0.82
	Total	**121**	**100.00**

Source: Computed.

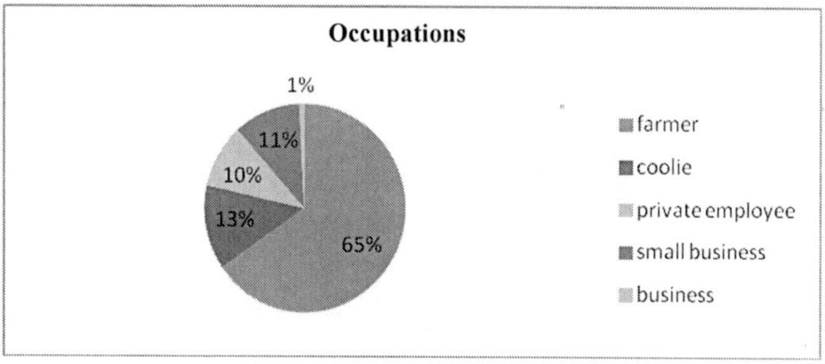

Table 18: Details of the Sanitation Services Available in the Respondents Houses

Sl. No.	*Sanitation Services*	*No. of Respondents*	*Percentage*
1.	Yes	95	78.51
2.	No	26	21.49
	Total	**121**	**100.00**

Source: Computed.

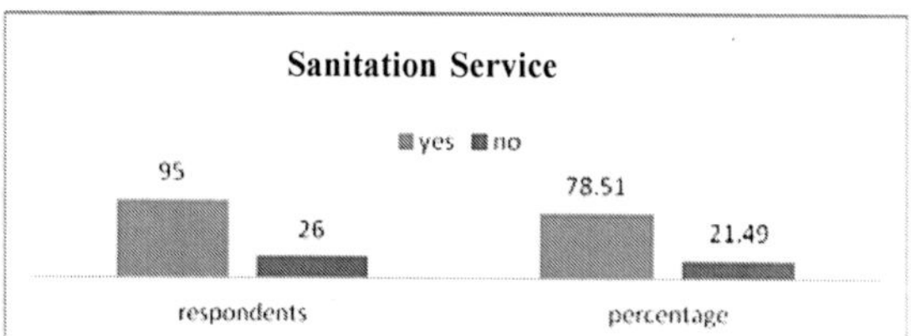

Table 19: Details of the Primary Source of Water for the Respondents

Sl. No.	*Primary source of water*	*No. of Respondents*	*Percentage*
1.	Public piped water system	75	61.99
2.	Private well	34	28.09
3.	Public well	12	9.92
	Total	**121**	**100.00**

Source: Computed.

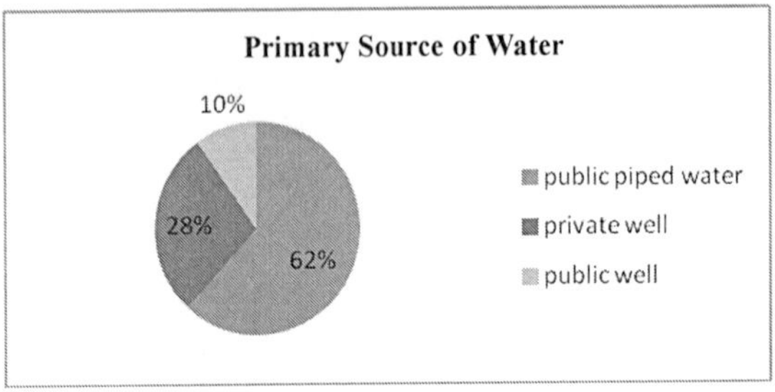

Table 20: Profile of the Type of Houses in which Respondents Live

Sl. No.	*Type of Houses*	*No. of Respondents*	*Percentage*
1.	Tiled House	37	30.58
2.	Others	84	69.42
	Total	**121**	**100.00**

Source: Computed.

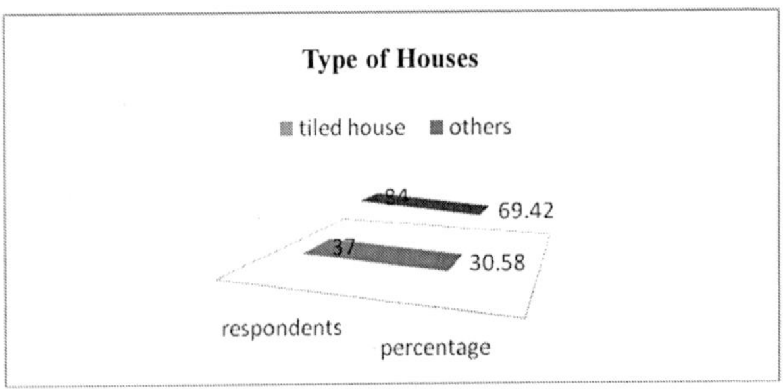

Table 21: Details of Land Holding of the Respondents

Sl. No.	*Land Holding*	*No. of Respondents*	*Percentage*
1.	Upto 2 acres	44	36.37
2.	2.1 to 5 acres	22	18.18
3.	5.1 acres and above	22	18.18
4.	Nil	33	27.27
	Total	**121**	**100.00**

Source: Computed.

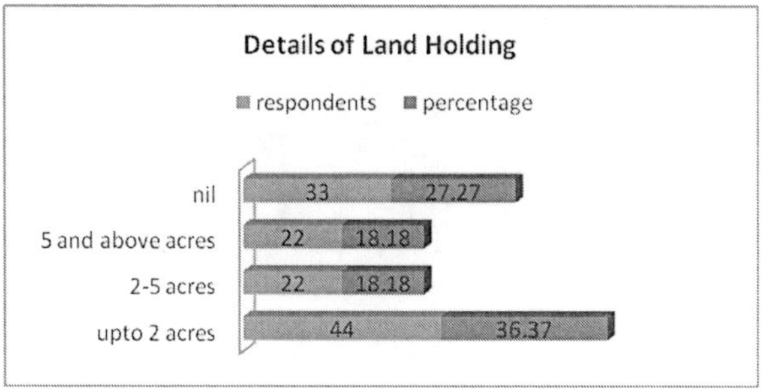

Table 22: Awareness of the Respondents on Gender Justice

Sl. No.	*Options*	*No. of Respondents*	*Percentage*
1.	Yes	91	75.20
2.	No	30	24.80
	Total	**121**	**100.00**

Source: Computed.

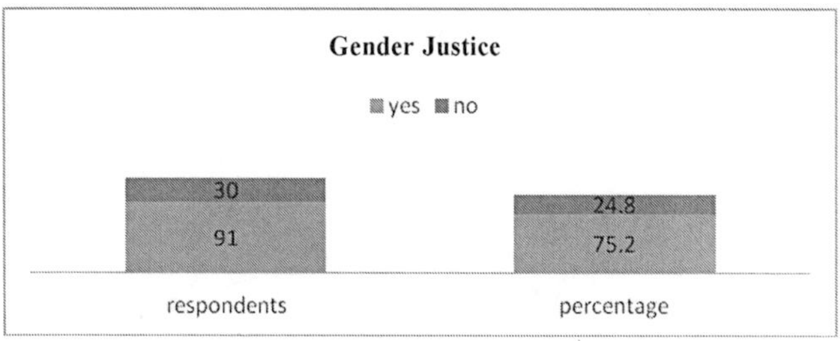

Table 23: Awareness of the Respondents on the Possibility of Working for Reducing Violence against Women

Sl. No.	*Violence against Women*	*No. of Respondents*	*Percentage*
1.	Yes	92	76.03
2.	No	29	23.97
	Total	**121**	**100.00**

Source: Computed.

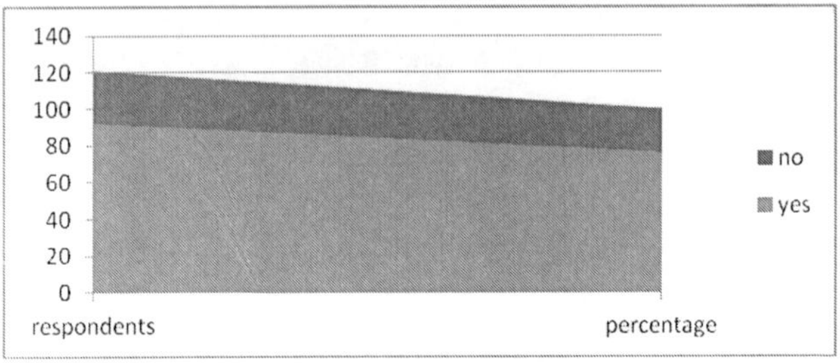

Table 24: Aspiration of the Respondents to make the Panchayat Performance

Sl. No.	*Pro-women Panchayat*	*No. of Respondents*	*Percentage*
1.	Yes	86	71.08
2.	No	35	28.92
	Total	**121**	**100.00**

Source: Computed.

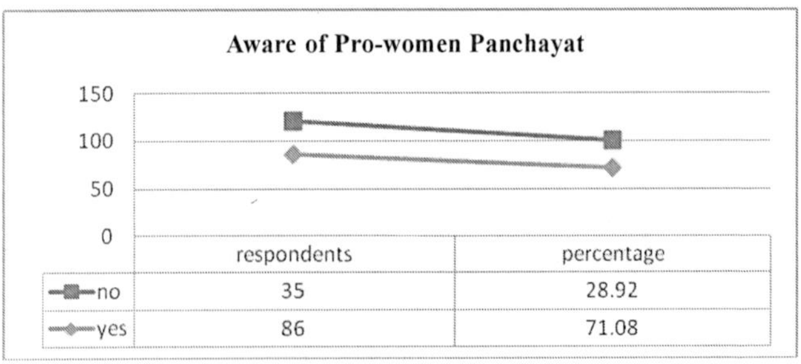

Table 25: Awareness of the Respondents on Gender Equality

Sl. No.	*Panchayat work for Gender Equality*	*No. of Respondents*	*Percentage*
1.	Yes	82	67.77
2.	No	23	19.00
3.	No answer	16	13.23
	Total	**121**	**100.00**

Source: Computed.

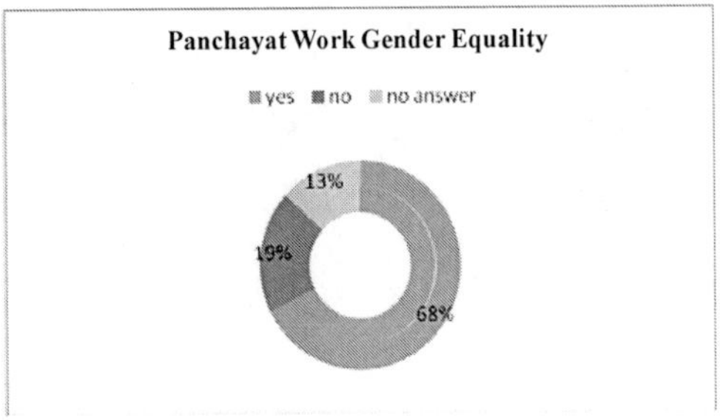

Table 26: Respondents Awareness on Health Conditions of Rural Women

Sl. No.	*Aware of women's Health Condition*	*No. of Respondents*	*Percentage*
1.	Yes	91	75.21
2.	No	30	24.79
	Total	**121**	**100.00**

Source: Computed.

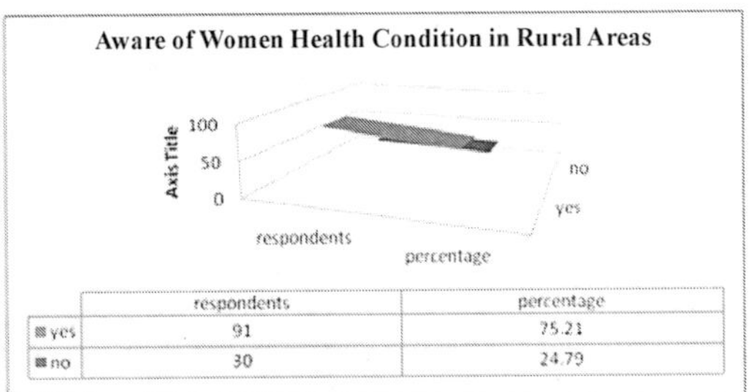

Table 27: Respondents' Awareness on Health Condition of Children in Rural Areas

Sl. No.	*Aware of children Health Condition*	*No. of Respondents*	*Percentage*
1.	Yes	91	75.21
2.	No	30	24.79
	Total	**121**	**100.00**

Source: Computed.

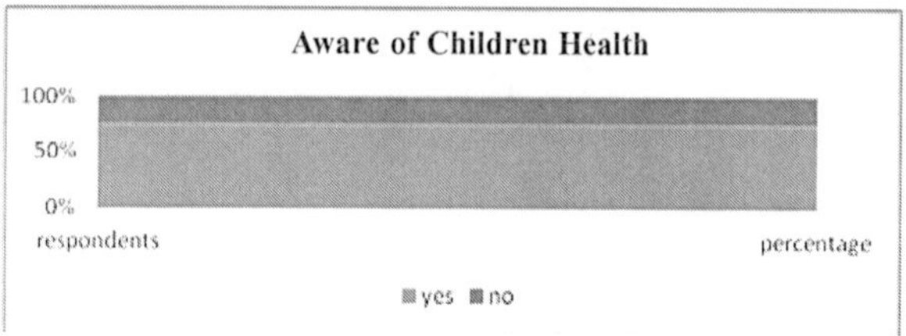

Table 28: Mobility of the Villagers

Sl. No.	*Villagers easily Accessible to the outsiders*	*No. of Respondents*	*Percentage*
1.	Yes	93	76.86
2.	No	28	23.14
	Total	**121**	**100.00**

Source: Computed.

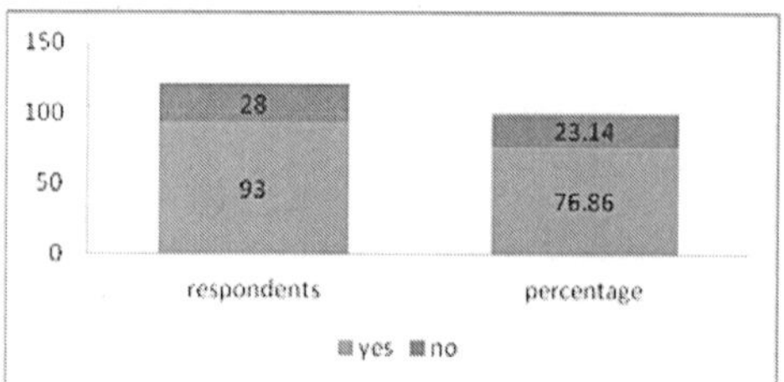

Table 29: Respondents Habit of Watching TV for News

Sl. No.	*Watching Television*	*No. of Respondents*	*Percentage*
1.	Yes	97	80.17
2.	No	24	19.83
	Total	**121**	**100.00**

Source: Computed.

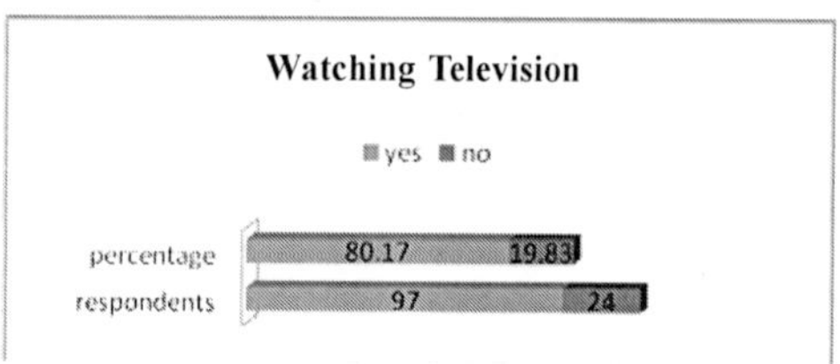

Table 30: Respondents Habit of Listening Radio for News

Sl. No.	*Listening Radio by respondents*	*No. of Respondents*	*Percentage*
1.	Yes	76	62.80
2.	No	45	37.20
	Total	**121**	**100.00**

Source: Computed.

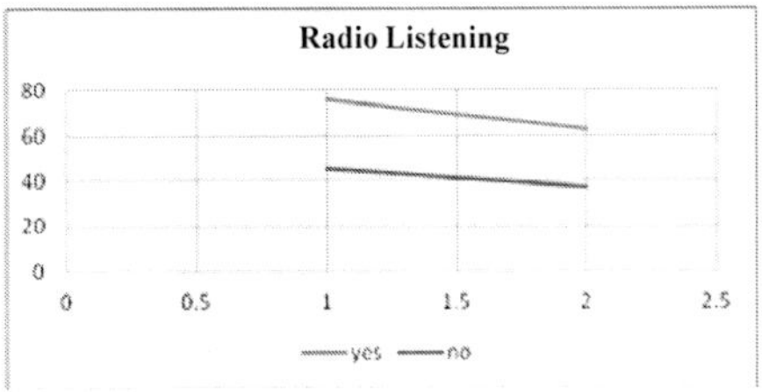

Table 31: Respondents Habit of Reading Newspapers

Sl. No.	*Reading Newspaper*	*No. of Respondents*	*Percentage*
1.	Yes	91	75.20
2.	No	30	24.80
	Total	**121**	**100.00**

Source: Computed.

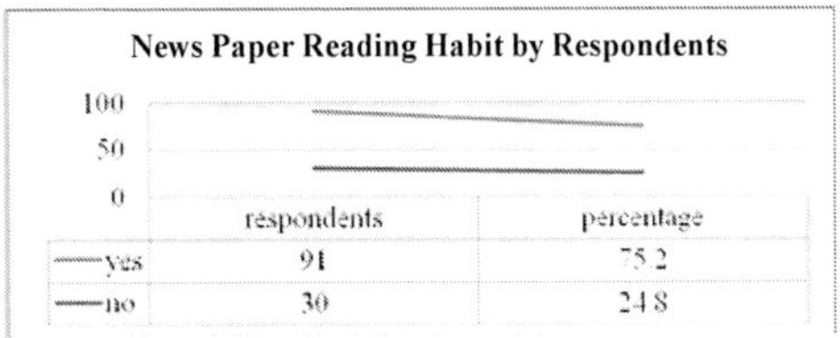

Table 32: Details of the Programme Watched by Respondents

Sl. No.	*Types of Programme*	*No. of Respondents*	*Percentage*
1.	Politics	14	11.58
2.	Current affairs	72	59.50
3.	Serials	11	9.09
4.	Others	24	19.83
	Total	**121**	**100.00**

Source: Computed.

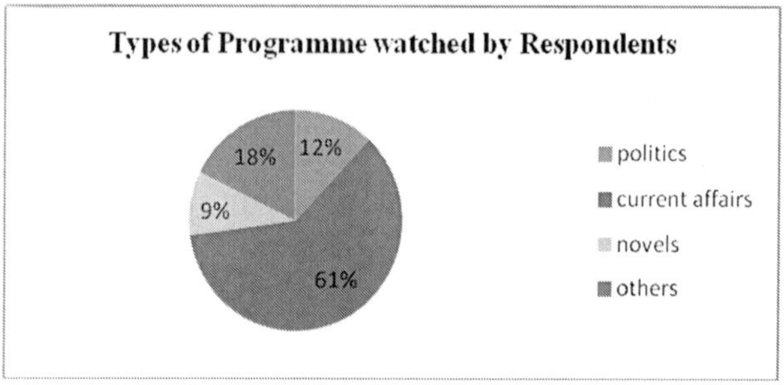

Table 33: Details of Gram Sabha Convened

Sl. No.	*Gram Sabha meeting in year*	*No. of Respondents*	*Percentage*
1.	2 times	11	9.09
2.	4 times	14	11.58
3.	5 and above	96	79.33
	Total	**121**	**100.00**

Source: Computed.

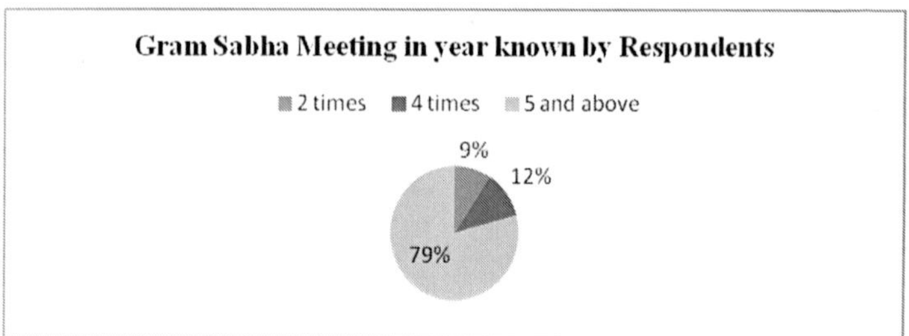

Table 34: Respondent Awareness of quorum of Gram Sabha Meeting

Sl. No.	*Options*	*No. of respondents*	*Percentage*
1.	Yes	87	71.90
2.	No	31	25.62
3.	No Answer	3	2.48
	Total	**121**	**100.00**

Source: Computed.

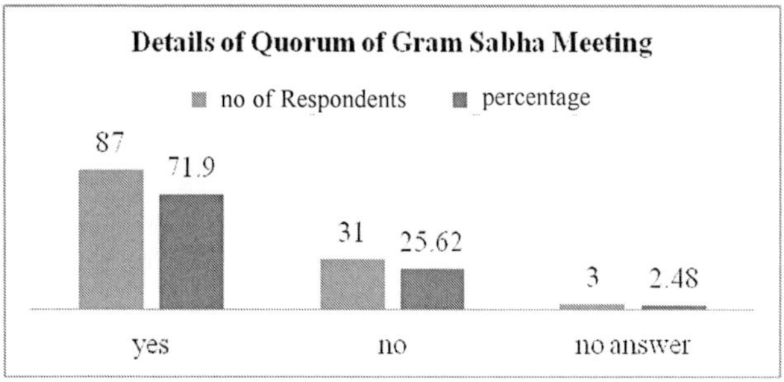

Table 35: Respondents' Awareness of the Procedures of Gram Sabha Meeting

Sl. No.	*Options*	*No. of Respondents*	*Percentage*
1.	Yes	108	89.25
2.	No	13	10.75
	Total	**121**	**100.00**

Source: Computed.

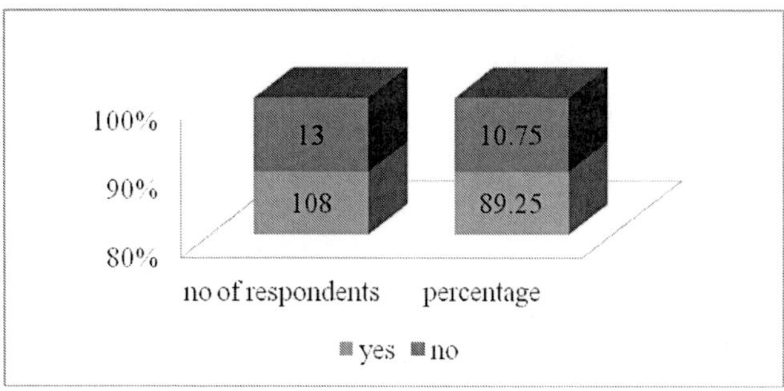

Table 36: Respondents' Knowledge on Implementing Resolutions

Sl. No.	*Options*	*No. of Respondents*	*Percentage*
1.	Yes	110	90.90
2.	No	11	9.09
	Total	**121**	**100.00**

Source: Computed.

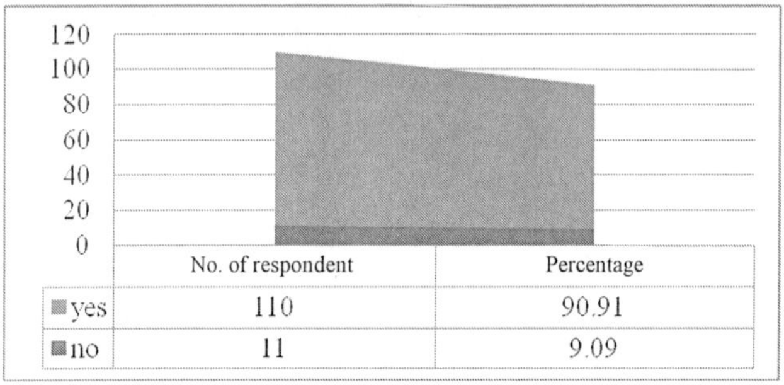

Table 37: Respondents' Awareness on Procedures for the Conduct of Panchayat Council

Sl. No.	*Options*	*No. of Respondents*	*Percentage*
1.	Yes	110	90.90
2.	No	11	9.09
	Total	**121**	**100.00**

Source: Computed.

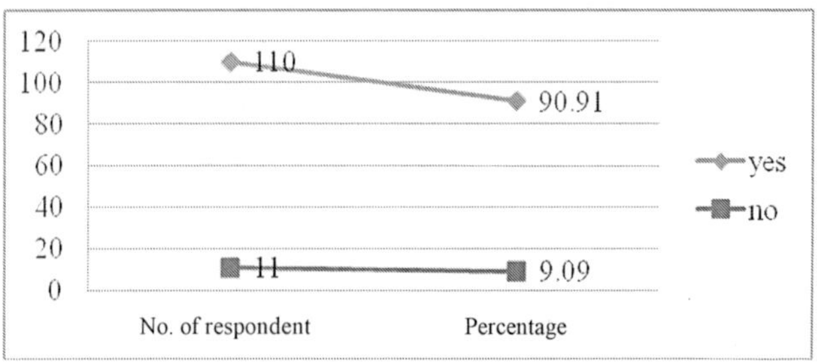

Table 38: Respondents' Knowledge on Decision Making in Panchayat Council

Sl. No.	*Options*	*No. of Respondents*	*Percentage*
1.	Yes	104	85.96
2.	No	17	14.04
	Total	**121**	**100.00**

Source: Computed.

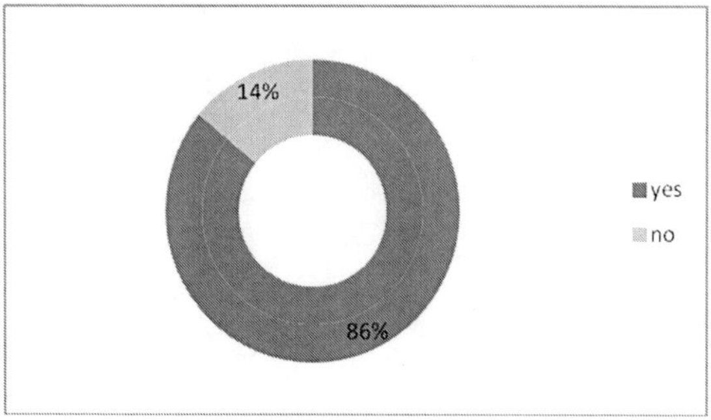

Table 39: Respondents' Knowledge on Planning Exercise at Panchayat Level

Sl. No.	*Options*	*No. of Respondents*	*Percentage*
1.	Yes	92	76.03
2.	No	29	23.97
	Total	**121**	**100.00**

Source: Computed.

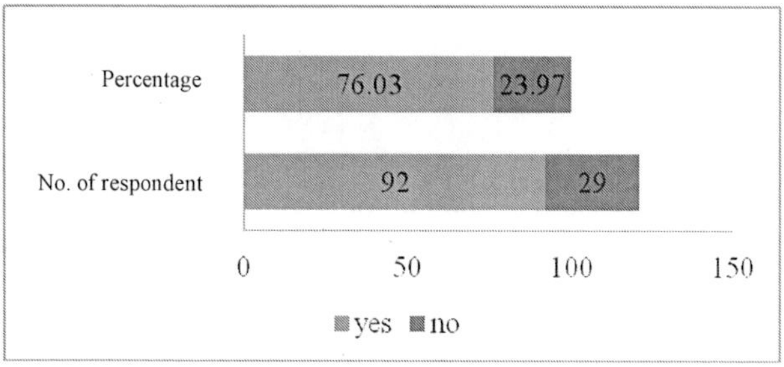

Table 40: Respondents Knowledge on Budget Preparation

Sl. No.	*Options*	*No. of Respondents*	*Percentage*
1.	Yes	107	88.42
2.	No	14	11.58
	Total	**121**	**100.00**

Source: Computed.

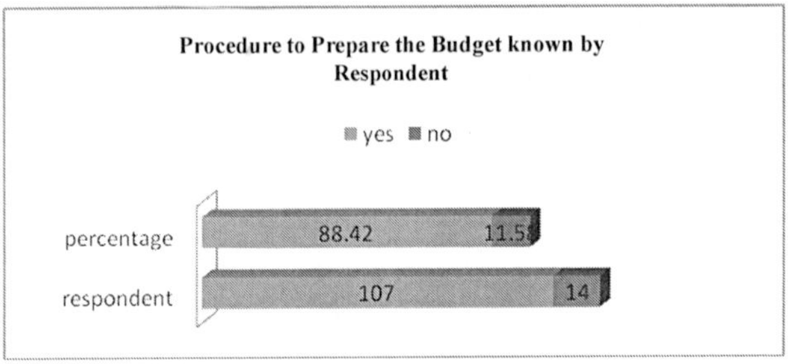

Table 41: Respondents' Knowledge on Tracking Finance

Sl. No.	*Options*	*No. of Respondents*	*Percentage*
1	Yes	108	89.25
2	No	13	10.75
	Total	**121**	**100.00**

Source: Computed.

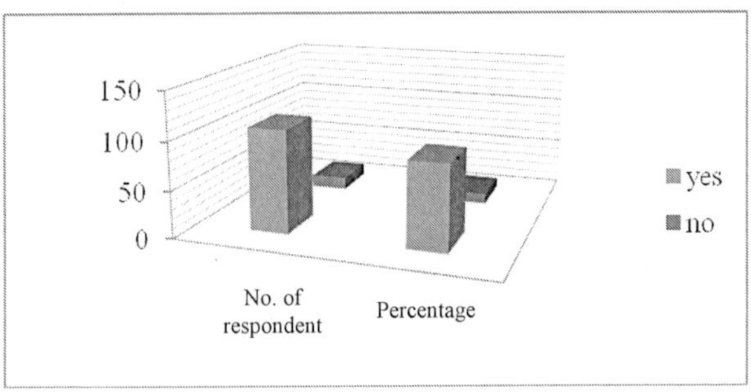

In terms of social and economic background, the respondents are not comfortable as majority of them are having very low income. Their social background was also poor. In terms of the land asset the respondents are having very less land asset. From the description in this chapter it is to be noted that the practice of elite capture has been reduced. People have been drawn from the poorest segments of the society. In terms of information asset the respondents have got access to basic information relating to governance and development.

Notes and References

1. Burn, S.M., "Women across Cultures: A Global Perspective" May Field: Mountain View, 2000.
2. Santha, E.K., "Political Participation of in Women in Panchayati Raj: Haryana Kerala and Tamil Nadu", New Delhi: Institute of Social Sciences, 1999.
3. Sekhon, Joti, "Democratic Theories and Women's Practices" Canadian Journal of Development Studies", XXII (special issue).
4. Mohanty, Bidyut, "Panchayati Raj Institutions and Women" in From Independence Towards Freedom: Indian Women Since 1947 (eds) Bharati Ray and Aparna Basu, New Delhi: Oxford University Press, 1999, pp. 19-33.
5. Rai, Manoj, Nambiar Mabini, Paul Sohini, Sangeeta Sing and Satinder S. Sahni (eds), "The State of Panchayats: A Participatory Perspective", New Delhi: Sanskrit, for PRIA, 2001.
6. Kishor, Sumita and Gupta Kamla, "Women's Empowerment in India and its States: Evidence from the NFHS" Economic and Political Weekly, February 14, 2004.
7. Palanithurai, G, "Role of Panchayat in Service Delivery: A Case Analysis" Punjab Journal of Politics, Vol. XXXI: 2007.
8. Verba Sidney, Nie Norman H and Kim o K, Participation and Political Equality: A Seven Nation Comparison, London: Cambridge University Press, 1978.
9. Palanithurai, G, People Perception of Politics: An Indian Perspective, New Delhi: Kanishka Publishers and Distributors, 1995.
10. Shah, Ghanshyam, Caste Association and Political Process in Gujarat, Bombay: Popular Prakashan, 1975.

Chapter - IV

Opportunity Structure

Opportunity structure is defined as the formal and informal context in which actors operate. When women determined to contest in the election, they have to work through several organisations and institutions both formally and informally. While working through organisations and institutions the women get adequate access to information channels to get needed information. Institutions which provide needed information to manage institutions of governance which ultimately empower them. Connecting themselves with institutions and organisations will enhance their internal strength and hence connectivity is considered crucial and critical for their empowerment. Institutions and organisations meant for governance, administration and development have to be used by the Elected Women Representatives. Empowering themselves and women depends on the utilisation of the institutions and organisations by the Elected Women Representatives. Hence questions have been asked on the following aspects: linkages with political parties, participation in political party activities, inclination to move up in the political career, conduct of the council meeting, conduct of Gram Sabha meetings, deliberative aspect of the meetings, managing their political campaigns, constant contact with political parties for political affiliation, contact with government officials, meeting them for official purposes, aware of procedures and practices of managing the institutions; managing commons, supervising the service delivery points; dealing with traditional institutions, dealing with parallel bodies, and other aspects, to get response from the Elected Women Representatives.

All the respondents were drawn from the reserved constituencies. Gram Panchayat in Tamil Nadu is freed from the political party based contests. Hence they are women contesting in the election in the reserved seat not based on party ticket. A question has been framed to elicit whether they are aware about reservation. For this question 15.70 per cent of the respondents replied that the seat is not reserved for women. It indicates that they are drawn and filled by some body without giving any information to them. It is to be noted here that barring a few majority of the women are drawn towards this space by many forces namely, their family, their community, their group and others. Women who have come to this space on their own are very limited. 57.02 per cent of the respondents had no political experience and never attended any political party meetings in the past. Political experience of an individual will enable him or her to tackle the problems arise in public space at ease. But 88.42 per cent of the respondents have managed their election by involving themselves. 87.60 per cent of the respondents categorically said they had no political ambition to more in career leader. Aspiration to move in the ladder of power is a drive engine for the individual to work hard and to earn respect in the community. It is necessary that the Elected Women Representatives should know what for reservation of seats has been done to women and Dalits in local bodies. Unless they understand and aware how could they perform the critical function. As per the Tamil Nadu Panchayat Act, 1994 all the Gram Panchayats have to discharge the responsibilities as stipulated in the Act. There is no difference between Elected Women Representatives and Elected Men Representatives. But Elected Women Representatives have to walk extra miles by discharging responsibilities. In public space we find large number of knowledgeable people but we could not find sensitive people. Sensitivity could be created among the people through training. As president of the Panchayat they convened the Gram Sabha meeting. During the meeting entire crowd has to be managed by the respondents. The meeting lasted for one to five hours. 43.8 per cent of the respondents managed the crowd for three hours. Nine per cent of the respondents managed the crowd for four to five hours. Regulating the meeting of Gram Sabha is not an easy affair. It requires Courage, communication skill, and information. Equally conducting Panchayat Council meeting is yet another tough task. It lasted for from one to four hours. 30.59 per cent of the respondents conducted the meeting for three hours. 41.32 per cent of them conducted the meeting for two hours. Since it is a small gathering, with set of agenda, the meeting has to be conducted formally with professional skill. Hundred per cent of the respondents are well aware that they are the chair persons of the Gram Sabha and they have to preside over the meeting. 74.38 per cent of the respondents replied that all the members tried to participate in the meeting. It means people have evinced keen interest. But the problem is to manage the crowd. All the respondents have expressed that they got the support of the ward members.

The Elected Women Representatives have to democratise the community and institutions and for which Gram Sabha and Panchayat Council have been created. Utility of the institutions depends on how they are handled and used. When they are asked about the participation of stakeholders in the meeting, 74 per cent of the respondents said all members participated in the Gram Sabha meeting. It is not possible. 14.8 per cent of the respondents said around ten members participated in Gram Sabha meeting. 10.74 per cent of them expressed that at least 25 people have participated in Gram Sabha meeting. Many do not have clarity on democratisation. Further many do not have needed awareness on the importance if participation. As a result, Gram Sabha has been converted into a grievance redressal centre. Continuous mobilisation of people and make them to participate in the deliberative process are process oriented activities. In a plural and unequal society making every segment to participate in the deliberative process is critical and difficult job.

In Tamil Nadu, the position of Gram Panchayat President is not affiliated with political parties. Yet, 41.32 per cent of the respondents replied that they sought the help of political parties. They felt that the community is not apolitical and hence people vote based on party line. Hence they approached the political parties for support. It is the culture in Tamil Nadu that leaders at Gram Panchayat level tend to join with political party as they could get recognition in the government offices and they feel that they could get identity only by joining the political parties. As they have got political identity they contact officials directly for official work. Generally it is perceived that if the Elected Women Representatives go to office, contact officials, organise meetings, preside over the meetings, speak in the meetings, express opinion independently by themselves, the above behavioural traits can be considered that the women leaders are independent and empowered. 85.96 per cent of the respondents expressed that they meet officials directly without any family aid. 90.91 per cent of the respondents expressed that they met the officials to get assistance to redress the grievances of the community. 85.96 per cent of the presidents said that officials have responded to their request positively as they are relevant to the scheme implementation as per the rule of the scheme. 88.43 per cent of the respondents replied that they regularly contacted the officials as scheme funds are always with sectoral departments. Barring a few Panchayat presidents, 99 per cent of the respondents constantly meet the project Director DRDA and Block Development Officer meant for Gram Panchayats. Almost all the respondents expressed that they take maximum efforts to bring women members to Gram Sabha. Eighty one per cent of the respondents said that in their Gram Sabha women members use to speak in the Gram Sabha meeting. Members of Gram Sabha used to bring volley of issues which are affecting their life. It ranges from livelihood to women issues. All development issues are brought to Gram Sabha not only for deliberation but for solution and redressal.

Agenda for Gram Sabha meeting has been finalised by the Panchayat Council. In Tamil Nadu, it is not known to many of the Panchayat presidents. Since Panchayat presidents had not taken effort to convene Gram Sabha meeting in the beginning, the state governments initiated the process. Hence the State Government issued continuously notice to Gram Panchayat to convene Gram Sabha meeting. Only 22.31 per cent of the respondents have really indicated that Gram Panchayat Council is responsible for preparing agenda for Gram Sabha meeting. 78.51 per cent of the presidents informed that the common property resources are being managed by the Gram Panchayats. At the Gram Panchayat level, all the common have to be maintained and managed by the Gram Panchayat as per the Tamil Nadu Panchayat Raj Act of 1994. 19.83 per cent of the respondents expressed that it is the responsibility of the Panchayat presidents to look after the commons. It is to be seen that our Panchayati system is leader centric that is why respondents said that it is the duty of the Panchayat presidents to take care of the commons. 73.56 per cent of the presidents replied that they regularly write letters to District Collector.

Elected Women Representatives Contact

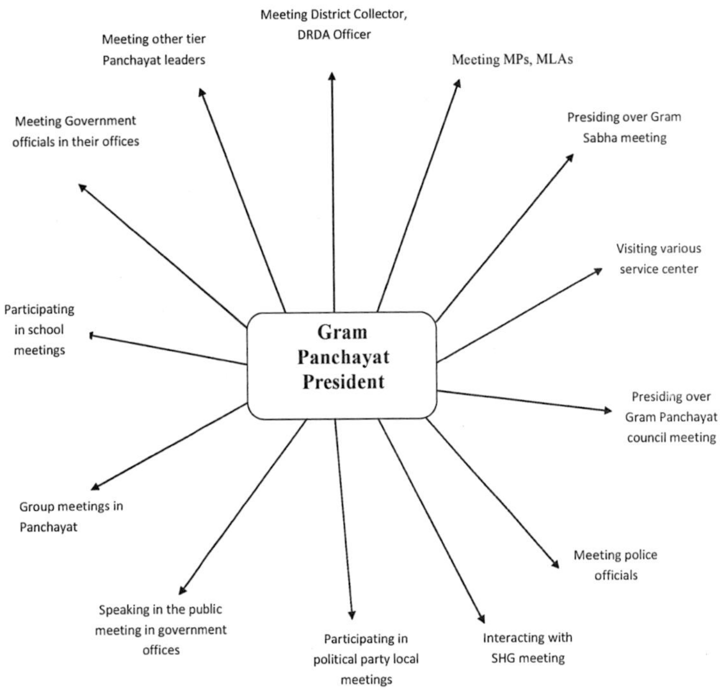

Nearly 37 sectoral departments are working with the rural communities. But the Panchayati presidents have informed us that they constantly in touch with only Rural Development Department. They mean that they are working with District Rural Development Agency. Beyond that they could not imagine. Only 14.89 per cent of the people are aware of the account to be maintained by the Panchayats. It gives the impression that someone is able to handle Panchayats. Yet, 87.60 per cent of the respondents informed us that they are fully informed of their roles and responsibilities to be discharged as Panchayati presidents. Establishing contact with officials of the Government Departments is very essential for effective functioning of the Panchayats. All centrally sponsored schemes barring MGNREGA are being implemented through the government departments. If the Panchayat presidents are not developing interaction with them they will not be able to get the benefits for the people from them. In reality Gram Panchayat presidents have established contact only with Rural Development Department not with other Sectoral Departments.

Panchayat is an institution of governance and administration. They are to be managed and administered as per the rules and regulations. In this regard only 14.89 per cent of the respondents know the exact number of accounts maintained in Panchayats. Others are not able to understand the accounts and it seemed that they are relying on the help of Panchayat secretary. 87.60 per cent of the Elected Women Representatives informed us that they are clear about their roles and responsibilities. When they are asked to specify they could not spell out the obligatory and discretional roles and responsibilities to be discharged by them. They were able to spell out a few regular activities. The respondents had visited public distribution shops, anganwadi and primary schools. They recorded that they are in good condition. But in the Gram Sabha meeting people made complaints. The Panchayat leaders never had the checklist to visit and inspect institutions.

Around 90 per cent of the respondents used to visit PDS shops, Anganwadi schools, attend public functions and 86 per cent of the respondents involved in school enrolment drive. Eighty four per cent of the respondents felt that there is always a strong presence of the traditional Panchayats in their respective Panchayats. Only 57 per cent of the respondents felt that parallel bodies are functioning in the Panchayat areas. Ninety per cent of the respondents informed that they maintain all the records in the office of the Panchayats and attending office regularly. Elected Women Representatives have informed that there is strong presence of traditional Panchayat. It means Panchayats have to struggle and more particularly women leaders have to face volley of problems. Strong presence of traditional Panchayat will create more problems to the elected women representatives. In the same tenor it will create problems for Dalit Elected Women Representatives. Elected Women Representatives expressed that they have to attend several public functions and they have to go to different offices for meetings. For all review meeting government officials demand the presence of Panchayat leaders. Hence they have to attend all the meetings. This kind of meetings and participation in these meetings will help the elected women representatives to gain confidence. Apart from these meetings the respondents have to go to Panchayat office regularly as they have to sign several documents since they maintain all the records in Panchayat office.

Legal Literacy

Panchayat leaders have to have legal literacy about the Panchayati Raj System based on the Amendment and conformity legislation passed by the Tamil Nadu legislature. Panchayat Act, Rules, Government orders, procedures relating to execution of government schemes and policy details are very essential for Panchayat leaders. They have to orient themselves in all the above aspects and this will enable them to perform their roles and responsibilities effectively. Normally the Panchayat leaders get all the details only through training and public interaction. Among the respondents 75 per cent of them replied that they are aware of the Tamil Nadu Panchayati Raj Act of 1994. Eighty eight per cent of the respondents expressed that they are aware of the rules and procedures. Eighty nine per cent of the respondents are aware of the schemes and programmes which are to be implemented through the village Panchayat. Eighty eight per cent of the respondents said that they are getting orders periodically from the government and they get to know all the details only through government offices.

Organisation Assets: Membership of Organisation/ Political Party and Group Leadership

For individual empowerment organisational support is sin quo non. Individuals who are involved in public activities and occupy public space necessarily tend to get the organisational support. Their membership and participation and its continuity will enable them to move in empowerment ladder. In this regard a battery of questions have been asked. 74.36 per cent of the respondents stated that they have affiliated themselves with political parties. 69.42 per cent of the respondents have expressed that they affiliated with political party as their families are attached with political parties for a long. Why people who are in position and offices tend to join political parties is the question to be answered. The existing governance culture demonstrates that unless the person goes with political identity, he or she can get response from the office otherwise he/she will be ignored. With regard to Gram Panchayat presidents they need the support of the political parties to gain visibility. Further they need the support of the ruling party to get maximum funds from the government for their Gram Panchayat. Now it becomes a condition that he/she has to have a political identity. 83.48 per cent of the presidents have expressed that periodically visit their party office and meet the party leaders. 76.86 per cent of them said that they alone go to party office and meet the party leaders. It is proved beyond doubt that they need the support of the political parties and hence the elected women representatives go to party offices. By going over they get psychological support as they belong that political party. They meet party office bearers and they discuss with the party office bearers about their problems. They get counselling and support from the party. When they go to party office they go alone and by which they demonstrate that they are independent and they have the clarity to receive direction from the party and implement the decisions. In such a way they get support from the political parties. Apart from the political affiliation they are having membership in many social organisations. Sometimes they are cultural or community based. Their membership is for the benefit of the individuals. The elected women representatives considered that these are the good opportunities to expand their base and get support. They are also part of some of the livelihood missions and organisations. At every level they tried to get support from the organisations. Many of them take office bearers position and thereby they get training in managing organisation, groups, associations and institutions. Seventy six per cent of them are members of social organisations. Most of them are in Self-Help Group. In the political organisations some of them are leaders of the parties at the grassroots and many are members of the party. 38.01 per cent of them replied that they get advantage out of it. Fifty seven per cent of them said that they are active members of SHG and they get adequate leadership training in SHG activities. 85.96 per cent of the respondents take independent decisions in the organisation.

Skill/Training/Capacity Building/Self Confidence

Capacity building is basic and essential requirement for the leaders of the institution. Without having any basic knowledge on governance and administration people are elected to position. The moment they occupy position they are expected to take up the role and responsibilities. Further they are expected to discharge their responsibilities. The members of parliament and legislative assembly are not taking up any direct responsibility in administration. But the local body leaders are involved in administration also. Hence they need proper training and orientation.

It is to be noted here that India has got 30 lakh representatives in local bodies. Of them 10 lakh are women. But we do not have a training policy or framework or a perspective either at the central government level or at state governments' level. We have no regular budgetary resource allocation for training local body leaders. There is no demand from the local body leaders that they need a training or orientation. Against this background training programmes are conducted. Even a small country like Singapore a leadership school had been established and it is a shame on our part that from India many leaders mostly youth from mainstream political parties have participated in leadership programmes offered by the leadership school in National University of Singapore. In our political discourse we do not find space for capacity building, training and orientation for our leaders in Parliament, Legislatures and Local Bodies (G. Palanithurai, 1991).

Ninety per cent of the Panchayat presidents said that had a clear cut perception about village development. They had a dream about their village. 85.96 per cent respondents are thorough on the responsibilities of the Panchayati presidents. 88.42 per cent of the panchayati presidents informed that they attend all the departmental works and meet officials. 80.17 per cent used to attend public meetings. Panchayat presidents have to participate in the meetings organised by the government departments. They have to speak in the meeting. They have to express their opinion on public issues. Most of them said that it is a difficult task. They never had such opportunity in life. Now they are facing such challenges. Now they are attending meeting, participating in them and speaking in the meeting. As they interact with many, they get perceptions of others and idea of others. Hence they express their opinions on issues. 90.91 per cent of the respondents replied that they have participated in the training programme. 90.91 per cent said they gained much in the training. Training is the need for the Panchayat leaders. Eighty six per cent of the respondents have said that they have administrative manual. They use to read the manual and follow the manual for Panchayat governance and Panchayat administration (G.Palanithurai, K. Vallinayakam, N.S. Chidambaram and K. Subaramaniam, 2007). 87.60 per cent of the presidents had expressed that they promised to the people that they will perform certain facilities if they return to office as Panchayati presidents. 86.78 per cent of respondents said that they used to attend the meeting along with men leaders. They participate in the meeting with equality. 87.60 per cent of the Panchayati presidents have expressed that they are satisfied with the position.

Problems faced by the Respondents

Since 1996, a number of studies have been conducted to elicit the problems faced by the elected women representatives. The studies have brought out volley of problems faced by the elected women representatives in the family, community, political party, government offices, public places (G. Palanithurai, 2002). Apart from the above the poor management and administrative skill added to the problems. Since they have formed their own elected women representatives' federation all the problems faced by them have been highlighted in the media for public consumption. Government of Tamil Nadu has taken series of steps to reduce their problems (G. Palanithurai and G. Uma and J. Vanishree, 2010). From the reply given by the elected women representatives, one could see the drastic improvement. Nearly one-tenth of the representatives have problems and all others are free from the problems.

Table 42: Respondents Awareness on Reservation of Seats for Women

Sl. No.	*Options*	*No. of Respondents*	*Percentage (Per cent)*
1.	Yes	102	84.30
2.	No	19	15.70
	Total	**121**	**100.00**

Source: Computed.

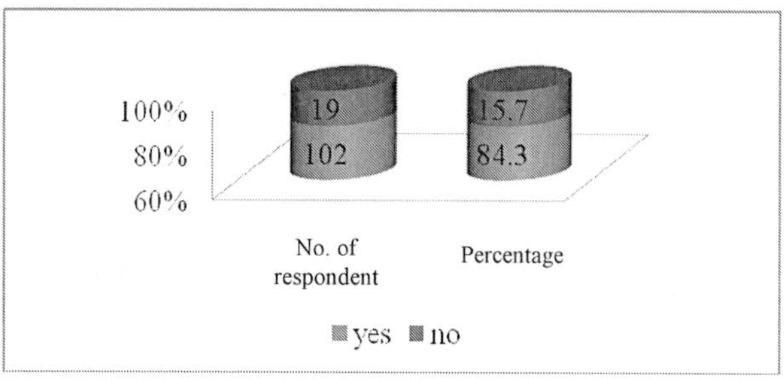

Table 43: Respondents' Participation in Political Activities

Sl. No.	*Options*	*No. of Respondents*	*Percentage*
1.	Yes	52	42.98
2.	No	69	57.02
	Total	**121**	**100.00**

Source: Computed.

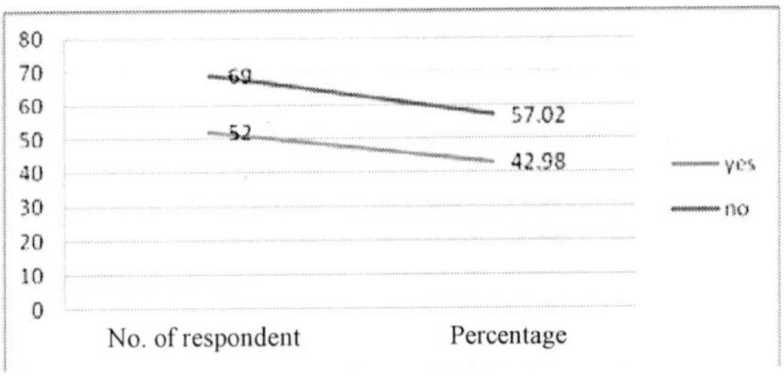

Table 44: Respondents' Participation in Campaign for Election

Sl. No.	*Options*	*No. of Respondents*	*Percentage*
1.	Yes	107	88.42
2.	No	14	11.58
	Total	**121**	**100.00**

Source: Computed.

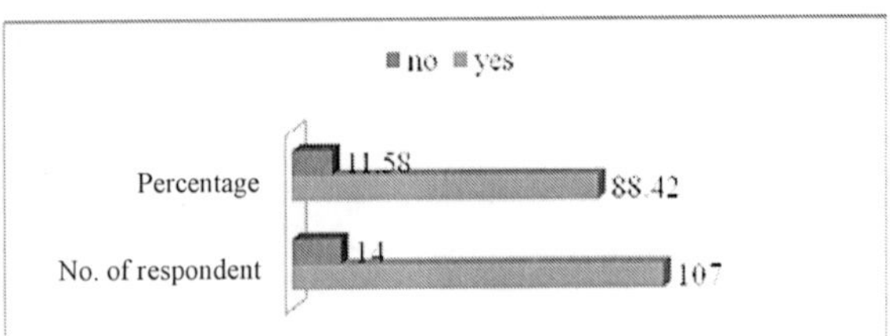

Table 45: Aspiration to Contest in MLA Election

Sl. No.	*Options*	*No. of Respondents*	*Percentage*
1.	Yes	15	12.40
2.	No	106	87.60
	Total	**121**	**100.00**

Source: Computed.

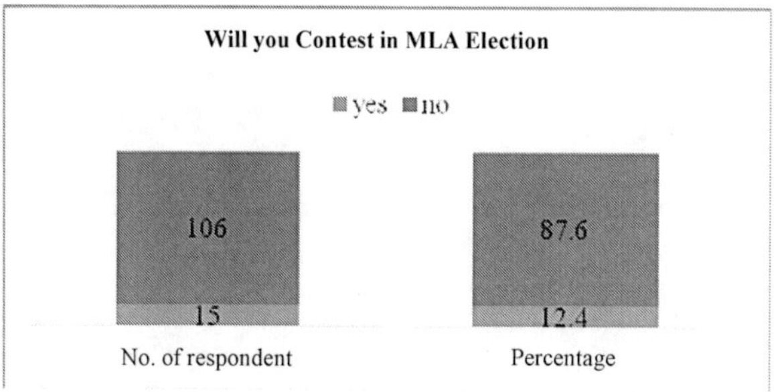

Table 46: Duration of Gram Sabha Meeting Conducted

Sl. No.	*Options*	*No. of Respondents*	*Percentage*
1.	1 hour	18	14.88
2.	Two hours	28	23.14
3.	Three hours	53	43.80
4.	Four hours	11	9.09
5.	Five hours	11	9.09
	Total	**121**	**100.00**

Source: Computed.

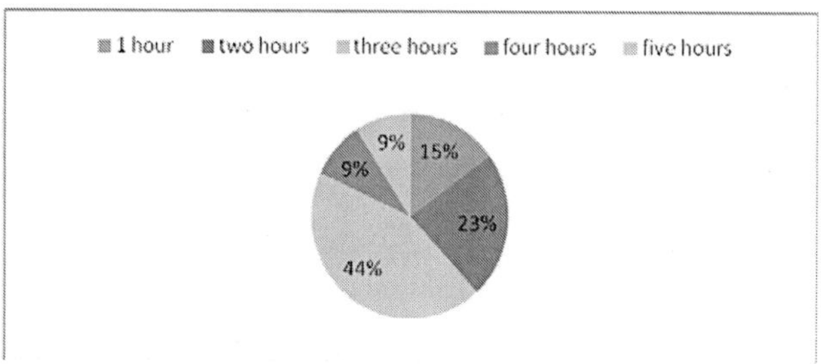

Table 47: Duration of Panchayat Council Meeting Conducted

Sl. No.	*Options*	*No. of Respondents*	*Percentage*
1.	One hour	33	27.27
2.	Two hours	50	41.32
3.	Three hours	37	30.59
4.	Four hours	1	0.82
	Total	**121**	**100.00**

Source: Computed.

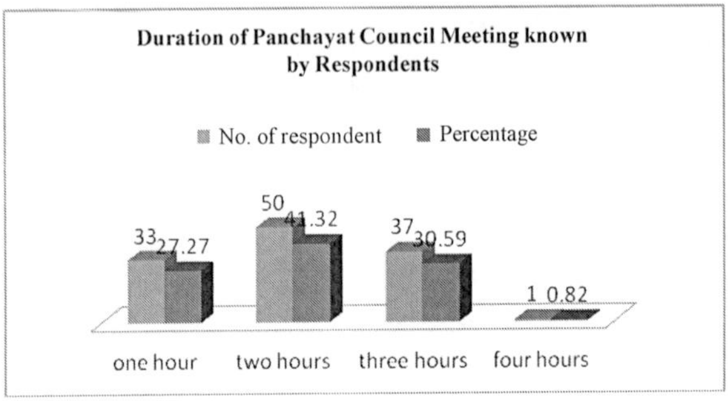

Table 48: Who Presides over the Meeting?

Sl. No.	*Options*	*No. of Respondents*	*Percentage*
1.	President	121	100.0
2.	Others	00	00
	Total	**121**	**100.0**

Source: Computed.

Table 49: Active Participation of Members

Sl.No.	*Options*	*No. of Respondents*	*Percentage*
1.	All members	90	74.38
2.	1 to 5 members	18	14.88
3.	8 members	13	10.74
	Total	**121**	**100.00**

Source: Computed.

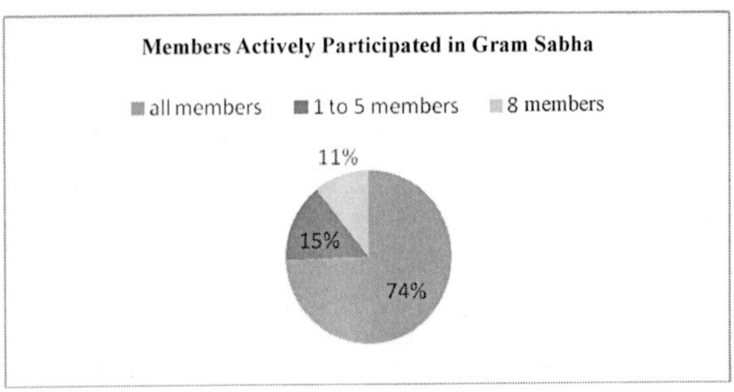

Table 50: Respondents Contact with Political Parties for their Election

Sl. No.	*Options*	*No. of Respondents*	*Percentage*
1.	Yes	50	41.32
2.	No	71	58.68
	Total	**121**	**100.00**

Source: Computed.

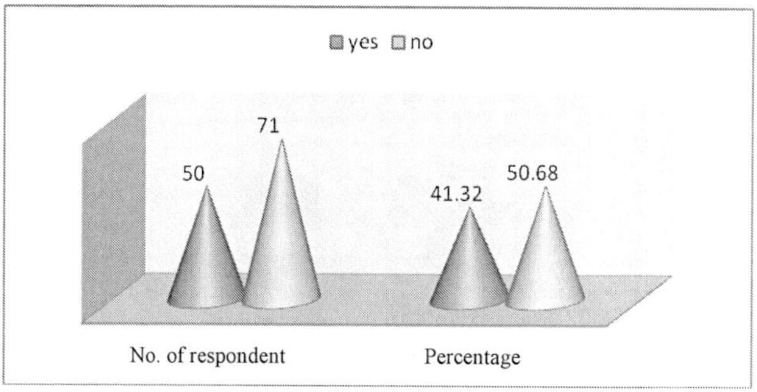

Table 51: Directly Contact Officials by the Respondents

Sl. No.	*Options*	*No. of Respondents*	*Percentage*
1.	Yes	104	85.96
2.	No	17	14.04
	Total	**121**	**100.00**

Source: Computed.

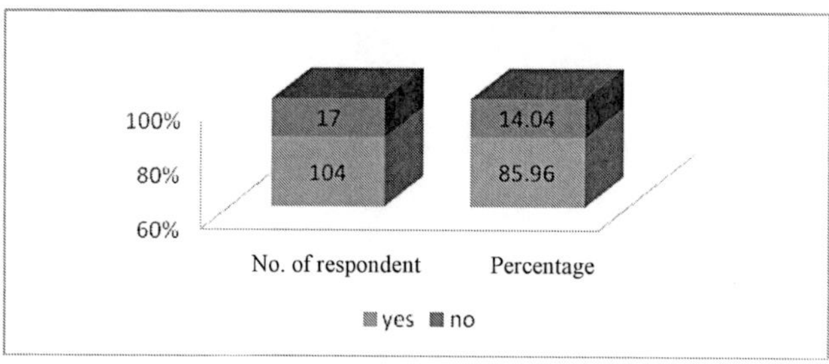

Table 52: Approaching Government Officials to Solve Problem in the Panchayats

Sl. No.	*Options*	*No. of Respondents*	*Percentage*
1.	Yes	110	90.91
2.	No	11	9.09
	Total	**121**	**100.00**

Source: Computed.

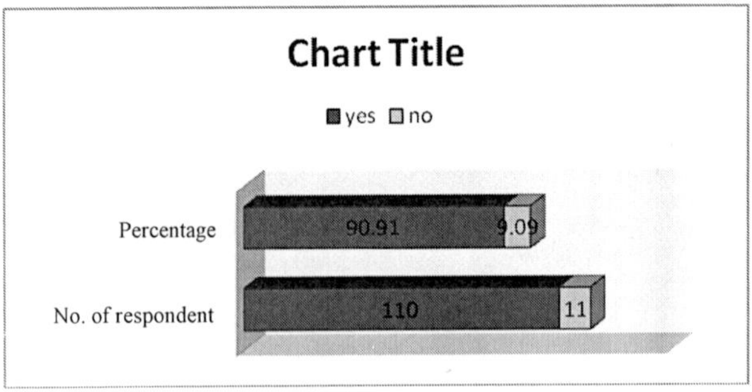

Table 53: Getting Positive Response from the Officials

Sl. No.	*Options*	*No. of Respondents*	*Percentage*
1.	Yes	104	85.96
2.	No	17	14.04
	Total	**121**	**100.00**

Source: Computed.

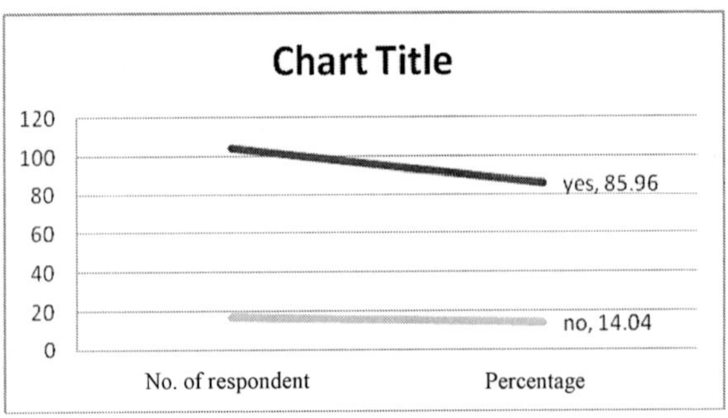

Table 54: Approaching Officials Regularly

Sl. No.	*Options*	*No. of Respondents*	*Percentage*
1.	Yes	107	88.43
2.	No	14	11.57
	Total	**121**	**100.00**

Source: Computed.

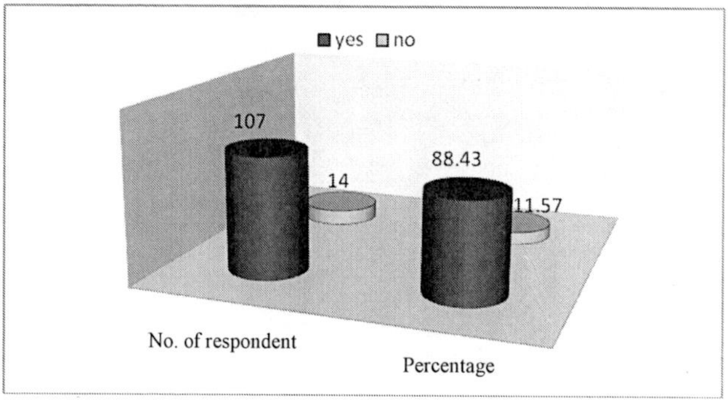

Table 55: Details of their Contact Officials

Sl. No.	*Options*	*No. of Respondents*	*Percentage*
1.	Project officer	16	13.22
2.	BDO	104	85.96
3.	Health officials	1	0.82
	Total	**121**	**100.00**

Source: Computed.

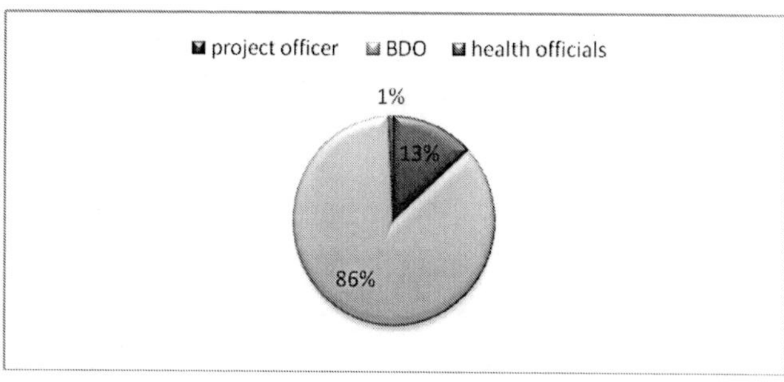

Table 56: Ensuring Maximum Presence of Women in Gram Sabha Meeting

Sl. No.	*Options*	*No. of Respondents*	*Percentage*
1.	Yes	121	100.0
2.	No	00	00
	Total	**121**	**100.0**

Table 57: Speakers in Gram Sabha Meeting

Sl. No.	*Options*	*No. of Respondents*	*Percentage*
1.	Women	98	81.00
2.	Dalit	1	0.82
3.	Men	3	2.48
4.	All	19	15.70
	Total	**121**	**100.00**

Source: Computed.

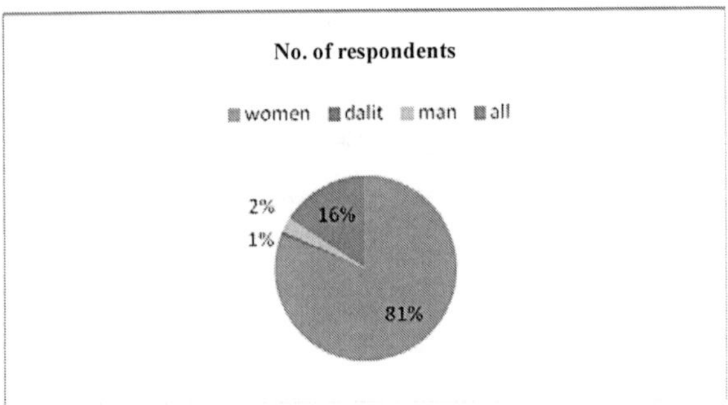

Table 58: Predominant Issues in Gram Sabha Meeting

Sl. No.	*Options*	*No. of Respondents*	*Percentage*
1.	Women	22	18.20
2.	Public service	17	14.04
3.	Road	1	0.83
4.	Water supply	12	9.91
5.	Agri, Livelihood, Social issues	1	0.83
6.	Other Development issues	68	56.19
	Total	**121**	**100.00**

Source: Computed.

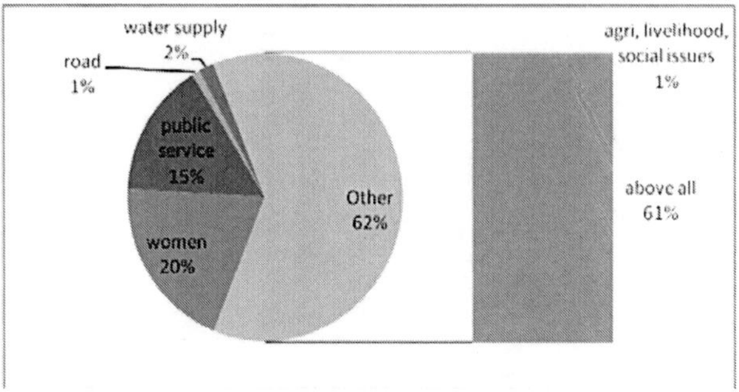

Table 59: Managing the Commons

Sl. No.	*Options*	*No. of Respondents*	*Percentage*
1.	Village Panchayat	95	78.51
2.	President	24	19.83
3.	Others	1	0.83
4.	No answer	1	0.83
	Total	**121**	**100.00**

Source: Computed.

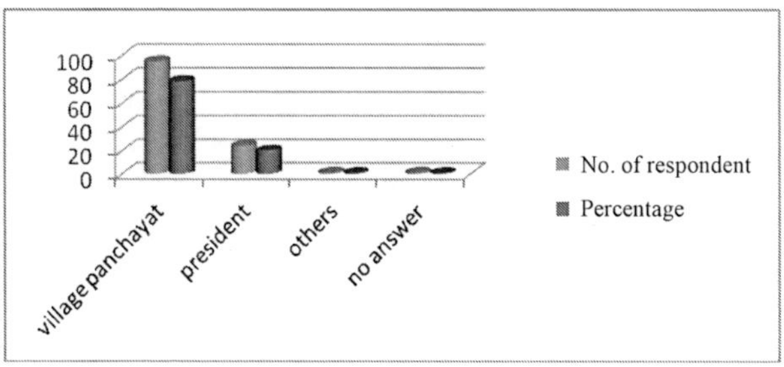

Table 60: Preparing Agenda for Gram Sabha Meeting

Sl. No.	*Options*	*No. of Respondents*	*Percentage*
1.	Government	46	38.01
2.	Panchayat leader	48	39.68
3.	Panchayat council	27	22.31
	Total	**121**	**100.00**

Source: Computed.

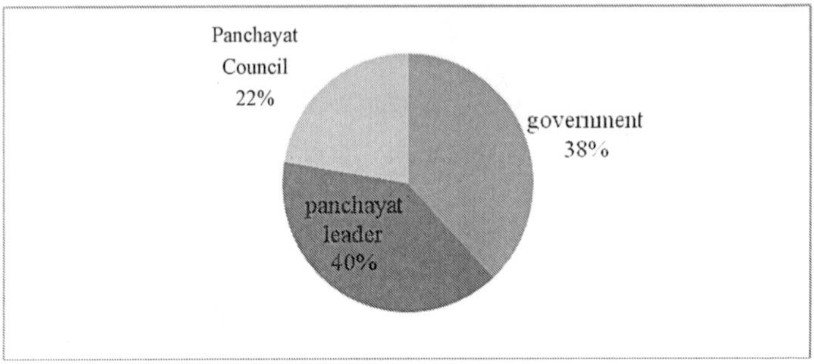

Table 61: Development Contact

Sl. No.	*Options*	*No. of Respondents*	*Percentage*
1	Rural Development	79	65.28
2	DRDA	37	30.59
3	Other Departments	5	4.13
	Total	**121**	**100.00**

Source: Computed.

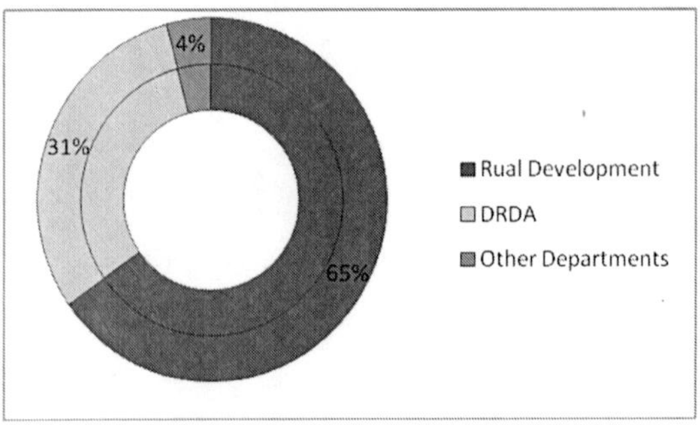

Table 62: Panchayat Accounts

Sl. No.	*Options*	*No. of Respondents*	*Percentage*
1.	5 Accounts	18	14.89
2.	6 Accounts	72	59.50
3.	7 Accounts	20	16.52
4.	More than 8 Accounts	11	9.09
	Total	**121**	**100.00**

Source: Computed.

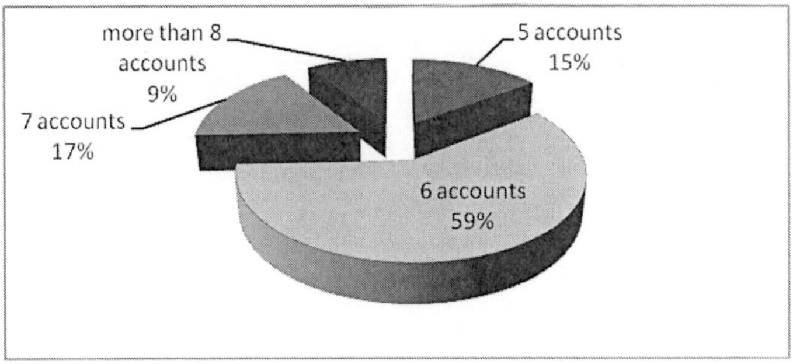

Table 63: Aware of the Roles

Sl. No.	*Options*	*No. of Respondents*	*Percentage*
1.	Yes	106	87.60
2.	No	15	12.40
	Total	**121**	**100.00**

Source: Computed.

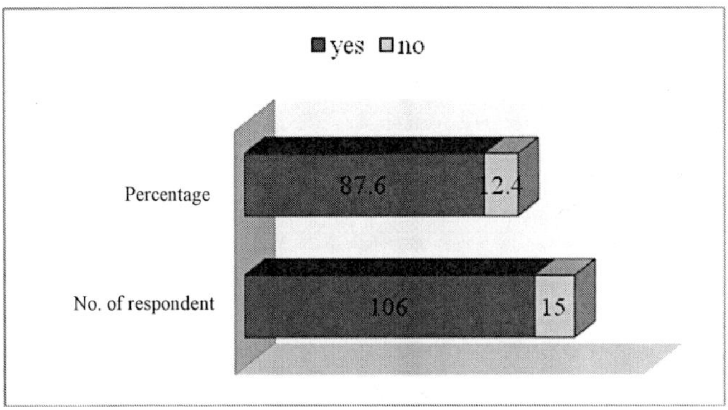

Table 64: Sending Letters

Sl. No.	*Options*	*No. of Respondents*	*Percentage*
1.	Yes	89	73.56
2.	No	32	26.44
	Total	**121**	**100.00**

Source: Computed.

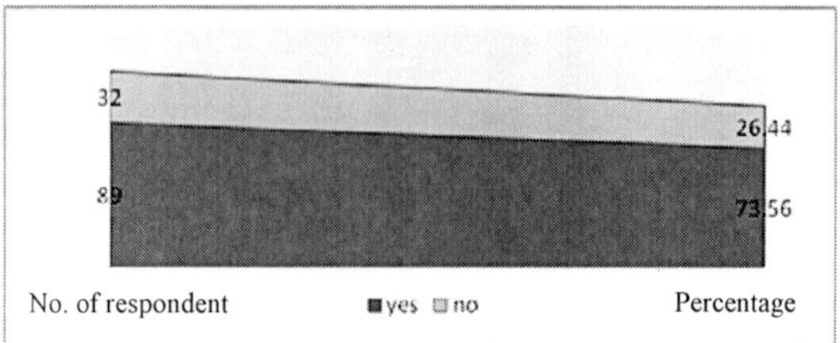

Table 65: Respondents Visit to Anganwadi

Sl. No.	*Options*	*No. of Respondents*	*Percentage*
1.	Yes	110	90.91
2.	No	11	9.09
	Total	**121**	**100.00**

Source: Computed.

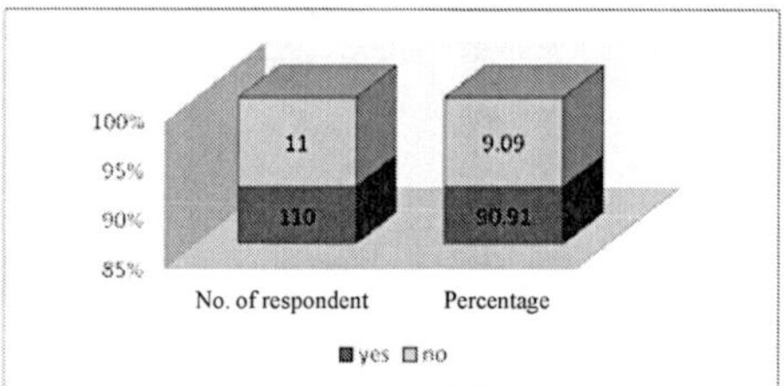

Table 66: Respondents Visit to PDS Shop

Sl. No.	*Options*	*No. of Respondents*	*Percentage*
1.	Yes	110	90.91
2.	No	11	9.09
	Total	**121**	**100.00**

Source: Computed.

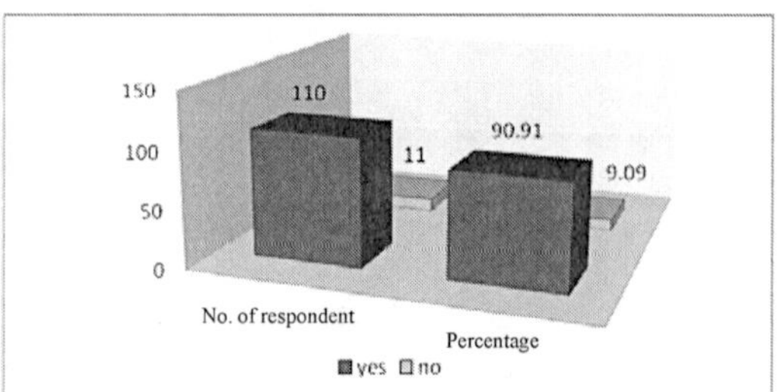

Table 67: Respondents' Visit to Schools

Sl.No.	*Options*	*No. of Respondents*	*Percentage*
1.	Yes	121	100.0
2.	No	00	00
	Total	**121**	**100.0**

Source: Computed.

Table 68: Respondent Attend the Function

Sl. No.	*Options*	*No. of Respondents*	*Percentage*
1.	Yes	109	90.09
2.	No	12	9.91
	Total	**121**	**100.00**

Source: Computed.

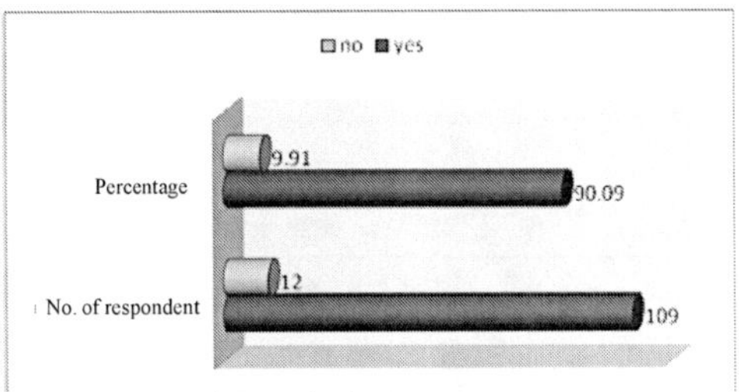

Table 69: Respondents Involvement in Enrollment Drive

Sl. No.	*Options*	*No. of Respondents*	*Percentage*
1.	Yes	105	86.78
2.	No	16	13.22
	Total	**121**	**100.00**

Source: Computed.

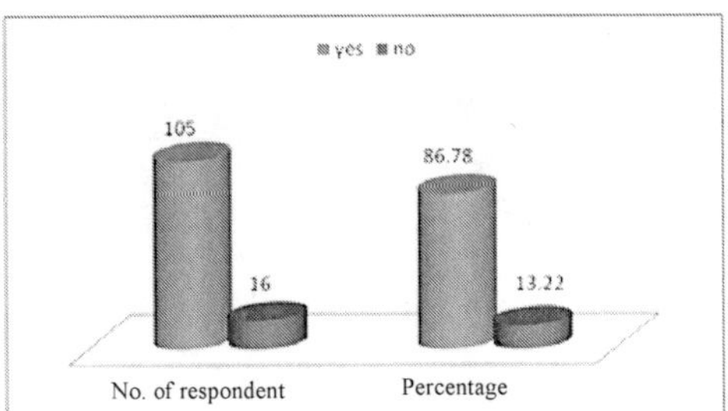

Table 70: Presence of Traditional Panchayats

Sl. No.	*Options*	*No. of Respondents*	*Percentage*
1.	Yes	102	84.30
2.	No	19	15.70
	Total	**121**	**100.00**

Source: Computed.

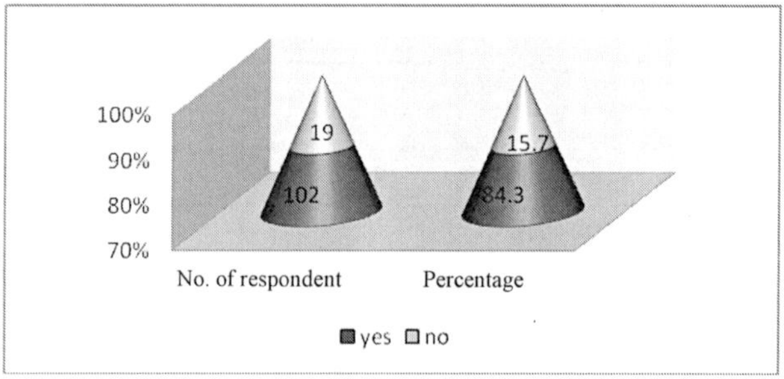

Table 71: Parallel Body Presence in Panchayats

Sl. No.	*Options*	*No. of Respondents*	*Percentage*
1.	Yes	70	57.86
2.	No	51	42.14
	Total	**121**	**100.00**

Source: Computed.

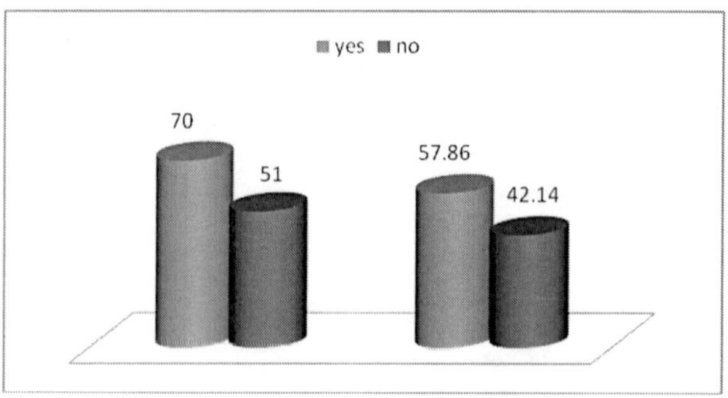

Table 72: Attending all the Officials Meeting

Sl. No.	*Options*	*No. of Respondents*	*Percentage*
1.	Yes	121	100.0
2.	No	00	00
	Total	**121**	**100.0**

Source: Computed.

Table 73: Going to Panchayat Office Regularly

Sl. No.	*Options*	*No. of Respondents*	*Percentage*
1.	Yes	110	90.91
2.	No	11	9.09
	Total	**121**	**100.00**

Source: Computed.

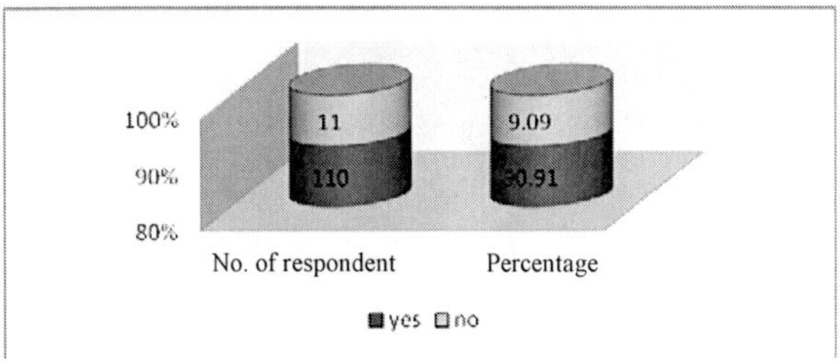

Table 74: Maintain Officials' Record

Sl. No.	*Options*	*No. of Respondents*	*Percentage*
1.	Office	110	90.91
2.	Other place	11	9.09
	Total	**121**	**100.00**

Source: Computed.

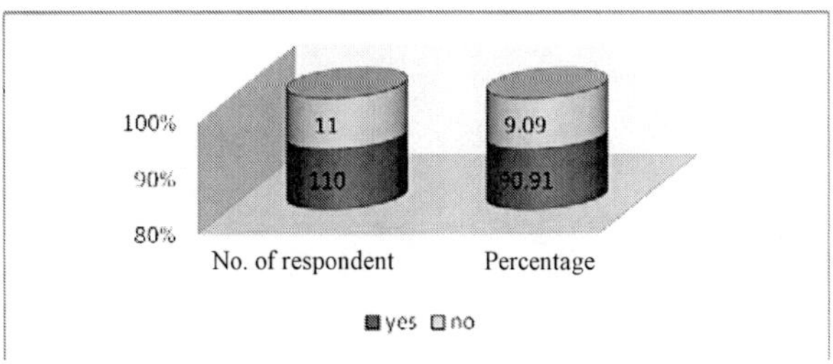

Table 75: Aware of Panchayat Act of Tamil Nadu

Sl. No.	*Options*	*No. of Respondents*	*Percentage*
1.	Yes	91	75.20
2.	No	30	24.80
	Total	**121**	**100.00**

Source: Computed.

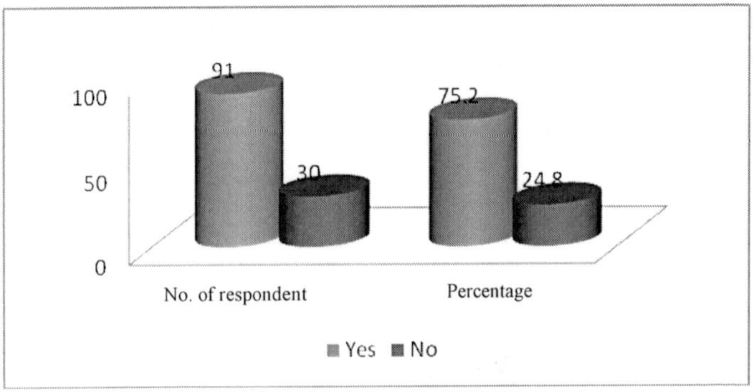

Table 76: Aware of Rules and Procedures of the Panchayats

Sl. No	*Options*	*No of Respondents*	*Percentage*
1.	Yes	107	88.42
2.	No	14	11.58
	Total	**121**	**100.00**

Source: Computed.

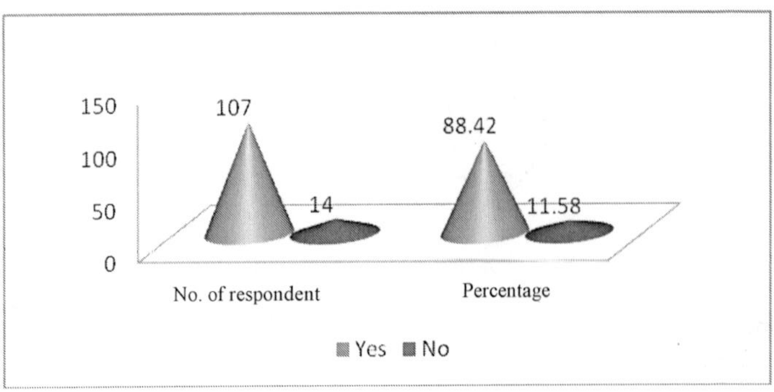

Table 77: Aware of the Schemes of Rural Development

Sl. No.	*Options*	*No. of Respondents*	*Percentage*
1.	Yes	108	89.26
2.	No	13	10.74
	Total	**121**	**100.00**

Source: Computed.

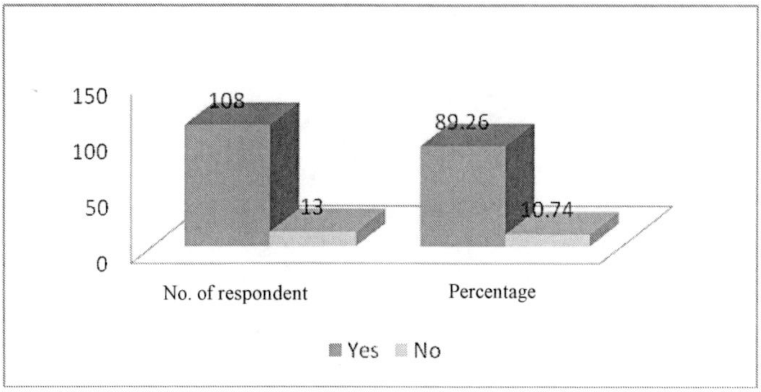

Table 78: Aware of the Reservation of Seats for Women

Sl. No.	*Options*	*No. of Respondents*	*Percentage*
1.	Yes	105	86.78
2.	No	16	13.22
	Total	**121**	**100.00**

Source: Computed.

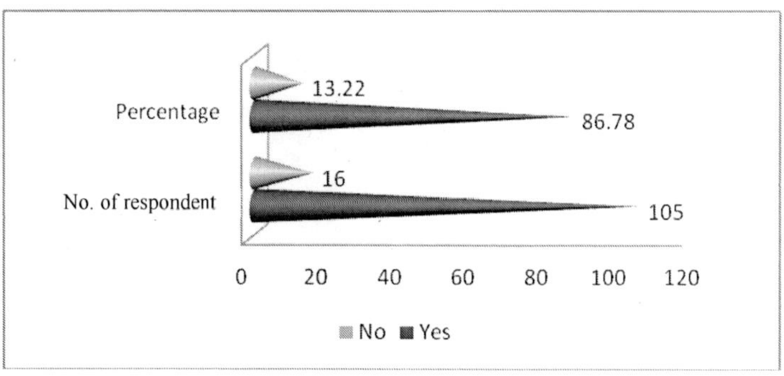

Table 79: Getting the Government orders properly

Sl. No.	Options	No. of Respondents	Percentage
1.	Yes	107	88.42
2.	No	14	11.58
	Total	**121**	**100.00**

Source: Computed.

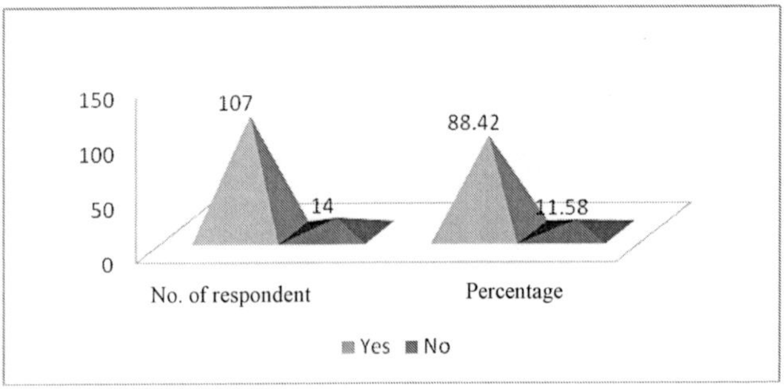

Table 80: Respondents Affiliation with political party

Sl. No.	Affiliated with political party	No. of Respondent	Percentage
1.	Yes	90	74.39
2.	No	31	25.61
	Total	**121**	**100.00**

Source: Computed.

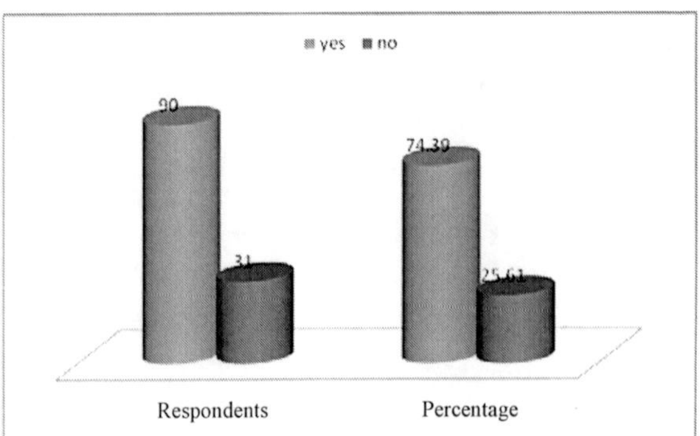

Table 81: Respondents' Families Affiliation with Political Party

Sl. No.	*Options*	*No. of Respondents*	*Percentage*
1.	Yes	84	69.42
2.	No	37	30.58
	Total	**121**	**100.00**

Source: Computed.

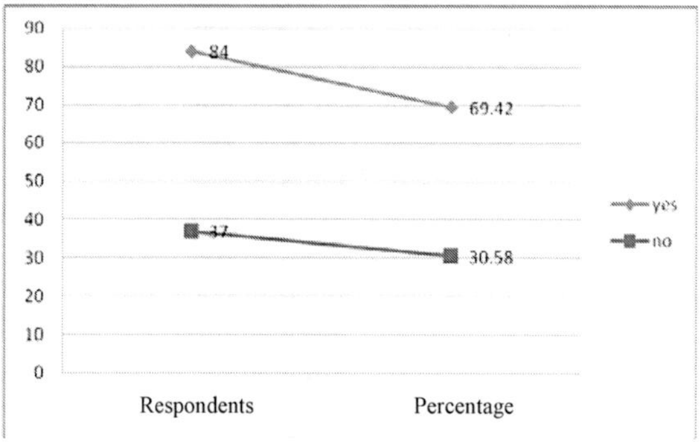

Table 82: Respondent's Meeting with Political Leaders

Sl. No.	*Options*	*No. of Respondents*	*Percentage*
1.	Yes	101	83.48
2.	No	20	16.52
	Total	**121**	**100.00**

Source: Computed.

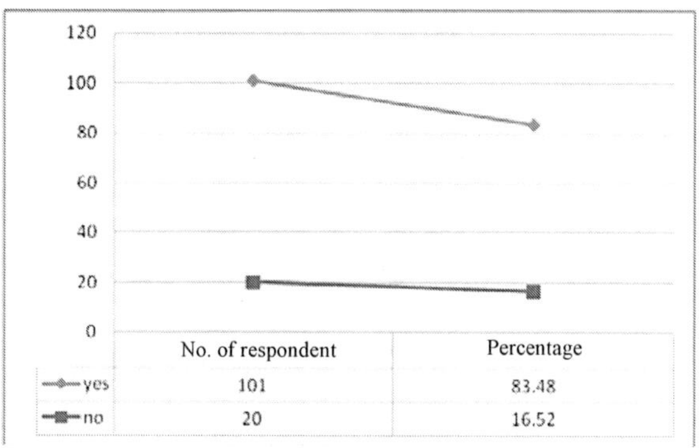

Table 83: Attending Meeting in Various Places

Sl. No.	Options	No. of Respondents	Percentage
1.	Yes	93	76.86
2.	No	28	23.14
	Total	**121**	**100.00**

Source: Computed.

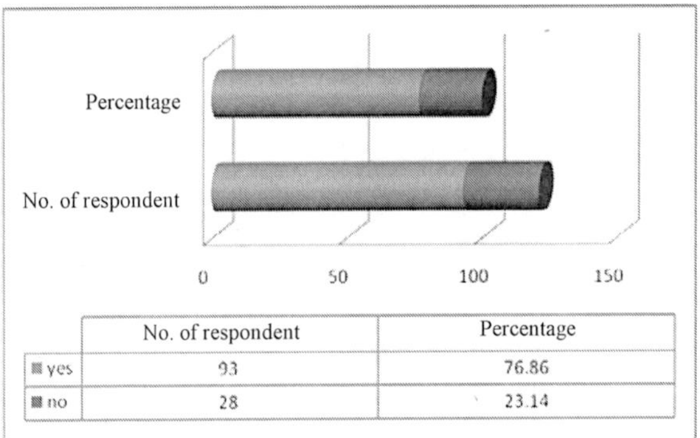

Table 84: Member of Social Organisations

Sl. No.	Options	No. of Respondents	Percentage
1.	Yes	27	22.31
2.	No	94	77.69
	Total	**121**	**100.00**

Source: Computed.

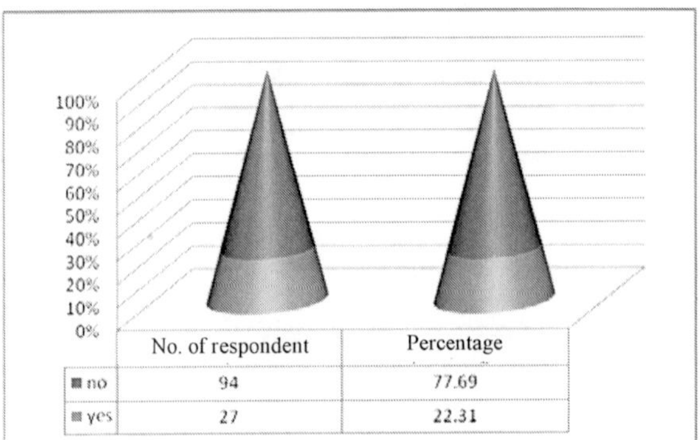

Table 85: Member of any Livelihood Organisations

Sl. No.	*Options*	*No. of Respondents*	*Percentage*
1.	Yes	92	76.03
2.	No	29	23.97
	Total	**121**	**100.00**

Source: Computed.

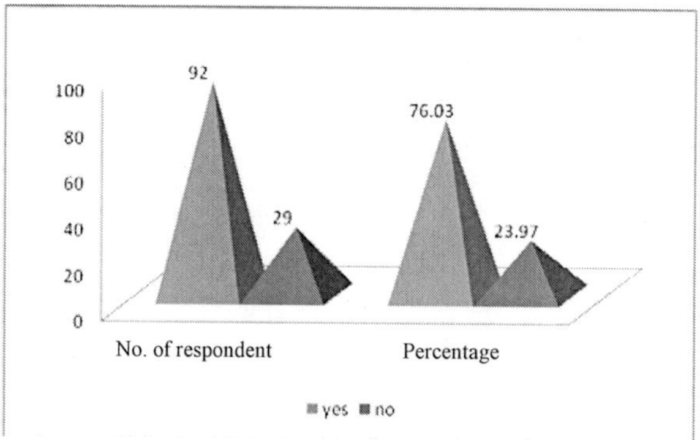

Table 86: Respondent Position in the Organisation

Sl. No.	*Options*	*No. of Respondents*	*Percentage*
1.	President	28	23.14
2.	Member	75	61.99
3.	No answer	18	14.87
	Total	**121**	**100.00**

Source: Computed.

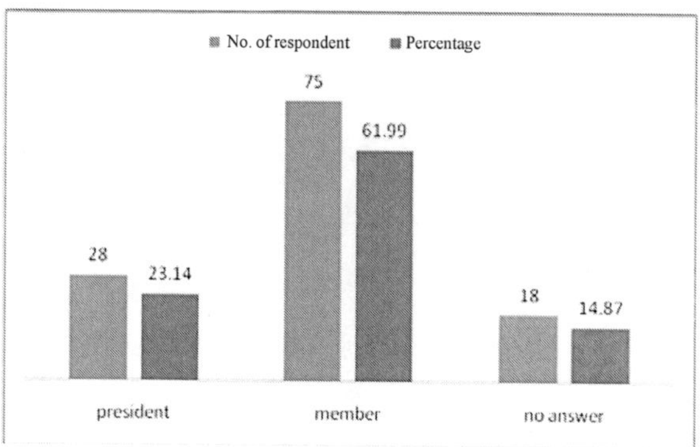

Table 87: Getting Benefits from Organisation Individually

Sl. No.	*Options*	*No. of Respondents*	*Percentage*
1.	Yes	46	38.01
2.	No	75	61.99
	Total	**121**	**100.00**

Source: Computed.

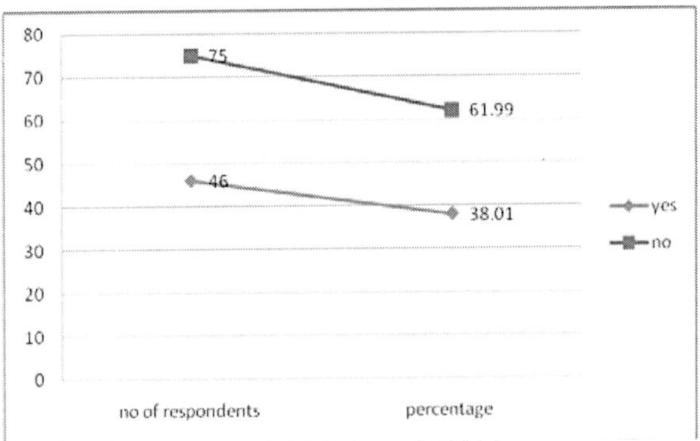

Table 88: Respondent Involvement in SHG Movement in Tamil Nadu

Sl. No.	*Options*	*No. of Respondents*	*Percentage*
1.	Yes	69	57.02
2.	No	52	42.98
	Total	**121**	**100.00**

Source: Computed.

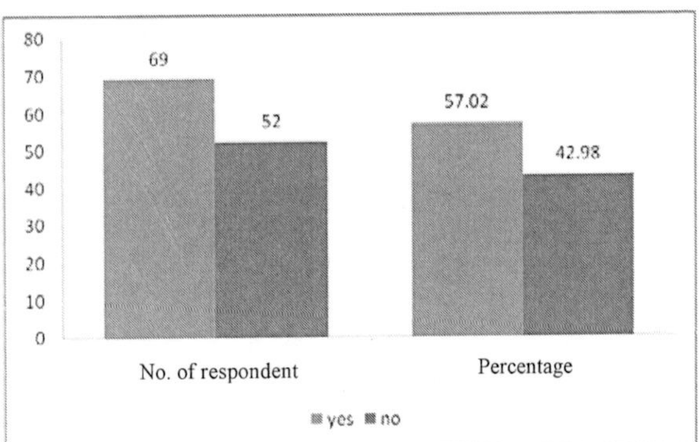

Table 89: Taking Decisions Individually

Sl. No.	*Options*	*No. of Respondents*	*Percentage*
1.	Yes	104	85.96
2.	No	17	14.04
	Total	**121**	**100.00**

Source: Computed.

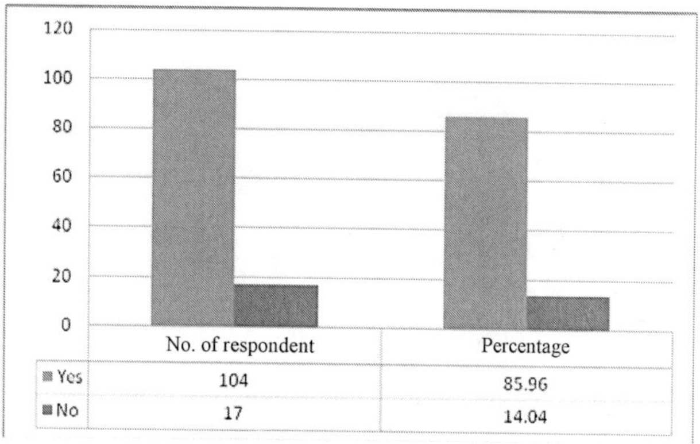

Table 90: Respondents Dream of Village Development

Sl. No.	*Options*	*No. of Respondents*	*Percentage*
1.	Yes	109	90.09
2.	No	12	9.91
	Total	**121**	**100.00**

Source: Computed.

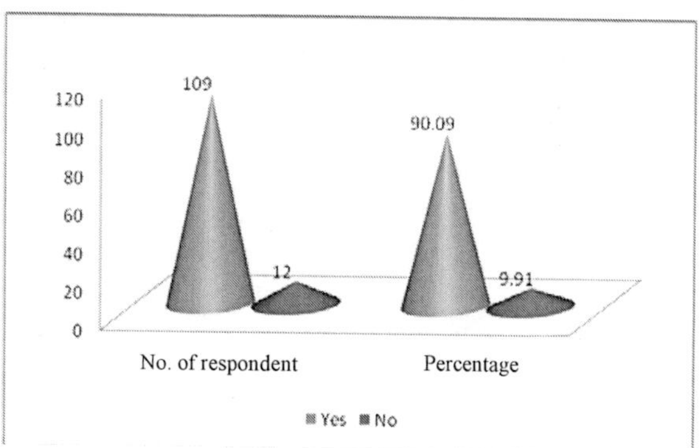

Table 91: Thorough on Responsibilities

Sl. No.	*Options*	*No. of Respondents*	*Percentage*
1.	Yes	104	85.96
2.	No	17	14.04
	Total	**121**	**100.00**

Source: Computed.

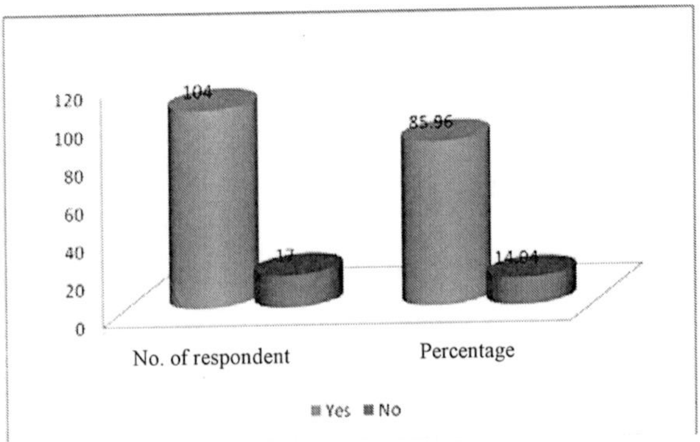

Table 92: Speaking to Officials Directly

Sl. No.	*Options*	*No. of Respondents*	*Percentage*
1.	Yes	109	90.09
2.	No	12	9.91
	Total	**121**	**100.00**

Source: Computed.

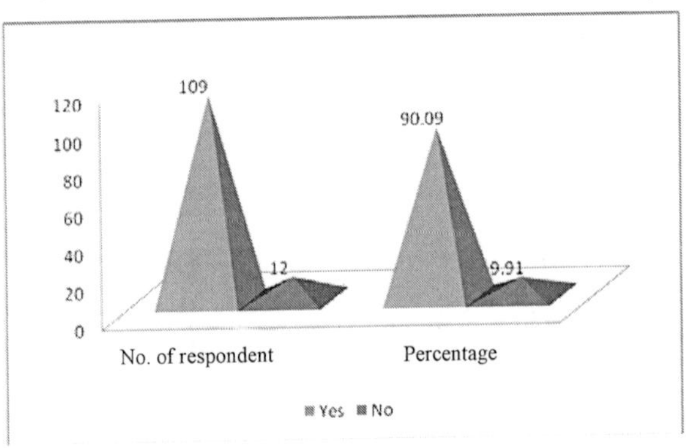

Table 93: Respondents Speak in Public Meetings

Sl. No.	*Options*	*No. of Respondents*	*Percentage*
1.	Yes	97	80.17
2.	No	24	19.83
	Total	**121**	**100.00**

Source: Computed.

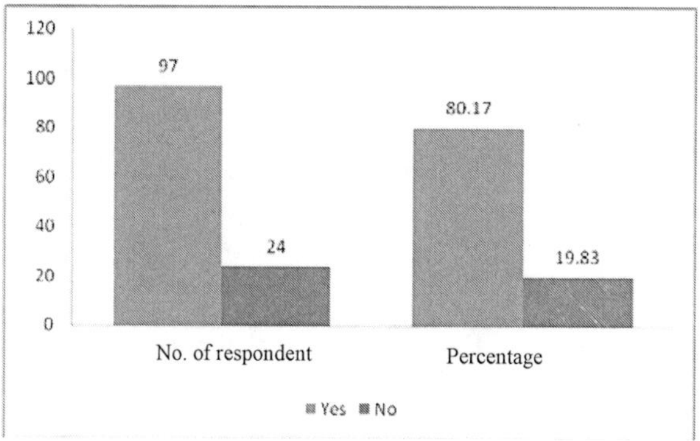

Table 94: Attending Training Programme by Respondents

Sl. No.	*Options*	*No. of Respondents*	*Percentage*
1.	Yes	110	90.91
2.	No	11	9.09
	Total	**121**	**100.00**

Source: Computed.

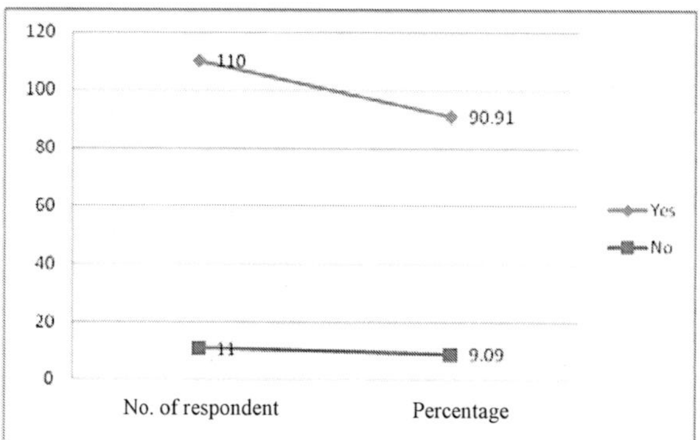

Table 95: Trainings have Enhanced the Capacity

Sl. No.	*Options*	*No. of Respondents*	*Percentage*
1.	Yes	110	90.91
2.	No	11	9.09
	Total	**121**	**100.00**

Source: Computed.

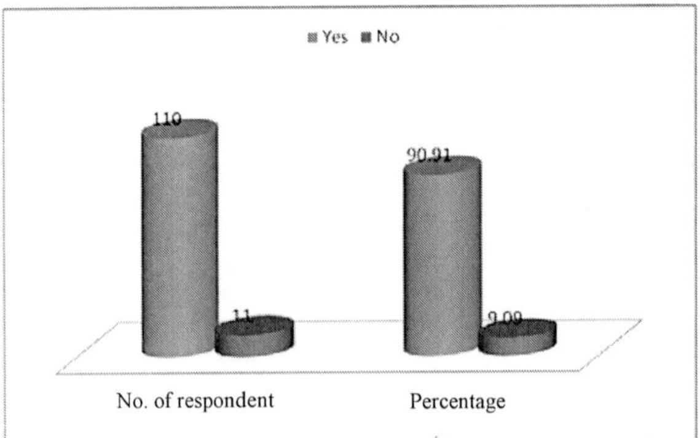

Table 96: Availability of Administrative Manual

Sl. No.	*Options*	*No. of Respondents*	*Percentage*
1.	Yes	108	89.26
2.	No	13	10.74
	Total	**121**	**100.00**

Source: Computed.

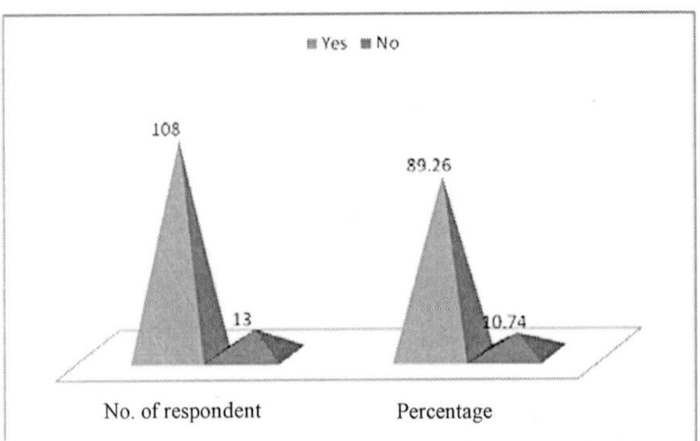

Table 97: Giving Promise to the People to Seek their Votes

Sl. No.	*Options*	*No. of Respondents*	*Percentage*
1.	Yes	106	87.60
2.	No	15	12.40
	Total	**121**	**100.00**

Source: Computed.

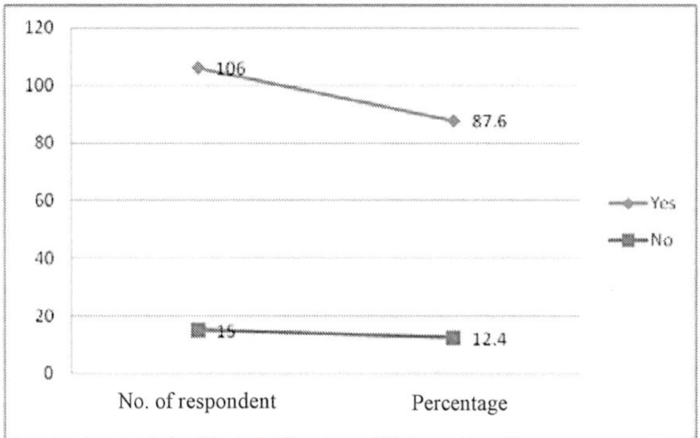

Table 98: Participate in all the meetings along with men leaders

Sl. No.	*Options*	*No. of Respondents*	*Percentage*
1.	Yes	105	86.78
2.	No	16	13.22
	Total	**121**	**100.00**

Source: Computed.

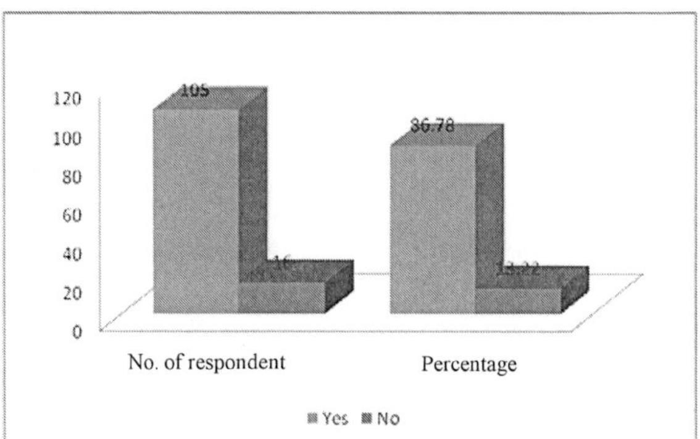

Table 99: Respondent's Job Satisfaction

Sl. No.	*Options*	*No. of Respondents*	*Percentage*
1.	Yes	106	87.60
2.	No	15	12.40
	Total	**121**	**100.00**

Source: Computed.

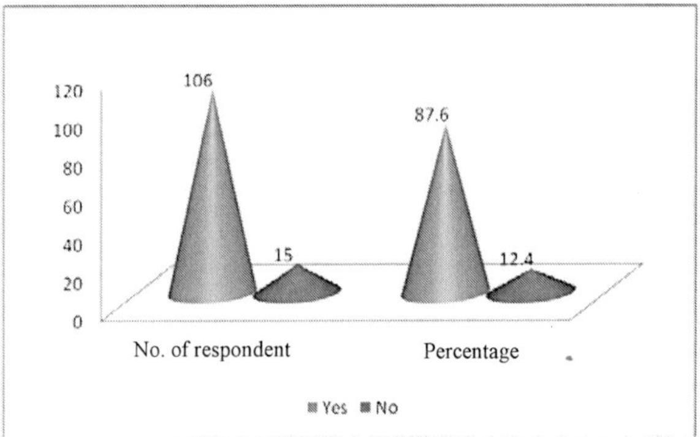

Table 100: Problems in Family Front

Sl. No.	*Options*	*No. of Respondents*	*Percentage*
1.	Yes	11	9.09
2.	No	110	90.91
	Total	**121**	**100.00**

Source: Computed.

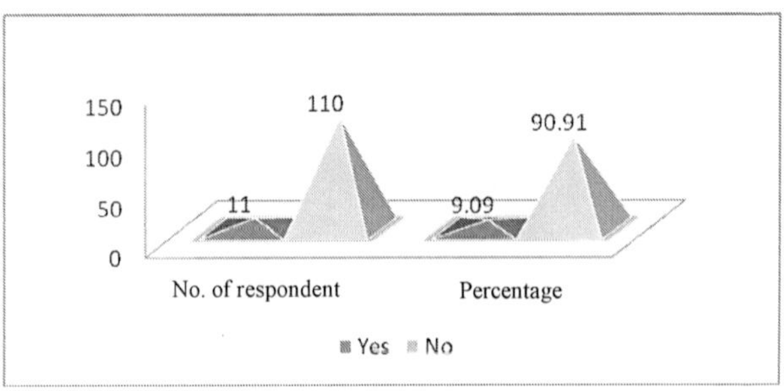

Table 101: Problems in Community Front

Sl. No.	Options	No. of Respondents	Percentage
1.	Yes	17	14.04
2.	No	104	85.96
	Total	**121**	**100.00**

Source: Computed.

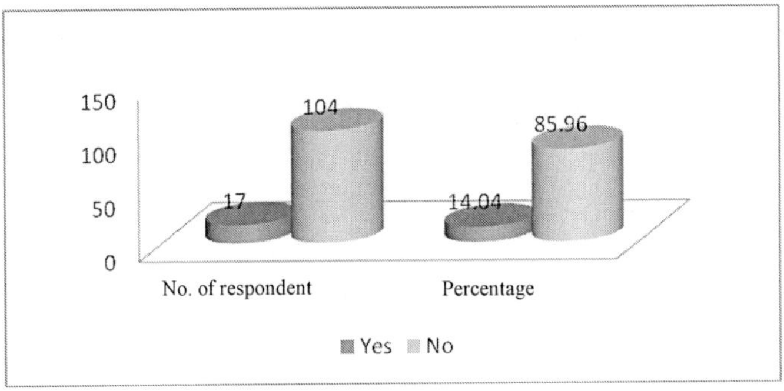

Table 102: Problems in Panchayat Council

Sl. No.	Options	No. of Respondents	Percentage
1.	Yes	11	9.09
2.	No	110	90.91
	Total	**121**	**100.00**

Source: Computed.

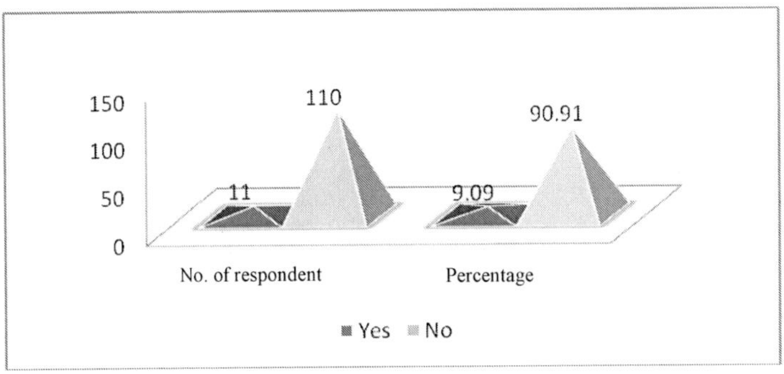

Table 103: Problems from the Family and Community while Contesting in the Election

Sl. No.	*Options*	*No. of Respondents*	*Percentage*
1.	Yes	12	9.91
2.	No	109	90.09
	Total	**121**	**100.00**

Source: Computed.

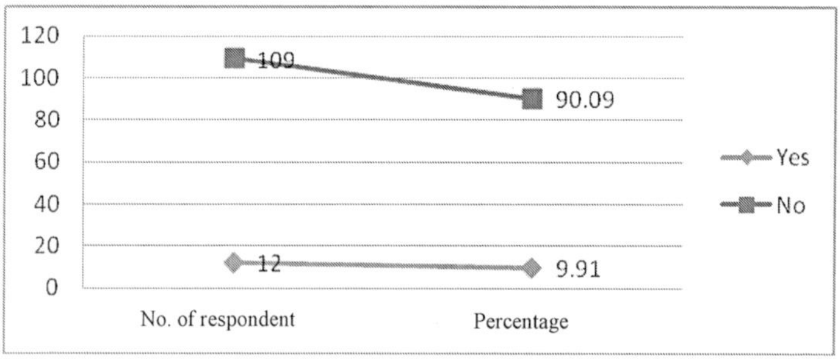

Table 104: Making Model a Village

Sl. No.	*Options*	*No. of Respondents*	*Percentage*
1.	Yes	101	83.48
2.	No	20	16.52
	Total	**121**	**100.00**

Source: Computed.

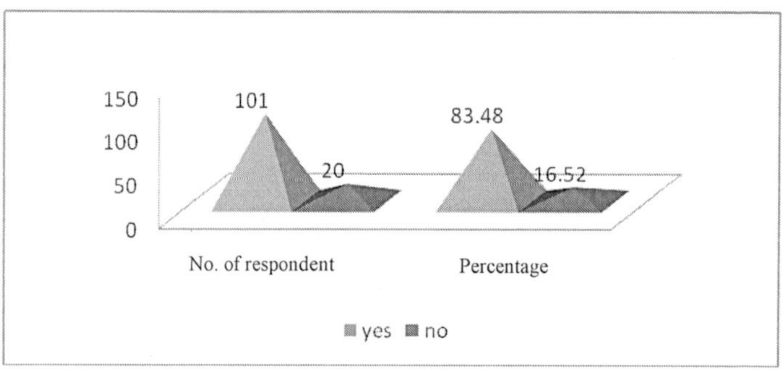

Table 105: Taking Steps in Income Generation for Poor

Sl. No.	*Options*	*No. of Respondents*	*Percentage*
1.	Yes	105	86.78
2.	No	16	13.22
	Total	**121**	**100.00**

Source: Computed.

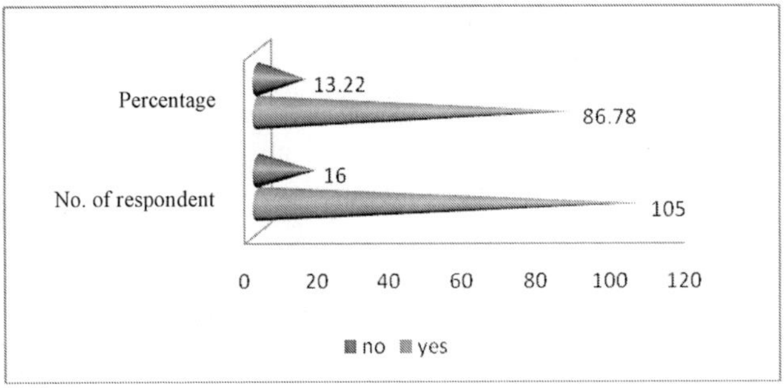

Opportunity structure is nothing but an enabling environment to make use of the opportunity. Enabling environment has to be created by the state governments and what are the steps to be taken by the government has been given in the following diagrams:

Once above imperative requirements are fulfilled by the state, evaluation of the performance comes. Evaluation has to be done by following indicators:

Reservation of seats for women is an opportunity. Equipping themselves through various efforts on the part of individuals and institutions is to manage the grassroots institutions and it is part and parcel of opportunity structure. So far the processes of equipping themselves have been explained. By handling the governing institutions and establishing contact with political institutions the Elected Women Representatives build their capacity, skill and capability. By doing so they prepare themselves to tackle the critical issues namely, the development issues of women and other marginalised. The opportunity structure is fully utilised by the elected women representatives. Yet they are not empowered.

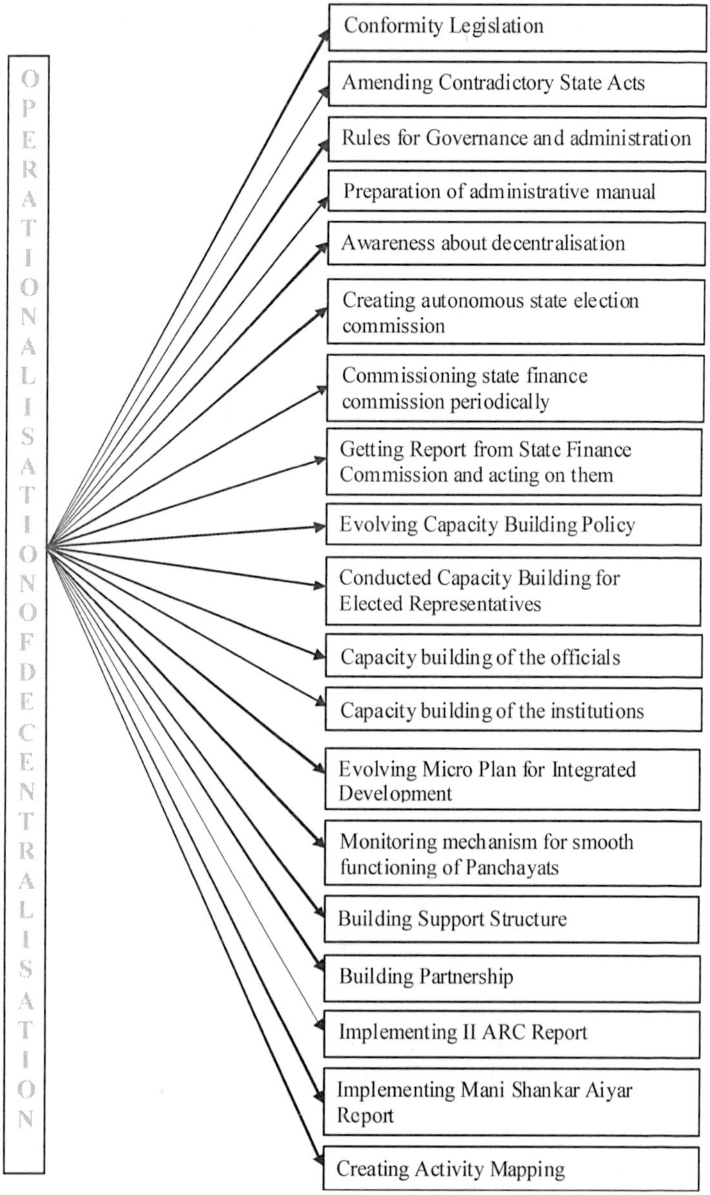

Figure II – Framework of Operationalisation of Decentralisation.

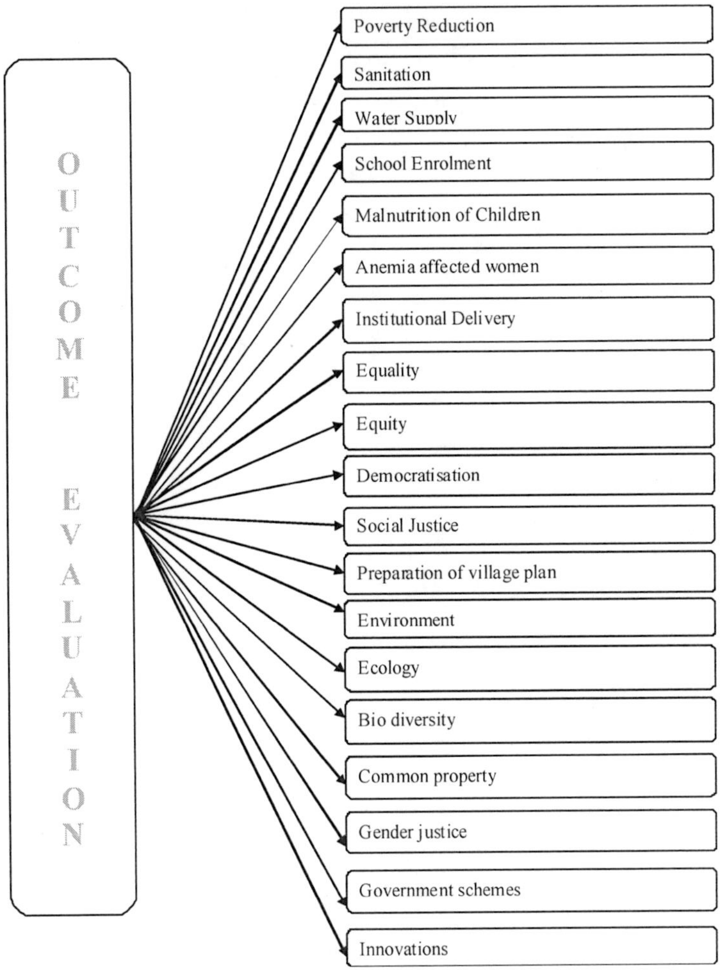

Figure III – Outcome Evaluation.

Notes and References

1. Palanithurai, G, Role Perception of Legislators, New Delhi: Konark Publication, 1991.
2. Palanithurai, G, Vallinayagam, K, Chidambaram N.S. and Subramaniam K, Handbook of Panchayati Raj Administration (Tamil Nadu), New Delhi: Concept Publishing Company, 2007.

3. Palanithurai, G, Problems Faced by the Elected Women Representatives (Monograph) Gandhigram: Rajiv Gandhi Chair Panchayati Raj Studies, 2002.

4. Palanithurai, G, Uma, G and Vanishree, J, Networking of Elected Women Representatives at Grassroots, New Delhi: Concept Publishing Company, 2010.

Chapter - V

Empowerment and Achievements

Normally achievements are considered as unique steps taken by the Elected Women Representatives distinctively different from others. There are obligatory responsibilities and duties assigned to the elected representatives whether they are men or women. All the assigned responsibilities have to be discharged by everyone. Since the respondents are the Gram Panchayat presidents, they have to perform the assigned responsibilities. They are explained here under:

Village Panchayat

A Village Panchayat or Gram Panchayat is constituted for a minimum of five hundred populations. But there are 60 Panchayats do not have even 500 populations. In the Village Panchayat the Ward Members and the President, are to be elected directly by the voters. The Vice-President of the Village Panchayat is elected indirectly from among the elected Ward Members of the Village Panchayat. The Village Panchayat has to look after the following subjects:

(a) Construction, repair and maintenance of Village Panchayat roads;

(b) Lighting of public roads and public places;

(c) Providing drainage facilities;

(d) Extension of village sites and the regulation of buildings;

(e) Sinking and repairing of wells, the excavation repair and maintenance of ponds or tanks and the construction and maintenance of water works for the supply of water;
(f) Maintenance of parks and reading rooms;
(g) Implementation of schemes such as Indira Awaas Yojona (IAY) and National Rural Employment Guarantee Scheme (NREGS);
(h) Cleaning of streets;
(i) Providing public latrines;
(j) Providing burial and burning grounds;
(k) Providing water for washing and bathing purposes and
(l) Such other duties notified by the government then and there.

Resources

Village Panchayat has got the following sources of revenue:

(a) *Tax Revenue:* Of the three tier Panchayats, Village Panchayat alone has got power to levy taxes. House tax, profession tax and Advertisement tax are the commonly levied taxes.
(b) *Non Tax Revenue:* Licensing fees for building plan and layout approval, fees charges on dangerous and offensive trades, water charges, fees on cart stands, fishery rentals, 2c pattas fees, income from markets and fairs, ferries, fines and penalties and so on.
(c) *Assigned and Shared Revenue:* It includes the in terms pooled at the state level (surcharge on stamp duty and entertainment tax) which are released by the Director of Rural Development and Panchayati Raj to all the three tiers of the Panchayats including the village Panchayats. Other items of assigned and shared revenues for the Village Panchayats include the seigiorage fees (100 per cent) and lease amount 50 per cent share on minor minerals and social forestry auctions amount.
(d) *Grants:* Central Finance Commission Grant, State Finance Commission Grant, Development Grants under centrally sponsored and state schemes.

Administrative Powers

Gram Panchayat have been empowered to give administrative sanction and executive individual works upto Rs 2 lakh from their general funds. It has been given powers to execute urgent works upto Rs 2000 at a time and upto Rs 5000 for a year without anybody's permission. The President can draw self cheque upto Rs 500 to meet contingent expenditure. It can attend to repairs and maintenance of hand pumps, power pumps and Rs 7500 per power pump per year without reference to engineer for preparation of estimates or passing of bills. In order to encourage the Village Panchayats to carryout innovative works in the villages Uthamar Gandhi Village Panchayat awards are being given to the best adjusted Panchayats based on their performance. A citation with Rs 5 lakh cash award is being given to each best adjusted best Gram Panchayats. They are minimum. Even while performing the task, the elected representatives can adopt different methods for execution to bring maximum outcome without flouting the established rules. Apart from the assigned responsibilities, the elected represen-tatives assume certain responsibilities and perform certain duties which are unique to their Panchayats (The Hunger Project, 2006, 2007, 2008, 2009, and 2010).

For the Panchayats who walk extra mile by performing their functions extraordinarily awards and recognitions are given. Panchayats are given awards and incentives for their best performance. This kind of incentivisation has enabled the Panchayats to compete with each other for achieving unique things in Panchayats. They are being recognised for their initiatives. The respondents around 90 per cent replied that they know the incentives, recognitions and awards are given for the outstanding performances. They replied that they are taking earnest efforts. But only 14 per cent said that they got awards and recognitions from the state and central governments. Later when it was verified that they got certificates from the organisations for their participation in the programme without knowing the details they have informed us that they have received awards. Nearly 74 per cent of the respondents replied that they have created durable assets created through their actions. All the assets they have indicated are the assets created through MGNREGA scheme. Only 25 per cent of the elected women representatives replied that they have created assets worth gathering income for the Panchayats. Eighty two per cent of the respondents informed that they are being invited for public functions and they are attending all the functions. Fifteen per cent of the elected women representatives have informed us that they have visited other places to get to know the development takes place there. It is interesting to note that 17 per cent of the elected representatives have gone to foreign countries. Some of them related to study visit as they are helped by the civil society organisations. Ninety per cent of the elected representatives responded that they have disseminated the knowledge which they have gained through training, government offices and exposure visits. Eighty nine per cent of the respondents replied that they have created awareness among the people about sanitation, water management, and prenatal and post-natal care. Many of them tried do it through Gram Sabha meeting. Some of them have done through Self Help Group meetings. Since government departments are driving the Panchayats to help them to disseminate development information to the public, they do it periodically and for which government is also helping. Gram Sabha is a major vehicle for such a kind of task. It is almost a crowd management. Eighty eight per cent of the representatives said that they are able to manage the crowd. It is very interesting to note that 57 per cent of the respondents said that their family workload has been reduced. It is a major problem among the SHG women and elected women representatives that the workload of the family is a problem. Now it has been reduced continuously. With regard to the condition of the roads, facilities in the schools, attendance of teachers in the school and activities of the anganwadi workers, and ANM 90 per cent of the respondents informed that they are fine. One could see lot of improvements after the interventions of the Panchayats. As per the responses of the respondents the Panchayat have performed the assigned duties well and as a result, all service delivery activities have been carried out very well. In all the villages after the interaction with the elected women representatives the investigators have extensively visited the Panchayat areas and interacted with the public by adopting different methods with regard to the services of the Gram Panchayat.

Critical Functions

It is expected that the critical mass has to perform the critical functions. The elected women representatives have to address the issues of discriminatory practices based on caste and gender. It requires commitment, perspective, strategy and skill. How these issues are tackled by the Elected Women Representatives is being elicited from them. Thirty eight per cent of respondents informed that they have directly intervened on untouchability practices and tackled it. Twenty four per cent of them expressed that they have eradicated the double tumbler system. Twenty eight per cent of them have intervened in many of these activities. In the same way 68 per cent of them have replied that they have taken up the gender issues for redressal. Eighty seven per cent of the respondents said that they have intervened on the issues of women and Dalit. All women who are coming to Gram Sabha meeting are allowed to speak. Among women there are Dalit women, and they are also encouraged to speak in Gram Sabha meetings. Eighty five per cent of the representatives informed that they had a practice of mobilising people for common action. They have further informed that they have used all institutional mechanisms to redress the grievances of the people. Ninety per cent of the respondents felt that there is possibility to get justice for women in the judicial system. Thirty one per cent of the Elected Women Representatives have approached judiciary for redressal of grievance of women. While reading the above one should not come to a conclusion that everything is fine in Tamil Nadu. Here the boxes bring the other side of the stories.

Box – A: Traditional Panchayats in Maharashtra
A 42 year old Dalit widow Rekha Arun Chavan was tripped and beaten up in her own village (Malegaon) in Maharashtra, a most industrialised state, for the reason that her son Amol allegedly eloped with a Maratha girl Anita Desai. This incident happened in his own village of the Maharashtra Chief Minister Prithviraj Chavan. People who were involved in beaten up the poor widow had admitted and they argued that the community has taken such a decision. It was taken in "Tanta Mukti Samiti" (a traditional committee to resolve caste disputes in every village in Maharashtra) and accordingly the Dalit widow was given a

punishment. The poor widow asked a question "would they have tortured me the same way had I not been a Dalit?" The whole incident took place in front of many that too in the presence of other Dalit men and women. Nobody prevented and interfered when she was beaten up by the caste Hindus. It is to be noted here that in Maharashtra there is a practice under Mahatma Gandhi Tanta Mukti Goan Yojana (Dispute free village scheme) and under which disputes are resolved locally by a committee. The head of the committee is also from the Desai family. Though police case has been registered, the fact remains that the Dalits are still tortured and it is being done through a committee system and for which government scheme is helpful. In this regard it is to be concluded that the discriminatory practices are in the Indian villages with different levels of intensity.

[*The Hindu*, 14th January, 2012, p. 14]

Box – B: Paradox

It is to be noted here that the Government of Tamil Nadu had made a declaration that the untouchability problem persists in 384 villages in Tamil Nadu. Annually the Government of Tamil Nadu is allocating resources for awareness creation on this issue among the people. Annually Rs 50 lakh are allocated and yet the problem continues. Here another paradoxical issue is to be highlighted. Government of Tamil Nadu made an announcement that the villages where there is no untouchability will be given Rs 1 lakh as award money. In 2010, only 31 Gram Panchayats got the award and it means in the whole of Tamil Nadu only 31 Gram Panchayats are able to apply for this award. It gives a clear impression that in most of the places in one form or other untouchability continues. In Tamil Nadu, on untouchability issue 1050 cases have been registered. Normal conviction rate is only five per cent in Tamil Nadu.

Box – C: Performance of Dalit Panchayat Leaders

A large number of Gram Panchayat Leaders belonging to Dalit community performed their roles and responsibilities very well. Because they were all trained fully oriented and enabled them to excel in their performance. These successes are attributed towards the role of training institutions and the support service provided by the training and research institutions. Further they were all talented leaders addressed the issues of the Dalits through a new framework of governance without antagonising the dominant communities. Many have crossed all the barriers. In all these places where Panchayat leaders have excelled, the other communities are positive towards the activities of the Panchayats. The leaders' vision, commitment, skill, strategy and capacity are critical to their functioning. All the success stones have been recorded and documented for wider dissemination.

Box – D: Dalits Prohibited from using public well

Kodikulam, a village located under the foothills of Yanamalai (elephant hill) near here is a gifted place. It boasts of an age old public well that provides tasty water round the year. People from far and wide throng the place with cans and drums to fetch the water home. But the Dalits of the village cannot dare even to go nearer to the well.

The SCs (scheduled castes) cannot go beyond this point, "Says a 61 year old farmer, A. Akkniveeranan, pointing to a distance of about 150 meters away from the well. They (Dalits) can ask any of us to fetch the water for them and we will oblige. But they cannot do it on their own. This practice has been there for ages and it cannot be changed", he adds with no shilly – shallying.

The caste Hindus of the village, occupied predominantly by people belonging to Kallar and Moopanar community, do not hesitate to talk about the discrimination of Dalits even to journalists. The well has been associated with four small temples built close to it and religious sentiments were given as a reason to keep the Dalits away from it.

They (Dalits) will not be spared. Honeybees will sting them if they try to go near the well, "says Packiam, an aged widow. Concerning with her, 26-year old P. Suresh, a construction labourer, says." The youngsters of our village will be in these temples all round the clock. Some of us even sleep here in the nights to prevent anyone from defiling this holy place.

The well is surrounded by trees that are home to thousands of honeybees. Strangers must be careful while nearing the well as the might suffers a sting or two. The villages have intentionally left the honey combs untouched as it serves their purpose of discriminating the Dalits, "the bees do not sting us and we will not allow anyone to clear the honeycombs", says C.K. Aurtha Paiyyar , a 19 year old youth.

A lawyer practicing in the Madras High Court Bench here and residing at Othakadai neighbours fetch water from that well for drinking purpose. They travel in two wheelers to the village, which could be accessed either through the Government Agricultural College or from the Madurai-Chennai four-lane, and bring the water filled in cans.

"Once when I had gone there, some children asked me if I could give them some water to drink. I asked them why they do not take it themselves. They said they were not supposed to go there. Then, I understood and felt very sad for the poor children. This atrocity is being practiced there for ages and nobody is able to raise their voice for the fear of earning the wrath of the dominant caste", he says seeking anonymity.

Box – E: "Kudiparayan"

There is a system of bounded labour called "Kudiparayan" in some of the villages in Pudukkottai Disrict. 'Kudiparayan' is an individual from a Dalit family who has to serve the family of a dominant community and by which all manual works have to be carried out by Kudiparayan. The wage is not as per the minimum wage act of Government of Tamil Nadu. It is lesser than that of the approved rate. Normally Kudiparayan used to borrow money from the family where he is working. Hence he cannot demand. During festivals some free doles will be given. The same Kudiparayan has to perform the assigned duties which cannot be carried out by any other caste. This practice is in practice Pudukkottai district. Apart from those villages; this practice is in vogue in Sooranviduthi, Vaanjanviduthi and

Dakshinapuram. Duties such as digging death messages, drum beating for death, removing dead animals are assigned to them. Dalits cannot refuse to do it and if they do so, they will be tortured through social boycott and as a result their livelihood will be affected.

Box – F: Caste differences are legitimised

In many places, graveyard for each and every village has been created in both rural and urban areas. It is noticed in the survey that this creation of separate graveyard in the districts of Madurai, Thanjavur and Pudukkottai. Kappalar a village in Madurai district is an example of having 14 cremation yards for its 14 castes. Apart from the above there is a Samathuva Mayanam (common graveyard) in the same village at Kappalar. This can be used by all legally. But Dalits are not using it as they fear caste violence will erupt over this issue. There are Panchayats known for its achievements in resolving such a crises of graveyard for Dalits by providing such a kind of facility by issuing a government scheme – Annaithu Garamma Anna Marumalarchy Thittam. A separate graveyard for Dalits. The debate is on whether the act of Panchayat is correct legally. One argument is that the Panchayat has to perform the social justice function by resolving the dispute. Naturally the Panchayat has to make all the other communities to accept the dead bodies of the Dalit to the buried in the Common graveyard. Then only the untouchability will disappear. But in reality the caste discrimination is in the blood of every one and it cannot be done way with all of a sudden. It will take time and yet the problem has to be solved hence Panchayat leaders instead of making other communities to accept the common graveyard to be used by all including the Dalits, a separate graveyard is created for Dalits.

Box – G: Wall to divide people on Caste lines

In many places it was a practice to erect a stone or brick wall to segregate the Dalits from the caste Hindus in Tamil Nadu. It was brought to light and agitations have been launched. A 600 meters long wall separated Dalits from caste Hindus at Uthamapuram village in Madurai district. It was brought to light only by the Gram Panchayat president who happened to be a Dalit. It is because a mass movement. The left political parties took up the case and fought for it. The state government has acted promptly and removed the wall.

Box- H: Opportunities are being missed

It is sad to note that there are representatives from Dalit communities in Parliament and State Legislatures. Apart from the above there are representatives from Dalit communities in Local Bodies. We have IAS officials from those communities. Yet they are not raising their voice against the neglect of state and central ministries in implementing special component plan for SC and ST. Despite letter from the Prime Ministers Office and Planning Commission the negligence of implementing the special component plan for SC/ST on the part of the central and ministries has not been either raised by the Legislators from that community or by the sensitive media. In the same way NREGA (programme) implementation can be used effectively for the Dalit land reclamation. But in reality, it does not happen all over the country barring a few places. It was not noticed and raised by our representative of the people. Many of the schemes meant for Dalits have not been implemented properly and huge unspent amount are being diverted. This was also not noticed and raised by the representatives of the people. Even the Dalit representatives have not developed Dalit component plan in local bodies.

Box – I: Humiliation faced by the Dalit Women Panchayat Leaders

Valli Deivanai (42) president of Pasavapatti village Panchayat in Cheurimalai Block Erode District accused that she faced discrimination continuously in the village because she is a Dalit. She was not allowed to sit in the Chair provide for Panchayat president. Subsequently, beneficiary selection for all government schemes had been done dubiously, and she had been forced to sign documents as dictated by the Vice-President and Vice-Presidents of District Panchayat. The list prepared by them was not proper. Even while finalysing old age pension beneficiaries; ineligible persons were included in the list.

A, Kalaimani Dalit women village Panchayat presidents of Karu Vadatheru Panchayat allegedly Flag on the Republic Day. He was not permitted by the Vice-president to hoist the tricolour. She lodged a complaint in the Police Station and submitted a petition to the District Collector.

Panchayat update, Vol. XIX No. 2, February 2012

All the above boxes are taken from yet another study of the Author (G. Palanithurai, 2013)

BOX-J: Caste Hindu Discriminate Dalit in MGNREGS

Caste Hindu of Putharenthal village of Ramanathapuram District refuses to work in the areas of Dalits settlement under the Mahatma Gandhi National Rural Employment Guarantee scheme (MGNREGA). This village appeared in the newspaper a few years ago for a rift between Dalits and Caste Hindus. Putharenthal Gram Panchayat allocated the work in the lands adjacent to the Dalits settlement but the caste Hindu refused to work in those areas. The caste Hindus refused to procure essential commodities from the ration shops which are located in the Dalit settlement. Workers in the ration shop carry the commodities from the shop and sell the same to the caste Hindus in a different place. The caste Hindus insisted that a new ration shop has to be constructed for them in their area. Caste Hindus do not allow the Dalits to enter into their residential areas. The discriminatory practice had been referred to National Human Rights Commission.

Dalits have given petition – *The New Indian Express,* 10th July, 2012

BOX-K: Caste row at Nagapalayam
Dalits in Nagapalayam town Panchayats in Erode district lodged a complaint to the district collector that the dominant caste groups constructed a wall and preventing the dalits to have access to the main road directly. The Dalit children have to take a circuitous route to reach the school. By giving a petition to the RDO, the Dalits got a solution as the RDO opened a pathway in the wall. The dalits were satisfied. In order to create a tension a few dominate caste groups took the dead today and reached the cremation ground through the lane created for the Dalits. Though there is a straight route to cremation ground, the caste Hindus took the dalits lane to carry the body. While carrying the body dominated caste people threatened the Dalit women by showing the lethal weapons. Hence the dalits lodged a complaint to the collector. The RDO who resolved the arising earlier ordered an enquiry and based on the report action will be taken.
The New Indian Express, 10th July, 2012

Service Delivery

Bringing women and Dalit to public institution as representatives is with the basic objective of tackling the issues of women and Dalit with a sense of commitment and a perspective. Apart from the above delivering service to all is yet another core function. Supporting the elected representatives and strengthening local bodies are with the intension of providing quality service. Cent per cent of respondents have informed that they take decision independently. All important decision is taken by the Panchayat presidents. Eighty three per cent of the respondents said that they are taking lead in the decision-making and get the approval of the Panchayat council. Eighty nine per cent of the respondents replied that they used to contact the health department staff for help. Ninety per cent of the respondents replied that they paid attention on educational training needs of the people. Fifty eight per cent of the respondents informed that they have made complaints to the higher authorities when they face problems in service delivery. Sixty six per cent of the respondents replied that they made complaints one or two times. Seventy four per cent of the respondents felt that they complied with the complaints of the respondents. Ninety per cent of the people expressed their happiness over the achievements in resolving the problems by taking them to the higher officials.

Table 106: Working for Award

Sl. No.	*Options*	*No. of Respondents*	*Percentage*
1.	Yes	101	83.48
2.	No	20	16.52
	Total	**121**	**100.00**

Source: Computed.

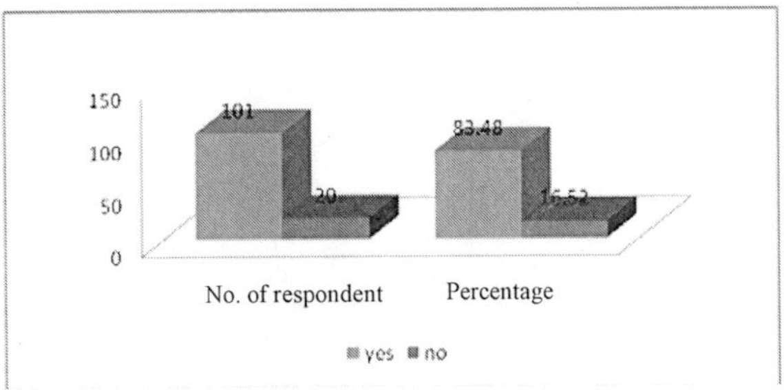

Table 107: Got Awards

Sl. No.	*Options*	*No. of Respondents*	*Percentage*
1.	Yes	17	14.04
2.	No	104	85.96
	Total	**121**	**100.00**

Source: Computed.

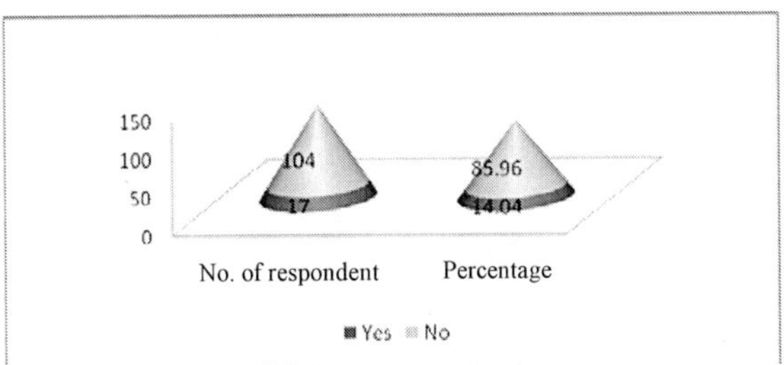

Table 108: Creating Commons

Sl. No.	*Options*	*No. of Respondents*	*Percentage*
1.	Yes	90	74.39
2.	No	31	25.61
	Total	**121**	**100.00**

Source: Computed.

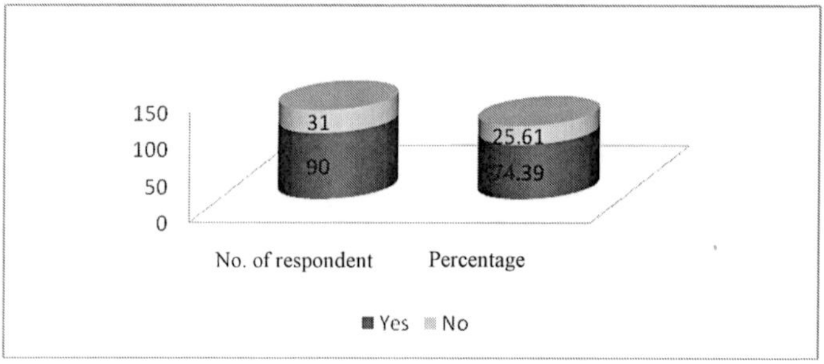

Table 109: Creating Assets for Revenue Generation

Sl. No.	*Options*	*No. of Respondents*	*Percentage*
1.	Yes	31	25.61
2.	No	90	74.39
	Total	**121**	**100.00**

Source: Computed.

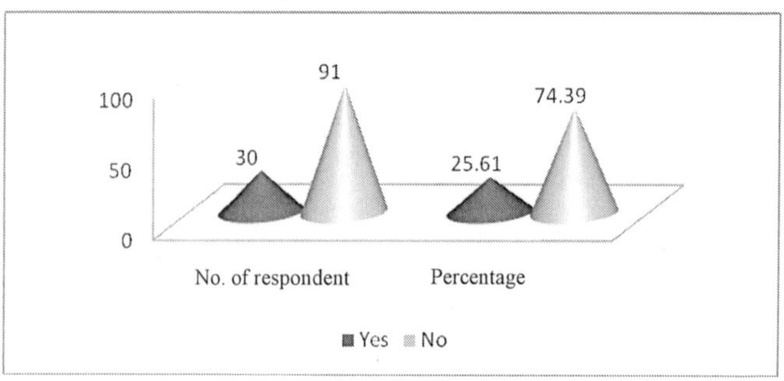

Table 110: Participating in Public Function

Sl. No.	Options	No. of Respondents	Percentage
1.	Yes	100	82.64
2.	No	21	17.36
	Total	**121**	**100.00**

Source: Computed.

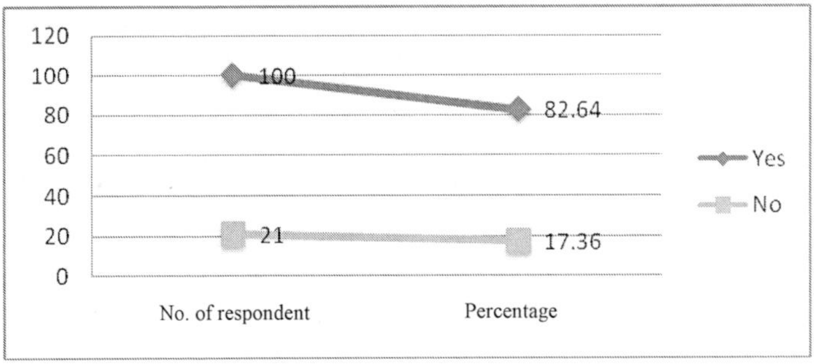

Table 111: Visiting Other States

Sl. No.	Options	No. of Respondents	Percentage
1.	Yes	19	15.70
2.	No	102	84.30
	Total	**121**	**100.00**

Source: Computed.

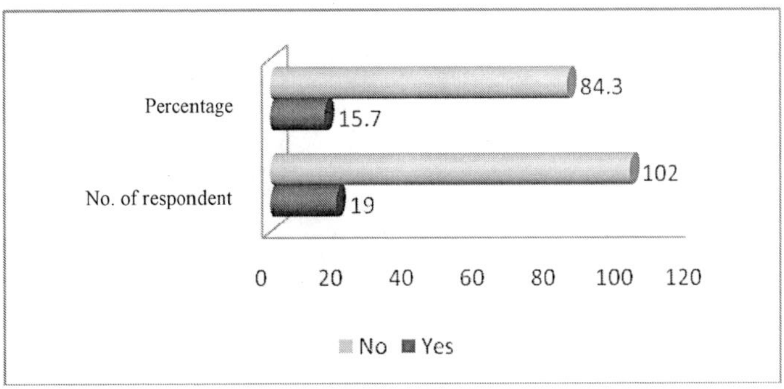

Table 112: Visiting Abroad

Sl. No.	*Options*	*No. of Respondents*	*Percentage*
1.	Yes	21	17.36
2.	No	100	82.64
	Total	**121**	**100.00**

Source: Computed.

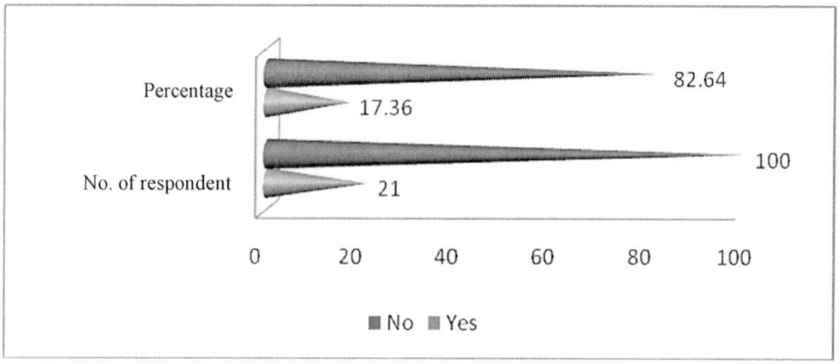

Table 113: Did you Disseminate the Knowledge Gained in the Trainings to the People?

Sl. No	*Options*	*No. of Respondents*	*Percentage*
1.	Yes	108	89.26
2.	No	13	10.74
	Total	**121**	**100.00**

Source: Computed.

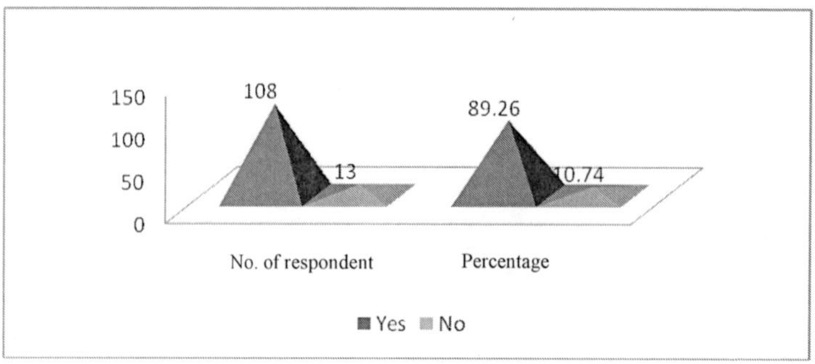

Table 114: Conducting Awareness to the People

Sl. No.	*Options*	*No. of Respondents*	*Percentage*
1.	Yes	108	89.26
2.	No	13	10.74
	Total	**121**	**100.00**

Source: Computed.

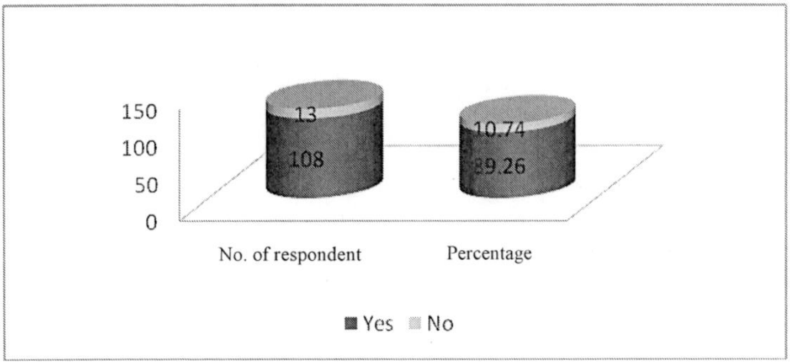

Table 115: Able to Manage the Crowd

Sl. No.	*Options*	*No. of Respondents*	*Percentage*
1.	Yes	107	88.42
2.	No	14	11.58
	Total	**121**	**100.00**

Source: Computed.

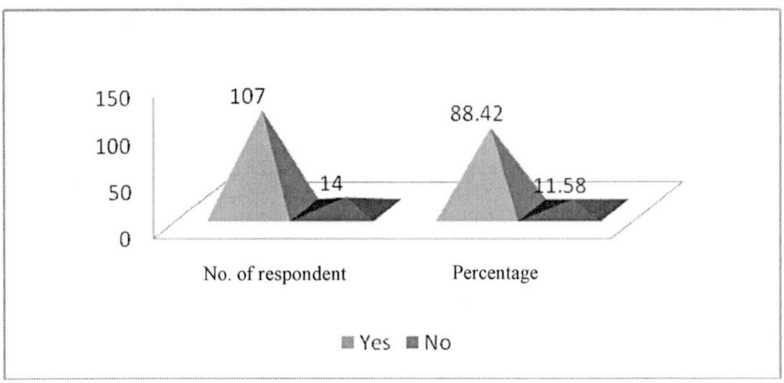

Table 116: Workload in Family Reduced

Sl. No.	*Options*	*No. of Respondents*	*Percentage*
1.	Yes	69	57.02
2.	No	52	42.98
	Total	**121**	**100.00**

Source: Computed.

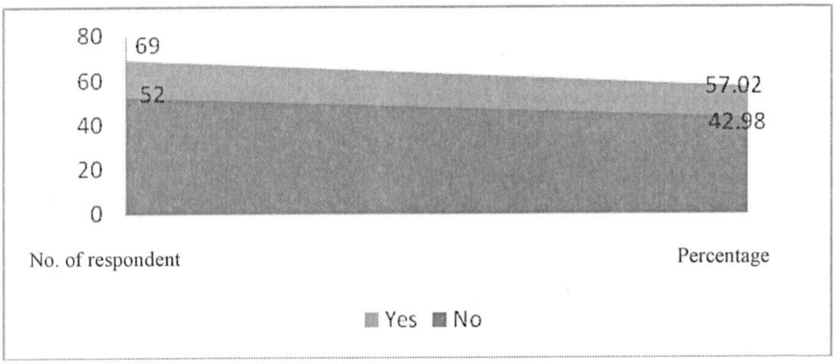

Table 117: Needed Facilities are in the Schools

Sl. No.	*Options*	*No. of Respondents*	*Percentage*
1.	Yes	120	99.18
2.	No	1	0.82
	Total	**121**	**100.00**

Source: Computed.

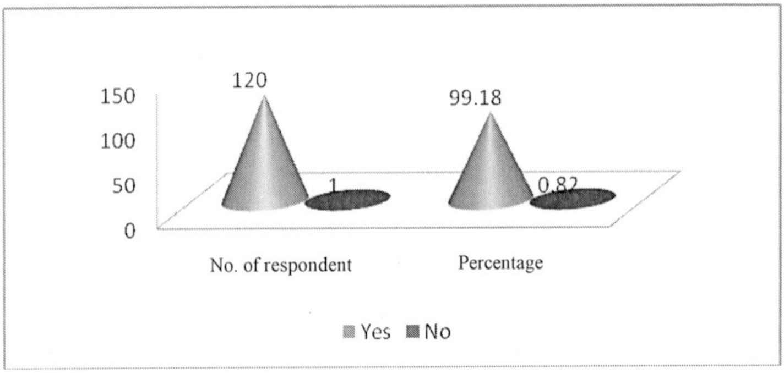

Table 118: Provided Drinking Water

Sl. No.	*Options*	*No. of Respondents*	*Percentage*
1.	Yes	108	89.26
2.	No	13	10.74
	Total	**121**	**100.00**

Source: Computed.

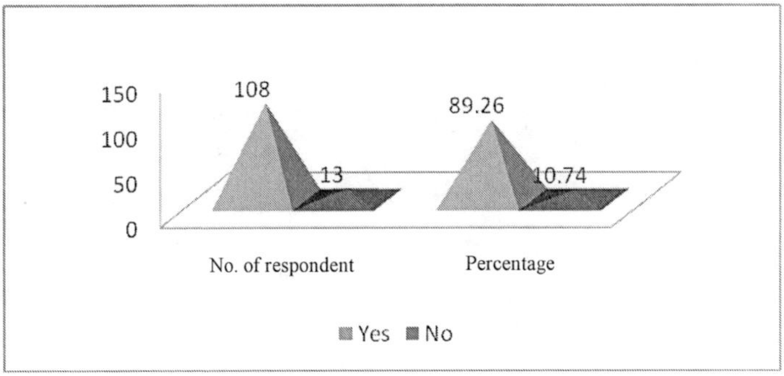

Table 119: Streets are Clean

Sl. No.	*Options*	*No. of Respondents*	*Percentage*
1.	Yes	120	99.18
2.	No	1	0.82
	Total	**121**	**100.00**

Source: Computed.

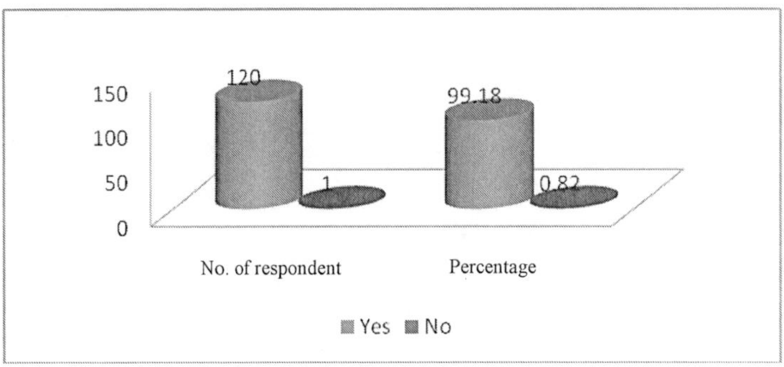

Table 120: ANM Regularly Visiting the Village

Sl. No.	*Options*	*No. of Respondents*	*Percentage*
1.	Yes	108	89.26
2.	No	13	10.74
	Total	**121**	**100.00**

Source: Computed.

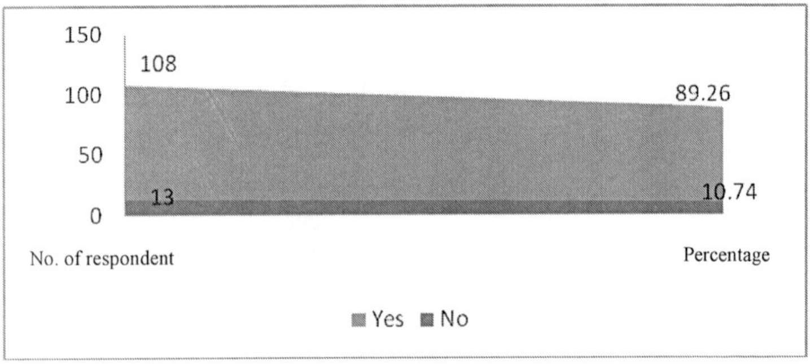

Table 121: Roads are in Good Condition

Sl. No.	*Options*	*No. of Respondents*	*Percentage*
1.	Yes	102	84.30
2.	No	19	15.70
	Total	**121**	**100.00**

Source: Computed.

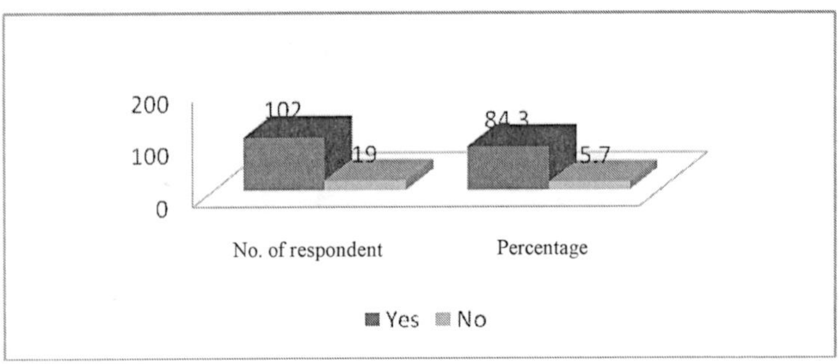

Table 122: Attending Social Justice Activities

Sl. No.	*Options*	*No. of Respondents*	*Percentage*
1.	No answer	24	19.83
2.	Untouchability	46	38.01
3.	Temple entry/eradicate double tumbler	30	24.80
4.	Nil	10	8.27
5.	Other issues	11	9.09
	Total	**121**	**100.00**

Source: Computed.

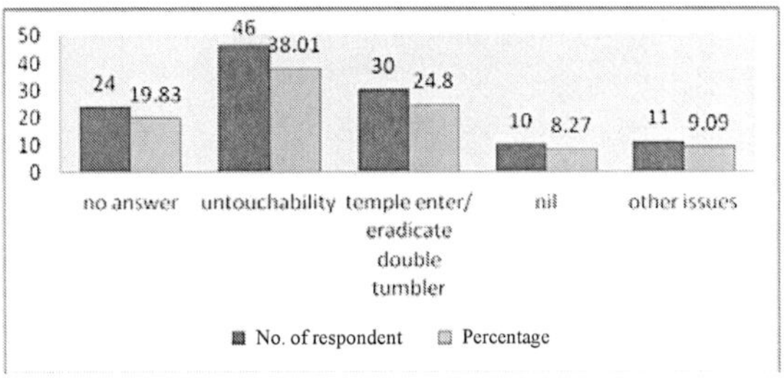

Table 123: Attending Gender Justice Activities in the Panchayat

Sl. No.	*Options*	*No. of Respondents*	*Percentage*
1.	Yes	83	68.60
2.	No	38	31.40
	Total	**121**	**100.00**

Source: Computed.

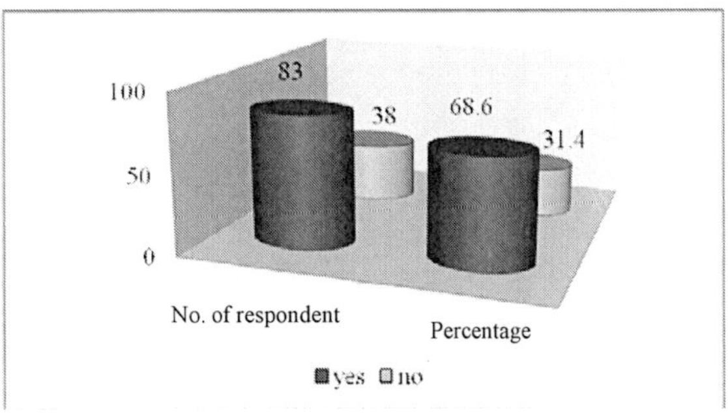

Table 124: Ensuring Maximum Justice to the Women and Dalit

Sl. No.	*Options*	*No. of Respondents*	*Percentage*
1.	Yes	106	87.60
2.	No	15	12.40
	Total	**121**	**100.00**

Source: Computed.

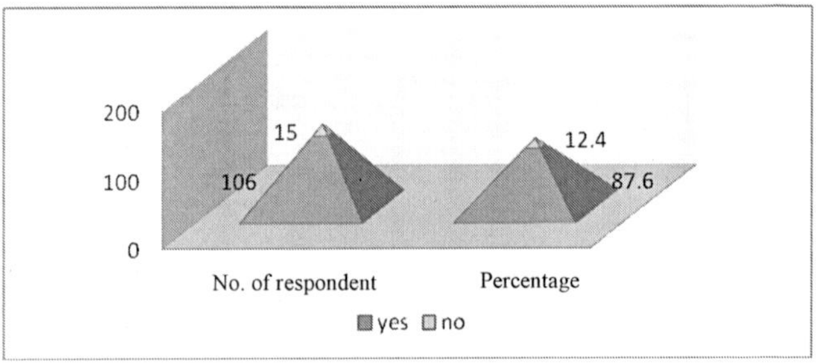

Table 125: Women of Gram Sabha are Permitted to Speak out Women Issue?

Sl. No.	*Options*	*No. of Respondents*	*Percentage*
1.	Yes	121	100.0
2.	No	00	00
	Total	**121**	**100.0**

Source: Computed.

Table 126: Dalit Women Members of Gram Sabha are Permitted to Speak

Sl. No.	*Options*	*No. of Respondents*	*Percentage*
1.	Yes	109	90.09
2.	No	12	9.91
	Total	**121**	**100.00**

Source: Computed.

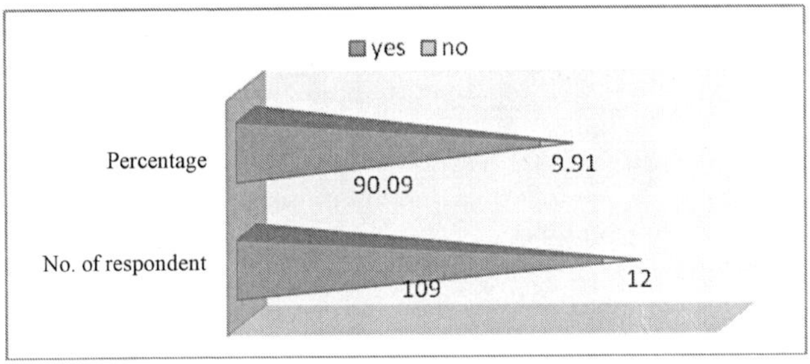

Table 127: Organising People for Common Problem

Sl. No.	*Options*	*No. of Respondents*	*Percentage*
1.	Yes	104	85.96
2.	No	17	14.04
	Total	**121**	**100.00**

Source: Computed.

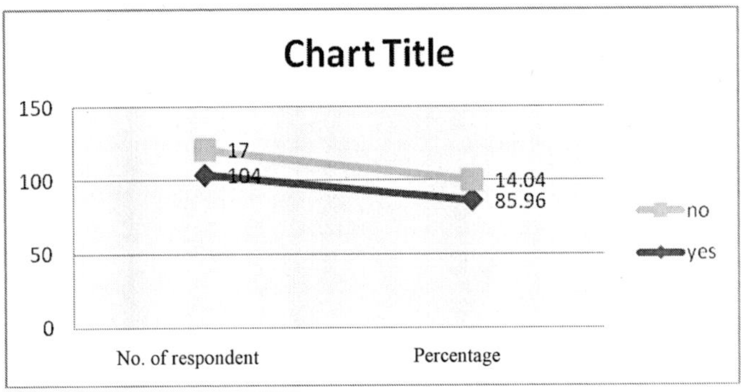

Table 128: Experience in Organising People

Sl. No.	*Options*	*No. of Respondents*	*Percentage*
1.	Yes	110	90.91
2.	No	11	9.09
	Total	**121**	**100.00**

Source: Computed.

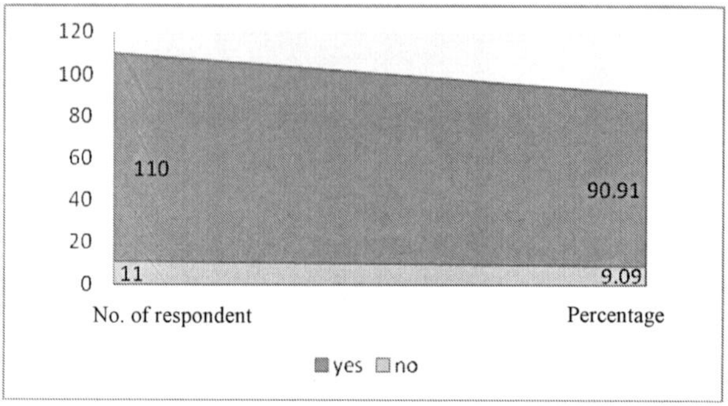

Table 129: Equal Rights are Enjoyed by Men and Women

Sl. No.	*Options*	*No. of Respondents*	*Percentage*
1.	Yes	110	90.91
2.	No	11	9.09
	Total	**121**	**100.00**

Source: Computed.

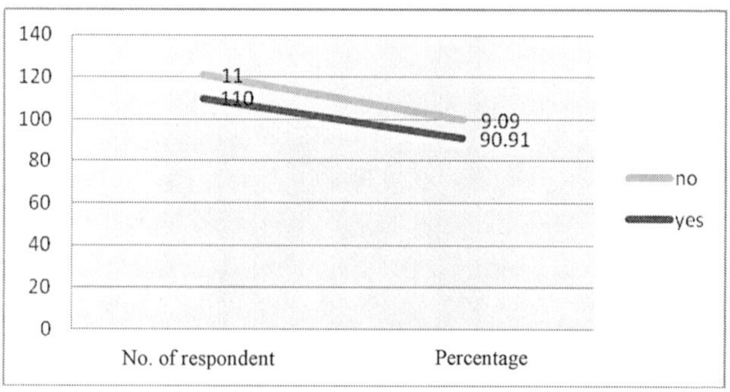

Table 130: Used the Legal Aid Cell

Sl. No.	*Options*	*No. of Respondents*	*Percentage*
1.	Yes	38	31.40
2.	No	83	68.60
	Total	**121**	**100.00**

Source: Computed.

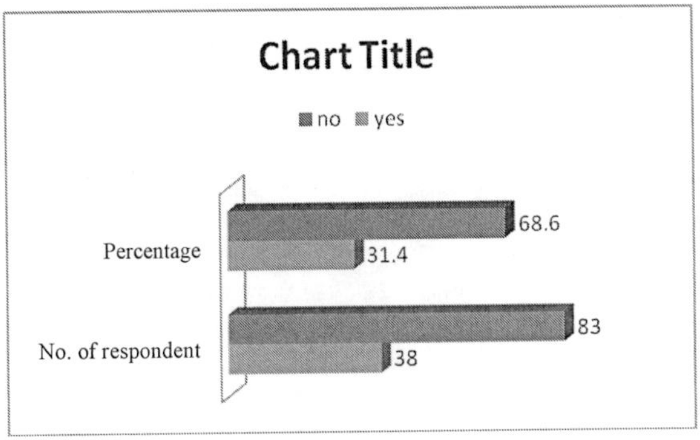

Table 131: Effective Delivery of Service on their Own

Sl. No.	*Options*	*No. of Respondents*	*Percentage*
1.	Yes	121	100
2.	No	0	0
	Total	**121**	**100.0**

Source: Computed.

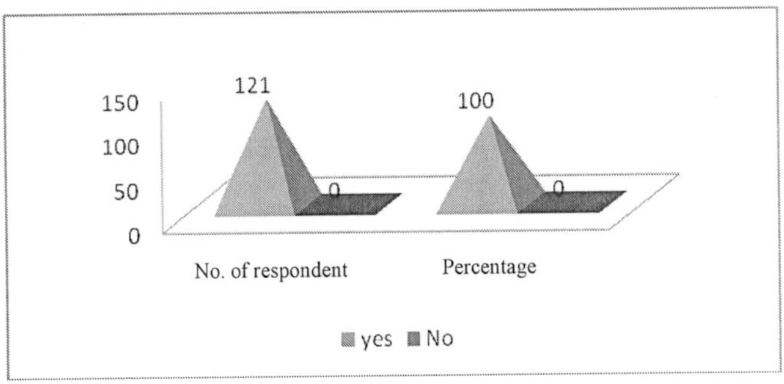

Table 132: Decisions are their Own

Sl. No.	*Options*	*No. of Respondents*	*Percentage*
1.	Myself	100	82.64
2.	No	21	17.36
	Total	**121**	**100.00**

Source: Computed.

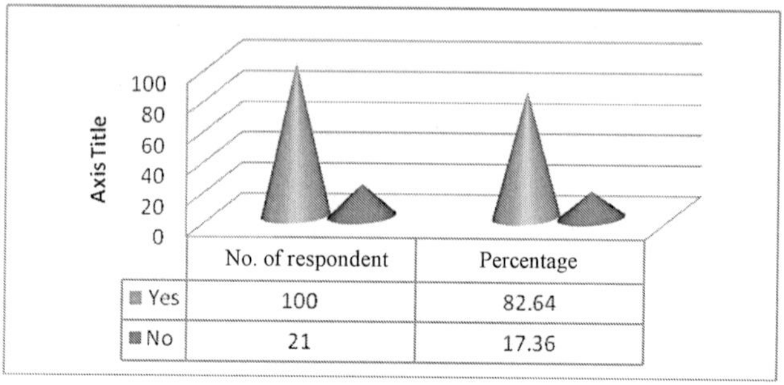

Table 133: Calling Health Professionals to Attend Healthcare Needs

Sl. No.	*Options*	*No. of Respondents*	*Percentage*
1.	Yes	108	89.26
2.	No	13	10.74
	Total	**121**	**100.00**

Source: Computed.

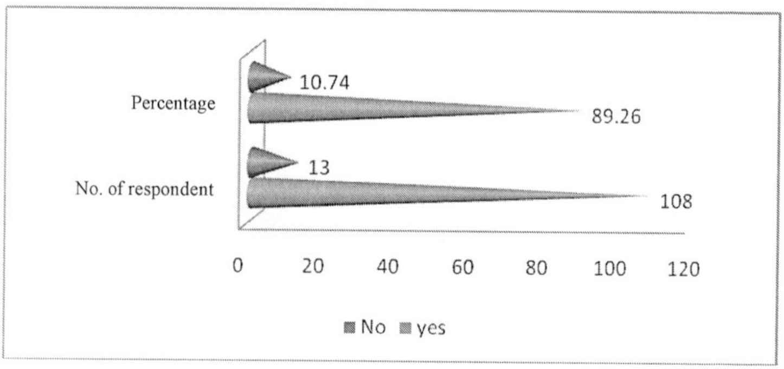

Table 134: Giving Complaints to the Authorities Regarding the Delivery of Services

Sl. No.	*Options*	*No. of Respondents*	*Percentage*
1.	Yes	71	58.68
2.	No	48	39.67
3.	Nil	2	1.65
	Total	**121**	**100.00**

Source: Computed.

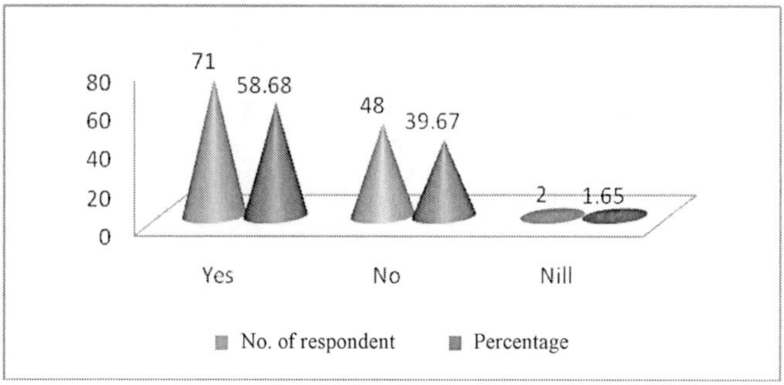

Table 135: Number of Times Complaint Made

Sl. No.	*Options*	*No. of Respondents*	*Percentage*
1.	1 to 2	81	66.94
2.	No	37	30.58
3.	Nil	3	2.48
	Total	**121**	**100.00**

Source: Computed.

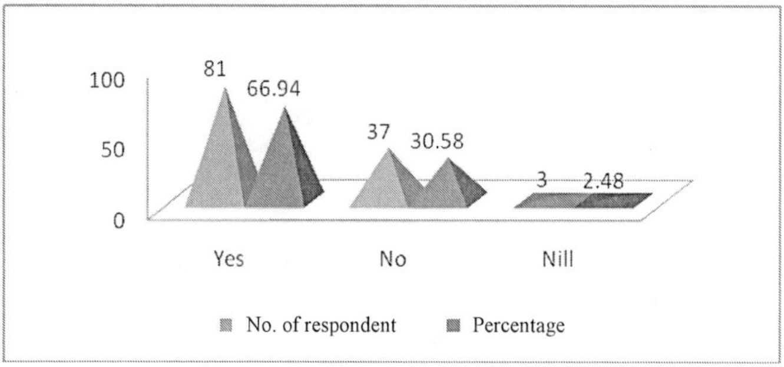

Table 136: Complaint were Responded

Sl. No.	*Options*	*No. of Respondents*	*Percentage*
1.	Yes	90	74.39
2.	No	31	25.61
	Total	**121**	**100.00**

Source: Computed.

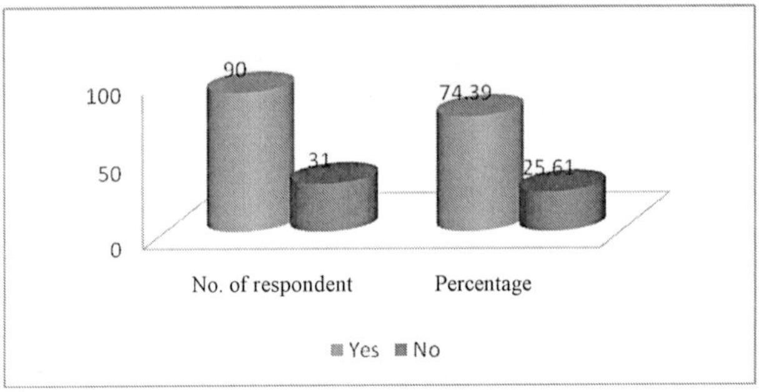

Table 137: Satisfied with the Delivery of Services

Sl. No.	*Options*	*No. of Respondents*	*Percentage*
1.	Yes	109	90.09
2.	No	12	9.91
	Total	**121**	**100.00**

Source: Computed.

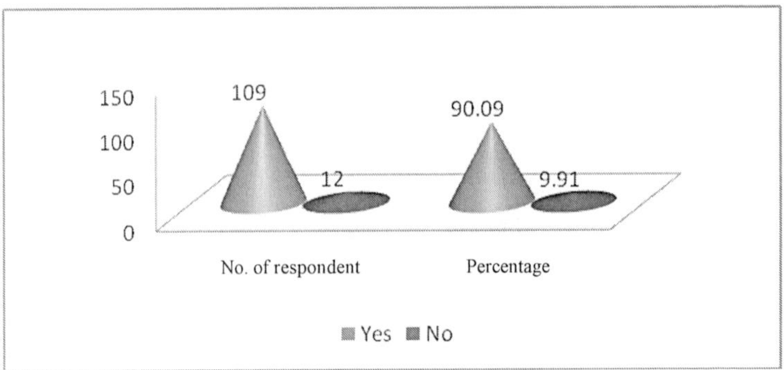

The elected representatives have to perform both assigned and assumed responsibilities. It is inferred from all the studies that the elected representatives have to perform the assigned duties otherwise they will face problem from the communities and from the officials. Normally elected representatives performances are evaluated from the outcome. In Tamil Nadu, our bureaucracy is very effective and the present status of social development is attributed for the achievements of the grassroots bureaucracy. Even before the

New Panchayati Raj system the performance of the state government through its bureaucracy was very high and ultimately it contributed for the high performance in Human Development. With regard to infrastructure development Tamil Nadu stands very high as it was the response of the government to the demands of the people (Catalyst Trust, 2008). Now Panchayats act very closely. In Tamil Nadu, during the DMK period every Gram Panchayat has got Rs 2500000 for infrastructure development. This scheme was called "Anaithu Grama Anna Marumalarchi Thittam". The amount was spent only for building infrastructure facilities as per the demands of the people. Subsequently during the AIADMK period, yet another scheme called "Thai Thittam" was introduced to build infrastructure in the hamlets of the Panchayats. Through this schemes on an average Rs 2500000 have been spent in a Gram Panchayat area. To cross-check the achievements public audit has to be conducted. It is being discussed in the next section.

Notes and References

1. The Hunger Project, Thus Spoke the Press: Select Articles on Elected Women Leaders in Village Panchayats, New Delhi: The Hunger Project, 2006, 2007, 2008, 2009, 2010.
2. The Catalyst Trust, Citizens Audit of Basic Services in Tamil Nadu Chennai: Catalyst Trust, 2008.

Chapter VI

Integrated Analysis

As per the framework used in this study to assess the empowerment, agency and opportunity structure are so essential. To analyse the agency, indicators have been fixed. The indicators are broader and covering the entire ground. The agency indicators are skills, capacity, vision, social status, economic background, level of confidence, personal initiatives, educational background, support structure, training undergone, political affiliation and mobility of the respondents. One set of indicators reflecting the individuals' assets and another set of indicators reflecting the background in which the actor is performing the assigned roles and responsibilities. In order to elicit response for all the indicators sixty seven questions had been framed and on which the respondents had been asked to respond. The broader assumption is that every respondent will be able to respond to all those questions. For some of the critical questions the respondents have not answered. If the respondents are aware and active in Panchayat they could have given answers. Mostly the questions are qualitative.

No doubt, in Indian context social background helps individuals for their empowerment if they belong to higher caste above the Dalits. Dalits are the only group struggling to get recognition. Dalit communities are always marginalised. They are neglected, marginalised and humiliated in the society over centuries. So to understand the whole process of transformation one has to trace it from socio-economic background of the individuals, groups and communities. When the survey was conducted to elicit responses questions have been asked on many aspects covering the entire range of subjects relating to the basic factors under the framework of analysis. They include their economic condition, educational background, wealth status, housing details, facilities in the house, income, expenditure, support gaining from local social and political organisations, information relating to Panchayati Raj management, opportunity to work for women and children through Panchayats, opportunity to read newspaper, view TV news, support of political party, capacity, skill, and capabilities. Their responses have been classified. It is to be noted here that among the respondents 35.54 per cent of them are from SC/ST communities, and 23.14 per cent are from the most background communities. It is inferred unequivocally that majority of the respondents belong to the poorest and socially backward segments of the society. Eighty per cent of the respondents had only school education and nine per cent did not have schooling also. Their educational background is also not so sound. Sixty five per cent of them are from farming background. Since they are in the rural areas majority are from the forming community. Among the respondents 27 per cent are landless and 36 per cent are having land up to two acres. Hence, their wealth status is also poor. While seeing the income and expenditure pattern of the respondents one can easily come to a conclusion that the background of the respondents is not positive towards empowerment. Because expenditure of the majority of the respondents exceeds their income. While the respondents were in the electoral contest, they are being supported by family members and other organisations. While looking at the socio-economic condition it is clear that majority of the respondents do not have second economic background and equally they are not well placed in the social hierarchy. In the local power dynamics, they have to struggle a lot to get recognition for themselves.

With regard to informational assets the Gram Panchayat Presidents have enough vision. Almost all the presidents of village Panchayats as respondents expressed that they wanted to make their Panchayats as model Panchayats. They have articulated their vision. More than 70 per cent of the respondents are aware of the potentials in Panchayati Raj. They have vision, and they have aspiration to perform and deliver services to the people. Every one said that in Panchayats violence against women could be reduced, and gender parity could be achieved through Panchayati Raj. They are aware of the health conditions of women and children and more particularly the poor women and children. All these information have been acquired through listening to All India Radio and watching TV with a specific purpose. Reading newspaper is the new habit that they have developed after assuming the responsibilities of the presidents. Apart from the above, they have attended a few training programmes and by which they acquire needed information and knowledge. In Tamil Nadu, every poor household is given a television set and information dissemination is not a problem. Whether they like or not information reached every one in Tamil Nadu. Since the respondents hold position, they have to meet officials and attend meetings and through the above interaction they get adequate information about development issues.

With regard to skill of the Elected Women Representatives the respondents are aware of the rules and regulations of the Panchayati Raj management as per the response of the respondents. How to convene Gram Sabha meeting, and how to convene the Panchayat Council meetings are known to them. They know the details regarding the implementation of the resolutions of Gram Sabha. They have attended the training programmes and got the details from the manual. Thus, in terms of social and economic background they are not well placed and in terms of informational asset, they are having the needed information.

Opportunity structure in the framework includes the space provided by the representative democracy to the individuals to assume responsibility for governance legitimately and how these opportunities are being used effectively and efficiently to empower themselves and to empower people those who are powerless. To make use of the opportunity structure people those who are in position should have sufficient knowledge and information about the machinery which is being handled by the representatives of the people. It is necessary that the representatives of the people should need an environment which is conducive for effective and efficient functioning. In this regard battery of questions have been raised to the Elected Women Representatives. In India, governance and administrative machinery and mechanism are so complex and they require adequate skill and capacity to handle them. In rural local bodies at the lowest tier the representatives have to work closely with people. Unless the representatives are skillful and knowledgeable, it is very difficult to manage the people and the governing institution. The Elected Women Representatives have to run the institutions and deliver services. In this process they have to face the people. They have to handle the participatory institutions. Their understanding about the handling of the institutions and skill to manage the same are crucial for service delivery. In this process the Elected Women Representatives have to face volley of problems.

It is inferred from the response of the respondents that around 15 per cent of the Elected Women Representatives are not aware that they are in the position as the seats are reserved for women. It gives an impression that they are drawn towards this position by somebody. One cannot expect effective management of the institutions from this segment. There is yet another issue to be discussed. Fifty seven per cent of the Elected Women Representatives had no political experience and never attended any political party discourses. They are absolutely raw representatives without any clear understanding of the political processes. It is to be noted here that politics is vibrant at the grassroots level. There is yet another issue one has to look in the political carrier of any representatives. In Indian context once a candidate enters into any contest for position he or she will continuously move in the power ladder. But contrary to expectation 87.60 per cent of the Elected Women Representatives responded that they do not have any career ambition in the political system. Aspiration of an individual is a propelling engine to motivate the human being to work hard and effectively to reach the goal. The Elected Women Representatives have to meet the demands of the people and fulfill the aspirations of the community and for which they have to manage the institution efficiently.

Gram Sabha meetings and Panchayat Council meetings are the space and opportunity for practicing deliberative democracy.

In a representative democracy, reflecting the opinion, views, needs and moods of the people is the role and responsibility of the representative. To reflect the views, opinions, needs of the people, nuances, methods and approaches are necessary. There is a method by which aspirations of the people could be articulated. Elected Women Representative should create an enabling environment for deliberation. While deliberating in the institutions the representatives have to discuss the issues of the people. They have to concentrate on the deliberative process of the discourse and discussion on the issues. Duration of deliberation, depth of deliberation process of deliberation, decision-making process of deliberation will reflect the maturity of the representatives and thereby one could see the impact of the above in the community. But to happen the above process both the leaders and representatives should have understanding and perception about deliberative aspects of democracy (Robert E. Goodin, 2012).

By creating Gram Sabha the representative democracy becomes representative and participatory democracy. Participation is ordinarily construed as attending meetings. Participation is a concept and when it is related to democracy it has got a specific meaning. Participation is not a mere verbal communication or mere attending the meeting but to commit and involve themselves in the process of taking decision on the issues affecting their life and implement the decision taken in the authoritative bodies. Gram Sabha is a training ground for citizens to orient themselves in deliberative democracy.

There are rules governing deliberation. In a multi-caste society, people from different segments facing different kinds of problems come to decision-making space. Against this background, they have to be facilitated to participate in the deliberation. When four hundred members are in one place for deliberation one cannot expect all the four hundred will participate in the deliberations. Members from different socio-economic strata have to be facilitated to participate in the meeting and deliberations. They may be from the youth, women, Dalits, farmers, Dalit women and other groups. While arriving at decision, care has to be taken to look at the issues based on the merit of deliberation and not on the number.

From the above background participatory process of Gram Sabha and Panchayat Council is analysed in this study. Totally one could see the formalities in the meeting. Getting resolutions adopted and getting signature became prominent and it becomes a ritual (G. Palanithurai and V. Ragupathy, 2006). All the bodies of the people have been made to function as per the direction of State Government. Though the Elected Women Representatives are aware of the rules of the game, they are unable to carry out the meetings in the best spirit of democracy.

The Elected Representatives have to have forward linkages and backward linkages. They have to interact with the community and get their problems through the process of their participation. Generated problems of the community have to be solved and for which forward linkages have to be established with the Government Departments. Thirty seven departments are working with the communities and those departments have to be contacted by the elected representatives for delivering services to the communities. 85.96 per cent of the elected representatives have responded that they meet officials directly. They meet the District Collector, Project Officer, District Rural Development Agency, Block Development Officer. Elected Women Representatives have to understand their roles clearly as they are in the land of role confusion and role conflict. Any geographical area is represented by many in different authoritative bodies as we have multilayered governance arrangement from Gram Sabha to Lok Sabha.

In India, peoples representative do not have adequate training capacity building exercises and orientations. As a result, we find always role conflict and role confusion. Most of the occasion elected representatives work on obligatory functions and assumed functions. Representatives who responded very well to the demands of the people and community got reelected. Mostly the elected representatives would work on discretionary functions. The elected representatives have to visit public offices and service delivery units. It is to be noted here that 90 per cent of the respondents expressed that they used to visit all PDS shops, schools, health centres. It is to be seen whether it has got any impact on the services. The Elected Women

Representatives have expressed that there is a strong presence of traditional and parallel bodies in the Panchayat areas. In terms of legal literacy, 75 per cent of the respondents expressed that they are aware of the Panchayat Act of Tamil Nadu, 1994 and schemes for Rural Development. The Elected Women Representatives were apolitical before their entry into Panchayati Raj governance. The moment they become representatives of the people after the election they tend to affiliate themselves with political parties. Unless they affiliate themselves with political parties, it is very difficult to manage the officials in the government departments. Mostly the elected women representatives join only the ruling party at the state. The Elected Women Representatives have taken up the critical issues of development and gender. The issues of marginalised have been taken up for redressal. From the analysis of the data generated from the respondents one can easily argue that the representatives are sensitive on the development issues of women, children and marginalised groups. By utilising the agency and opportunity structure they tried to address the issues. In the same way it is clear from the analysis of data that the skill and capacity of the respondents have contributed immensely for taking up the issues of the marginalised groups and more particularly women. The limiting factor in this process of achievements of the representative is the poor devolution of powers in Tamil Nadu. From the chapter two one can assess to what extent power has been devolved to Panchayats. In the absence of power and financial devolution one cannot expect a fair performance from the representatives. Despite their poor socio-economic conditions, and poor devolution of powers and resources, the elected women representatives have used the maximum of opportunities to deliver services to the people.

Means of Verification

Once the interaction with respondent was over the investigator has visited the village and got to know the conditions and services provided to the people by the Panchayats. To what extent the basic facilities are being provided, how streets are maintained, how water supply is being provided and how sanitation is maintained have been assessed. For many of the vital questions the response from the people was negative. There is no data for school enrollment, dropouts, malnourished children, anemia affected adolescent girls, and livelihood conditions of the poor. There is no micro plan document of the Village Panchayats. Dalits have not been permitted to enter into the common temples.

In all those Panchayats government driven programmes have been implemented. Every Panchayat president has to be a visionary and everyone should have a vision for development of the whole Panchayat. Panchayat has to perform its duties to transform the communities. Development function starts from awareness creation among the people in the village. People have to be mobilised for participation in the process of development and governance. The elected representatives should have the skill, capacity and capability to mobilise them for development and governance activities at the grassroots. They should have adequate information relating to governance and administration. They should know the art of tracking resource to Panchayats. Panchayat office should be made functional. All activities of the Panchayats should be people centric and not leader centric. At present grassroots institutions have been strengthened with a purpose of empowering people and make them to be responsible for development. Totally rural development paradigm has been changed. The new paradigm should focus on people centric, nature centric, human development centric, women centric, rights centric and inclusiveness centric activities.

The 73rd Amendment and the subsequent confirmative legislation in the state 1994 provided opportunity to create institutions at the grassroots for governance and development. In order to bring inclusiveness, space has been created legitimately for the excluded. It is a mandatory provision that women and the other marginalised have to be in governance. Hence hitherto excluded have moved into the power structure large in number as critical mass. The critical mass have to equip themselves. They have to build their support structure to face the problems. Their organisational ability and skill to mobilise people have to be enhanced. All the above aspects have been analysed individually. From the responses of the respondents one could infer that the agency assets are not very effective. Systematic efforts were not taken to build on the asset. Opportunity structure provides space, scope, and opportunity for transformation both for the respondents and their constituents. Conscious efforts are needed on the part of the respondents to transform themselves as transformative leaders with the ability and skill to manage change and bring transformation at the community level. Strategic efforts are needed for the elected leaders of the marginalised section to respond to the challenges emerging out of the society, polity, governance and administration. Empowering the elected women representatives in the new system is a process oriented action. This process starts from filing nomination for contesting in the election. When they are in office, their multiple roles push them in the task.

Elected Women Representatives have to manage the governance institutions, run the administration and initiate activities for rural transformation and development. In a hierarchical society equality and equity are the key background aspects to be kept in the backdrop of all the activities. Efforts are multidimensional. They are personal, organisational and institutional. Simultaneously they have to be taken and they are to be done integrally. To take up the critical function the Elected Women Representatives have to develop a development perspective and it is nothing but human development perspective. In the same way they have to develop or evolve a dignity perspective that is human dignity perspective. When initiatives are taken, they should be participatory which means, the representatives have to involve the stakeholders. While involving the stakeholders both in the process of decision-making and development, they have to be prepared to take on their destiny on their own. The task before them is huge complex and difficult. To perform the new task assigned to them and the available capacity on the part of the Elected Women Representatives is very less. The gap between the task assigned to them and the capacity of the Elected Women Representatives is vast. The gap has to be reduced and thereby the task assigned to the Elected Women Representatives will be performed effectively. The gap can be reduced by increasing the skill, capacity and capability of the Elected Women Representatives creating enabling environment to the Elected Women Representatives to perform the task. Mere creating a space for women will not alter the course of development.

Based on the responses and analysis of the responses of the respondents it is observed that almost all are drawn towards the space because of the reservation made in the constitution. They are driven by the family or community or other sources. Hardly we found the choice of the women to come to this public space. Having drawn towards the space the women have started moving into the process and taking efforts to dwell in the domain however deficiency they have. Apparently it is visible that efforts were on to build an environment to enable them to perform their task effectively. They tried to address the issues of development of women, Dalits, and children. While addressing the issues of women volley of problems have been faced by the Elected Women Representatives. Support structures are there in the system for the Elected Women Representatives. But the works of the structure remain to be studied. It is inferred that the performance of the Elected Women Representatives largely depends on the agency assets and opportunity structures. Further, it is inferred that to tackle the issues of the marginalised and women, the elected women representatives need skill capacity and support structure. It is to be noted here that there is a close relationship between the powers devolved and the performance of the elected representatives.

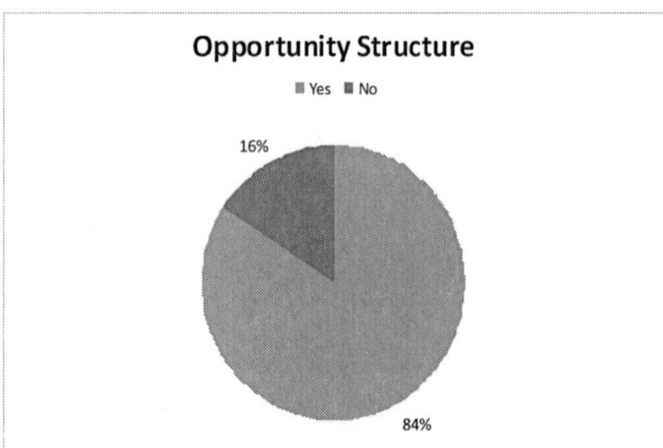

Sl. No.	Questions	No. of Respondents (121)*		Total No. of Respondents	Percentage		Total Percentage
		Yes	No		Yes	No	
1.	Respondents Awareness on Reservation of Seats for Women	102	19	121	84.30	15.70	100
2.	Respondents' Participation in Political Activities	52	69	121	42.98	57.02	100
3.	Respondents' Participation in Campaign for Election	107	14	121	88.42	11.58	100
4.	Aspiration to contest in MLA Election	15	106	121	12.40	87.60	100
5.	Respondents Contact with political Parties for their Election	50	71	121	41.32	52.68	100
6.	Directly contact officials by the respondents	104	17	121	85.96	14.04	100
7.	Approaching government officials to solve problem in the Panchayats	110	11	121	90.91	9.09	100
8.	Getting positive response from the officials	104	17	121	85.96	14.04	100
9.	Approaching officials regularly	107	14	121	88.43	11.57	100
10.	Ensuring maximum presence of women in Gram Sabha Meeting	121	00	121	100	00	100

(Contd...)

11.	Aware of the Roles	106	15	121	87.60	12.40	100
12.	Sending Letters	89	32	121	73.56	26.44	100
13.	Respondents visit to Anganwadi	110	11	121	90.91	9.09	100
14.	Respondents visit to PDS shop	110	11	121	90.91	9.09	100
15.	Respondents' visit to schools	121	00	121	100	00	100
16.	Respondent attend the function	109	12	121	86.78	13.22	100
17.	Presence of Traditional Panchayats	102	19	121	84.30	15.70	100
18.	Parallel Body presence in Panchayats	70	51	121	57.86	42.14	100
19.	Attending all the Officials Meeting	121	00	121	100	00	121
20.	Going to Panchayat office regularly.	110	11	121	90.91	9.09	100
21.	Maintain Officials' Record	110	11	121	90.91	9.09	100
22.	Aware of Panchayat Act of Tamil Nadu	91	30	121	75.20	24.80	100
23.	Aware of rules and procedures of the Panchayats	107	14	121	88.42	11.58	100
24.	Aware of the schemes of Rural Development	108	13	121	89.26	10.74	100
25.	Aware of the Reservation of seats for women	105	16	121	86.78	13.22	100
26.	Getting the Government orders properly	107	14	121	88.42	11.58	100

(Contd...)

27.	Respondents Affiliation with political party	90	31	121	74.39	25.61	100
28.	Respondents' families Affiliation with Political Party	84	37	121	69.42	30.58	100
29.	Respondent's meeting with political leaders	101	20	121	83.48	16.52	100
30.	Attending meeting in various places	93	28	121	76.86	23.14	100
31.	Member of Social organisations	27	94	121	22.31	77.69	100
32.	Member of any livelihood organisations	92	29	121	76.03	23.97	100
33.	Getting benefits from organisation individually	46	75	121	38.01	61.99	100
34.	Respondent involvement in SHG movement in Tamil Nadu	69	52	121	57.02	42.98	100
35.	Taking Decisions Individually	104	17	121	85.96	14.04	100
36.	Respondents Dream of village development	109	12	121	90.09	9.91	100
37.	Thorough on responsibilities	104	17	121	85.96	14.04	100
38.	Speaking to officials directly	109	12	121	90.09	9.91	100
39.	Respondents speaks in Public Meetings	97	24	121	80.17	19.83	100
40.	Attending Training Programme by Respondent	110	11	121	90.91	9.09	100
41.	Trainings have enhanced the capacity	110	11	121	90.91	9.09	100
42.	Availability of administrative manual	108	13	121	89.26	10.74	100

(Contd...)

43.	Giving promise to the people to seek their votes	106	15	121	87.60	12.40	100
44.	Participate in all the meetings along with men leaders	105	16	121	86.78	13.22	100
45.	Respondent's job satisfaction	106	15	121	87.60	12.40	100
46.	Problems in family front	11	110	121	9.09	90.91	100
47.	Problem in community front	17	104	121	14.04	85.96	100
48.	Problem in Panchayat Council	11	110	121	9.09	90.91	100
49.	Problems from the family and community while contesting in the election	12	109	121	9.91	90.09	100
50.	Making Model Village	101	20	121	83.48	16.52	100
51.	Taking steps in income generation for poor	105	16	121	86.78	13.22	100

Note: 121* (we have selected only 121 respondents for above mentioned data)

Sl. No.	Questions	No. of Respondents					Total No. of Respondents	Percentage					Total Percentage
		One hour	Two hours	Three hours	Four hours	Five hours		One hour	Two hours	Three hours	Four hours	Five hours	
52.	Duration of Gram Sabha Meeting conducted	18	28	53	11	11	121	14.88	23.14	43.80	9.09	9.09	100

	Questions	No. of Respondents				Total No. of Respondents	Percentage				Total Percentage
		One hour	Two hours	Three Hours	Four Hours		One hour	Two hours	Three hours	Four hours	
53.	Duration of Panchayat council meeting	33	50	37	1	121	27.27	41.32	30.50	0.89	100

	Question	No. of Respondents		Total No. of Respondents	Percentage		Total Percentage
		President	Others		President	Others	
54.	Who preside the over meeting?	121	00	121	100	00	100

	Questions	No. of Respondents			Total No. of Respondents	Percentage			Total Percentage
		All members	1 to 5 members	8 members		All members	1 to 5 members	8 members	
55.	Active participation of members	90	18	13	121	74.38	14.88	10.74	100

	Questions	No. of Respondents			Total No. of Respondents	Percentage			Total Percentage
		Project officer	BDO officer	Health officials		Project officer	BDO officer	Health officials	
56.	Details of their contacts	16	104	1	121	13.22	85.96	0.82	100

	Questions	No. of Respondents				Total No. of Respondents	Percentage				Total Percentage
		Women	Dalit	Men	All		Women	Dalit	Men	All	
57.	Speakers in Gram Sabha meeting	98	1	3	19	121	81.00	0.82	2.48	15.70	100

	Questions	No. of Respondents						Total No. of Respondents	Percentage						Total percentage
		Women	Public service	Road	Water supply	Agri	other		Women	Public services	Road	Water supply	Agri	Other	
58.	Predominant issues in Gram Sabha meeting	22	17	1	12	1	68	121	18.20	14.04	0.83	9.91	0.83	56.19	100

	Questions	No. of Respondents				Total No. of Respondents	Percentage				Total Percentage
		Village Panchayat	President	Others	No Answer		Village Panchayat	President	Others	No Answer	
59.	Managing the commons	95	24	1	1	121	78.51	19.83	0.83	0.83	100

	Questions	*No. of Respondents*			*Total No. of Respondents*	*Percentage*			*Total Percentage*
		Government	*Panchayat leader*	*Panchayat council*		*Government*	*Panchayat leader*	*Panchayat council*	
60.	Preparing agenda for Gram Sabha meeting	46	48	27	121	38.01	39.68	22.31	100

	Questions	*No. of Respondents*			*Total No. of Respondents*	*Percentage*			*Total percentage*
		Rural Development	*DRDA*	*Other Departments*		*Rural Development*	*DRDA*	*Other Departments*	
61.	Development contact	79	37	5	121	65.28	30.59	4.13	100

	Questions	*No. of Respondents*				*Total No. of Respondents*	*Percentage*				*Total percentage*
		5 accounts	*6 accounts*	*7 accounts*	*More than 8 accounts*		*5 accounts*	*6 accounts*	*7 ac-counts*	*More than 8 accounts*	
62.	Panchayat accounts	18	72	20	11	121	14.89	59.50	16.52	9.09	100

	Questions	*No. of Respondents*		*Total No. of Respondents*	*Percentage*		*Total Percentage*
		Office	*Other place*		*Office*	*Other place*	
63.	Maintain officials' record	110	11	121	90.91	9.09	100

	Questions	*No. of Respondents*			*Total No. of Respondents*	*Percentage*			*Total Percentage*
		President	*Member*	*No answer*		*President*	*Member*	*No answer*	
64.	Respondent position in organisation	28	75	18	121	23.14	61.99	14.87	100

Sl. No.	*Questions*	*No. of Respondents*		*Total No. of Respondents (121)**	*Percentage*		*Total Percentage*
		Yes	*No*		*Yes*	*No*	
65.	Working for Award	101	20	121	83.48	16.52	100
66.	Got Awards	17	104	121	14.04	85.96	100
67.	Creating Commons	90	31	121	74.39	25.61	100
68.	Creating Assets for Revenue Generation	31	90	121	25.31	74.39	100
69.	Participating in Public Function	100	21	121	82.64	17.36	100
70.	Visiting other States	19	102	121	15.70	84.30	100
71.	Visiting Abroad	21	100	121	17.36	82.64	100
72.	Did you disseminate the knowledge gained in the trainings to the people?	108	13	121	89.26	10.74	100
73.	Conducting Awareness to the people	108	13	121	89.26	10.74	100
74.	Able to Manage Crowd	107	14	121	88.42	11.58	100
75.	Workload in Family Reduced	69	52	121	57.02	42.98	100
76.	Needed Facilities are in the Schools	120	1	121	99.18	0.82	100
77.	Provided Drinking Water	108	13	121	89.26	10.74	100
78.	Streets are Clean	120	1	121	99.18	0.82	100
79.	ANM regularly visiting the village	108	13	121	89.26	10.74	100
80.	Roads are in good condition	102	19	121	84.30	15.70	100
81.	Attending gender justice activities in the Panchayat	83	38	121	68.60	31.40	100
82.	Ensuring maximum justice to the women and Dalit	106	15	121	87.60	12.40	100
83.	Women of Gram Sabha are permitted to speak out women issue?	121	00	121	100	00	100
84.	Dalit women member of Gram Sabha are permitted to speak	109	12	121	90.09	9.91	100
85.	Organising people for common problem	104	17	121	85.96	14.04	100
86.	Experience in organising people	110	11	121	90.91	9.09	100
87.	Equal rights are enjoyed by men and women	110	11	121	90.91	9.09	100
88.	Used the Legal Aid Cell	38	83	121	31.40	68.60	100
89.	Delivery of service effectively on their own	121	00	121	100	00	100
90.	Decisions are their own	100	21	121	82.64	17.36	100
91.	Calling Health Professionals to attend Health care needs	108	13	121	89.26	10.74	100
92.	Complaint were responded	90	31	121	74.39	25.61	100
93.	Satisfied with the delivery of services	109	12	121	90.09	9.91	100

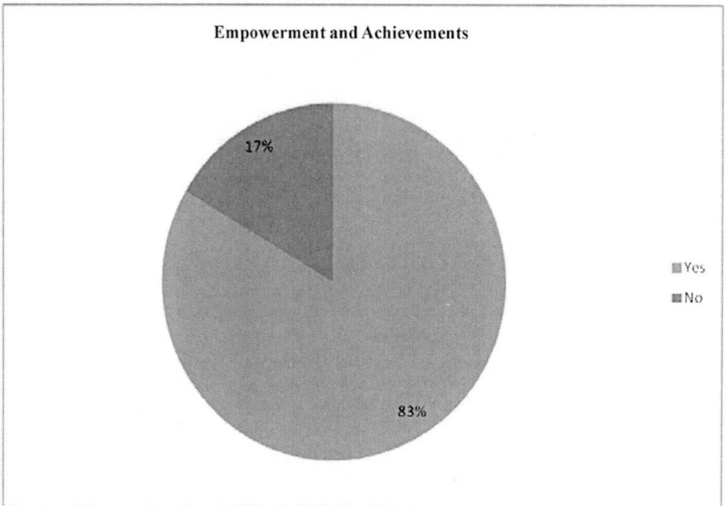

Sl. No.	*Correlation variables (Chapter V and Chapter VI)*	*Positive Answers by Respondents (per cent)*	*Negative Answers by Respondents (per cent)*	*Total Percentage*
1	Opportunity Structure	84	16	100
2	Empowerment and Achievements	83	17	100

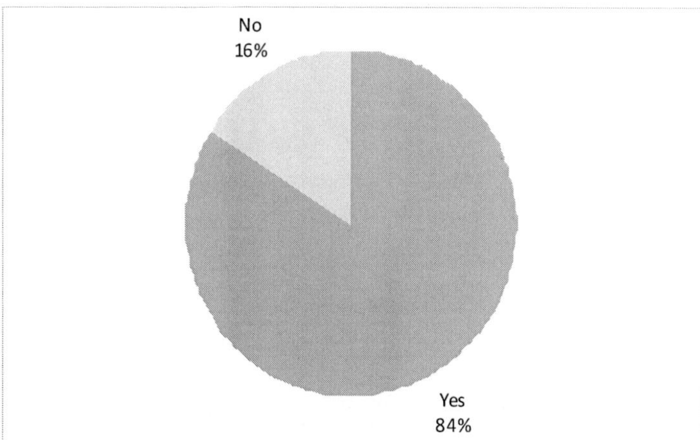

Correlations - Scatter Diagram

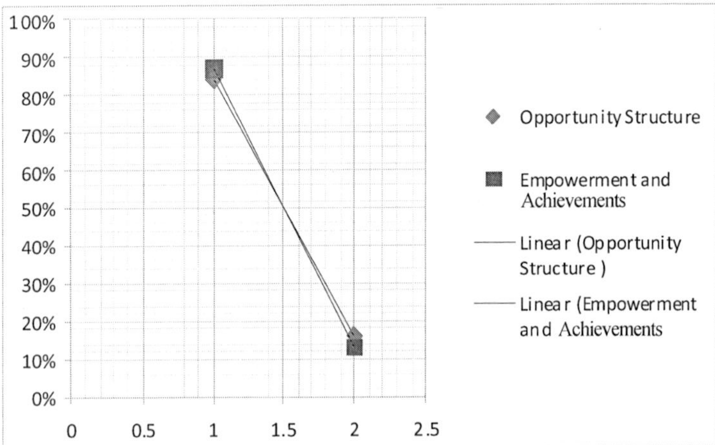

The above correlation is significant at -1 level.

Notes and References

1. Robert E. Goodin, Innovating Democracy: Democratic Theory and Practice after the Deliberative Turn United Kingdom: Oxford University Press, 2012.
2. Palanithurai, G and Ragupathy, V, Functional Efficiency of Gram Sabha, New Delhi: Concept Publishing Company, 2008.

Chapter VII

Conclusion

Variety of reasons are attributed for analysing the level of empowerment of women in India and more specifically now after the enactment of the 73rd Amendment to the Constitution of India. Of the reasons one is so important that the empowerment of women is directly related to the improvement of the health conditions of the entire family and more specifically women and children. Women empowerment is critical for the development of the country. Several researchers have tried to capture empowerment of women with varied perspectives and explanations. For this study the explanation and definition of Batliwala has been taken for analysis. Empowerment is the process by which the powerless gain greater control over the circumstances of their lives. It includes control over resource, gaining self confidence, increasing skill, capability, inner transformation of one's consciousness that enables the individuals to overcome the challenges and barriers. Here empowerment is to gain power to achieve goals. Goals here are the development of women and other marginalised segments of the society. This study makes an attempt to assess the process of empowerment of the Elected Women Representatives and to evaluate the impact of the empowerment on the issues of women and other marginalised.

To analyse and evaluate the above an analytical framework developed Ruth Alsop and Nina Heinsohn has been used. The framework envisages the degree of empowerment depends on the agency and opportunity structure. It further emphasises that development outcomes depend on the degree of empowerment. In simple terms the framework explains that the socio-economic conditions of the Elected Women Representatives and their efforts in building up their skill capacity and capability constitute the agency assets. Opportunity created in the power structure and the efforts made by the Elected Women Representatives to make use of the power structure constitute the opportunity structure. Both together decide the level of empowerment of the Elected Women Representatives. Development outcome of the institution namely, Panchayat depends on the level of empowerment of the Elected Women Representatives. To study the above, data have been drawn from the filed and they are analysed in different ways by using the simple statistical tools. From the study it is inferred that the socio-economic background of the Elected Women Representatives was not so sound. In a feudal social condition one cannot expect the political democracy to flourish and hence social condition coupled with economic status will decide the position of the individual in the society. For any group or individual social status is determined by the placement of his or her own caste in the hierarchy. If an individual is placed in the hierarchy at a higher level and the economic condition of the individual is sound, the empowerment level will be high. In this study it is found that the socio-cconomic conditions of the respondents are poor. Coming to the position as representatives from the marginalised section is a welcoming change. But they are occupying the position with severe constraints and deficiencies. Their preparation for performing the task is not as rigorous as it ought to be. Of course, all formalities have been completed for the preparation of the Elected Women Representatives to achieve development outcome in the institutions. In the same way while handling of the governance institutions and administrative organisations the Elected Women Representatives have not unleashed their potentials. The system drive delivered goods as government schemes are in operation. The uniqueness of the Elected Women Representatives have to be visualised in their functioning in Panchayats. Empowerment of the Elected Women Representatives is a process oriented one and not target oriented. In this study it is observed that they could not come up to the level to tackle the issues of women, children and other marginalised groups as expected. Of course they try to understand the conditions of the women and children. They try to attack the issues. But they could not produce the results as expected.

The given environment in the Panchayati Raj system is not conducive for taking up the critical issues for discourse and deliberation. Preparatory process of the Elected Women Representatives for governance is weak. Handling of the governance institution is as per the direction of the state government. The entire management of the institution is tightly controlled by the officials. Managing the institution and taking up the development issues for redressal by the Elected Women Representatives are crucial in Panchayati Raj system. Obviously, the Elected Women Representatives found it very difficult to tackle them as they are having lot of obstacles and barriers. Handling of the institutions requires special skill. The governance skill is lacking on the part of Elected Women Representatives. While looking at the status of the development more particularly development indicators of the Panchayats one could find the same trend as we find in other places. They are in position and governance takes place and yet one could not see the impact of women in governance. Critical mass has been formed and the critical mass tried to address the critical development issues. But one could not see the visible impact as expected. At the same time one could see the gradual empowerment of the Elected Women Representatives. One could see the impact in the years to come. The reason attributed for the slow process is the given social and economic conditions of the Elected Women Representatives and the preparatory process of the Elected Women Representatives to acquire needed skills and capacity to manage the institution.

Take Away for Policy Recommendation

While conducting any study the researcher is always conscious about its contribution. The contribution may be a confirmation of the established knowledge or a new dimension of the existing knowledge, or rejecting the established knowledgc, and finding a solution to the existing problem or suggesting a new policy dimension to the policy makers. It may be in many forms. It depends on the problem formulation. If a problem is generated from the field and thereby investigation is made, the study would bring solution to the problem in the society. If a problem is formulated from the existing theory, the study would bring either new knowledge or conform the existing knowledge or reject the existing knowledge.

The problem for investigation in this study is formulated from the field and hence it has to contribute solution to the problem in the society. The study is about the level of performance of the Elected Women Representatives and their competency, capacity, skill, capability, in managing the institution of governance at the grassroots. Local body institutions have been created with certain objectives and goals. To fulfill the objectives and goals people are drawn towards the institutions through the process of election while drawing people from different socio-economic segments of the society, the concept of reservation is being operated and thereby an inclusive approach is kept intact in building decision-making institutions. Having the institutions in place the lead question is, have they fulfilled the objectives? Have they got the needed capacity to perform the tasks? For all the above questions answers have been found out in this study by analysing the data collected from the field and conclusions have been drawn. From the conclusions arrived in this study following recommendations have been made.

I. For the successful functioning of the local bodies whether they are rural or urban, public awareness and public vigilance are the basic requirements. We have three tiers of governments namely, Central Government, State Governments, and Local Governments. Even the local governments are of two types. They are rural and urban local governments. The rural local government has got three tier structures. What are the functions to be performed by the central government, state governments, and local governments and more particularly the three tiers of Panchayats have to be known to the people. Activities chart have to be prepared and they are to be known to the people in the rural areas. Till date there is no exercise in the villages.

Even after twenty years of decentralisation exercises, people are not having clarity on the role to be performed by the Members of Parliament, Members of Legislative Assembly and Members of Local Bodies. People have role confusion. Hence they submit petitions to the Members of Parliament for water supply which is to be looked after by the local bodies. Equally the elected representatives have role confusion. It is a known fact that in our country there is no training for Members of Parliament and Members of State Legislatures. There is no exclusive training academy for legislators. For local body leaders we have training institutions but they are not having the institutional capacity to build the capacity of the elected representatives. To shape our local body leaders to perform the expected function it has to function as a leadership school as they are in the west or in Singapore Leadership Academy. A new leadership school is needed not only for local body leaders but also for all other representatives.

The existing training institution at the state level has to be made as Leadership School and they have to function independently and autonomously as universities. They should be made leadership schools meant for training and research. Every State Institute of Rural Development has to be converted into a Leadership School on par with Kennedy School of Government attached with Harward University. All the state Institutes of Rural Development have to be attached with the nearest university with full autonomy for their functions. Training fee has to be paid by the local bodies and hence they should have hold over the training institutions. Government can directly allocate the training resources to local bodies. In such a way training exercises have to be carried out.

We have thirty lakh and six thousand representatives from local bodies to National Parliament. But we do not have a training policy, training framework and regular resource allocation for capacity building. Hence we need to have a training policy, training approach, perspective and regular resource allocation.

Elected representatives have been given salary, perks and other privileges for both Members of Parliament and Members of State

Legislatures. But for local body leaders such a kind of remuneration has not been given. To the level of their service they have to be paid. No one will be in the public space for free service. One cannot expect that representatives of the people to do free service. Only in Kerala, the local body leaders are moderately paid salary to the elected representatives. In the same way remuneration has to be paid. It is a paid work. Poor women that too from a Dalit background comes to local body through a process of election and she has to perform her duties and discharge her responsibilities and what she will do for her livelihood, if she is not adequately compensated for her work.

Elected representatives should have a manual for their roles and responsibilities. Whether they are Members of Parliament, or Members of State Legislatures or Members of Local Bodies, they need to have a manual to discharge their responsibilities.

Twenty years have gone in decentralisation. Thirty million representatives are in position. The impacts of the institutions are multidimensional as people drawn from different social and economic segments of the society to the new institutions. Where are the local body institutions in terms of their stability, what are the strengths and weakness of these institutions? How they are performing their duties? How they are cost effective? What new dimensions are emerging in governance at grassroots? have to be studied by a group of scholars. It needs a new academy or an academic association as Indian Academy of Social Science or any other Academic Association covering all over India.

Governance and administration in India is complex as politics. To enable the local body leaders to perform their duties and responsibilities, governance and administration have to be simplified. Steps have to be taken to simplify both. To do the above both the Centre and State Governments have to implement the recommendations of Second Administrative Reform Commission, State Administrative Reform Commission and Centre and State Relations Commission.

In a Nutshell

(i) Still people not aware of the core responsibilities of the local bodies and hence massively awareness has to be created. Throughout the country higher learning institutions can be used to do such awareness.

(ii) In order to bring role clarity among the representatives; activity mapping has to be done for all the three governments.

(iii) For building the capacity of the elected representatives India needs leadership schools as in the west. The schools should be made autonomous and they should be attached with higher learning institutions preferably with universities.

(iv) Twenty years have gone after the introduction of the 73rd Amendment to the Constitution and hence its impact has to be studied through a team of scholars.

(v) An academy has to be constituted by drawing scholars from different disciplines to deepen the studies in grassroots transformation with a focus on decentralisation.

(vi) Administrative manual for local governance has to be prepared for every state and they should be given to the elected representatives.

(vii) India should have a training policy and training framework. Equally states should have training policy and training framework. Along with training policy both central and state governments should allocate a fixed resource every year for training in the budget itself.

(viii) Elected women representatives in local bodies have to be paid salary as it has been done to MLA and MP salary based on the responsibilities assigned to them.

(ix) Steps have to be taken to implement the report of the Second Administrative Reform Commission meant for local bodies by both central and state governments.

(x) In every state a watch dog committee has to be constituted to monitor the empowerment process of women through cutting edge activities of all the government departments.

Bibliography

1. Alsop Ruth and Nina Heinsohn, Measuring Empowerment in Practice: Structuring Analysis and Framing Indicators Working Paper 3510, Washington DC: World Bank, 2005.
2. Athreya, V.B. and Rajeswari K.S., Women's Participation in Panchayati Raj: A Case Study from Tamil Nadu, Chennai: M.S. Swaminathan Research Foundation, 1999.
3. Batliwala, Srilatha, "The Meaning of Women's Empowerment" Women's World, 23-34.
4. Buch, Nirmala, From Oppression to Assertion: A Study of Panchayats and Women in Madhya Pradesh, Rajasthan and Uttar Pradesh (Mimo) New Delhi, CWDS, 1999.
5. Burn, S.M, "Women across Cultures: A Global Perspective" May Field: Mountain View, 2000.
6. Caroline, Moser, "Gender Planning in Third World: Meeting practical and strategic gender needs" World Development, Vol. 17, No.11 (1989).
7. Chaney, Paul "Critical Mass, Deliberation and the Substantative Representation of Women: Evidence from the UK's Devolution Programme" Political Studies (2006) Vol. 54, 691-714.
8. Chathukulam, Jos and John MS, "Empowerment of Women Panchayat Members: Learning from Kerala" Asian Journal of Women Studies, Vol. 6, No. 4 (1985).
9. Damyanty Sridharan and Vesna Rodic (eds), Breaking the Political Class Ceiling: Women and Local Governance in South Asia, New Delhi: Fredrich Ebert Stiftung, 2004.

10. Dharampal, The Madras Panchayat System Vol. II A General Assessment, New Delhi: Impex India, 1972.
11. Gargarella, R, "Full Representation, Deliberation and Impartiality" in J. Elster (ed) Deliberative Democracy Cambridge: Cambridge University Press, 1998, pp.142-163.
12. Government of India, Powers and Functions of Panchayati Raj Institutions A Framework, New Delhi: Ministry of Rural Development, 1994.
13. Government of India, Renewing Local Self Government in Rural India, New Delhi: Ministry of Rural Development, 1994.
14. Government of India, Towards Equality: Report of the Committee on the status of women in India New Delhi: Government of India, 1975.
15. Government of Tamil Nadu, Democratic Decentralisation: Powers entrusted to Panchayati Raj Institutions, Chennai: Rural Development Department, 1999.
16. Government of Tamil Nadu, High Power Committee Report on Entrustment of Powers to three tier Local Bodies in Tamil Nadu, Chennai: State Planning Commission, 1998.
17. Gupta, Sen, "Poverty, Economic Growth and Gender Equity: The Asian and Pacific Experience" in Gender Economic Growth and Poverty Nocleen Heyzer and Gita Sen, New Delhi: Kali For women, 1994.
18. Gupta, Sen and Grown Caren, Development Crises and Alternative Visions: Third World Perspectives, New York: Monthly Review Press, 1987.
19. Jennie Litvack, Junaid Ahmed, Rethinking Decentralisation in Developing and Richard Bird Countries, Washington D.C.: The World Bank, 1998.
20. Kabeer, Naila, "Reflections on the Measurement of Women's Empowerment" in Discussing Women's Empowerment: Theory and Practice sida studies No. 3 Stockholm: Novum Grafiska AB, 2001.
21. Kishor, Sumita and Gupta Kamla, "Women's Empowerment in India and its States: Evidence from the NFHS" Economic and Political Weekly, February 14, 2004.

22. Kishor, Sunita, "Empowerment of Women in Egypt and Links to the Survival and Health of their Infants" in Harriet B. Presger and Gita Sen (eds) Women's Empowerment and Demographic Process, New York: Oxford University Press, 2000.
23. Mangubhai, Jayshree, Irudayam sj Aloysius and Sydenham Emma, Dalit Women's Right to Political Participation in Rural Panchayati Raj, The Netherlands: Justiatia et pax, 2009.
24. Ministry of Panchayati Raj, Study on Elected Women Representatives in Panchayati Raj Institutions, New Delhi: Ministry of Panchayati Raj, 2008.
25. Mohanty, Bidyut, "Panchayati Raj Institutions and Women" in From Independence Towards Freedom: Indian Women Since 1947 (eds) Bharati Ray and Aparna Basu, New Delhi: Oxford University Press, 1999, pp. 19-33.
26. Narashimhan, Sakuntala, Empowering Women: An Alternative Strategy from Rural India New Delhi, Sage Publications, 1999.
27. Norris, P. Lovenduski, J Blair's, Babes: Critical Mass Theory, Gender and Legislative Life (Working paper series) John F. Kennedy School of Government, Harvard University, 2001.
28. Palanithurai, G, Building Alliance and Capabilities among the Elected Women Representatives of Grassroots, Gandhigram: Rajiv Gandhi Chair for Panchayati Raj Studies, 2003.
29. Palanithurai, G, Elected Women Representatives and Emerging Alternative Governance, Gandhigram: Rajiv Gandhi Chair for Panchayati Raj Studies, 2005.
30. Palanithurai, G, Elected Women Representatives and Empowerment, New Delhi: Concept Publishing Company, 2012.
31. Palanithurai, G, Evaluation of the Process and Performance of Women and Dalit Leaders in Gram Panchayats, New Delhi: Concept Publishing Company, 2005.
32. Palanithurai, G, Experience of the Elected Women Representatives in Grassroots Institutions, Gandhigram: Rajiv Gandhi Chair for Panchayati Raj Studies, 2004.
33. Palanithurai, G, G. Uma and J.Vanishree, Networking of Elected Women Representaives, New Delhi: Concept Publishing Company, 2012.

34. Palanithurai, G, Governance: From the Perspective of Elected Women Representatives, Gandhigram: Rajiv Gandhi Chair for Panchayati Raj Studies, 2004.

35. Palanithurai, G., "Building Alliances and Capabilities among the elected women representatives of Grassroots institutions", Womens Link, Vol.10, No.1 (Jan-Mar 2004) pp.18-25.

36. Palanithurai, G., "Towards Participatory Governance at Grassroots: Synergisation of Rural Communities and Institutions" South Asian Journal of Socio Political Studies, Vol. 4, No.1 (Dec, 2003).

37. Palanithurai, G., Capacity Building for Local Body Leaders, New Delhi: Concept Publishing Company, 2001.

38. Palanithurai, G., Development Role Reversed: From Government to People, Gandhigram: Rajiv Gandhi Chair for Panchayati Raj Studies, 2003.

39. Palanithurai, G., Dwaraki B.R. and Narayanasamy S., (Eds), Major Issues in New Panchayati Raj System (Eds), New Delhi: Kanishka Publications, 1997.

40. Palanithurai, G., Empowering People for prosperity: A study in New Panchayati Raj System, New Delhi: Kanishka Publications, 1994.

41. Palanithurai, G., Evaluation of Process and Performance of Gram Panchayat Women and Dalit Presidents in Tamil Nadu, Gandhigram: Rajiv Gandhi Chair, 2003.

42. Palanithurai, G., Grassroots Democracy in Indian Society, New Delhi: Concept Publications, 1997.

43. Palanithurai, G., New Panchayati Raj System at Work: An Evaluation, New Delhi: Concept Publishing Company, 2000.

44. Palanithurai, G., New Panchayati Raj System at Work: An Evaluation, New Delhi: Concept Publications, 1999.

45. Palanithurai, G., New Panchayati Raj System: Status and Prospects, New Delhi: Kaniska Publications, 1996, pp. 57-64.

46. Palanithurai, G., Panchayats, Communities and Social Development, Gandhigram: Rajiv Gandhi Chair for Panchayati Raj Studies, 2003.

47. Palanithurai, G.,(Ed), Empowering People: Issues and Solutions, New Delhi: Kanishka Publications, 1996.
48. Palanithurai, G.,(Ed), New Panchayati Raj System Status and Prospects, New Delhi: Kanishka Publications, 1996.
49. Palanithurai, G, "Role of Panchayat in Service Delivery: A Case Analysis" Punjab Journal of Politics, Vol. XXXI: 2007.
50. Palanithurai, G and Ragupathy, V, Communities, Panchayats and Governance at Grassroots, New Delhi, Concept Publishing Company, 2007.
51. Palanithurai, G, Governance from the Perspective of Elected Women Representatives (Monograph), Gandhigram: Rajiv Gandhi Chair for Panchayati Raj Studies, 2004.
52. Palanithurai, G, People Perception of Politics: An Indian Perspective, New Delhi: Kanishka Publishers and Distributors, 1995.
53. Palanithurai, G, Synergisation of Traditional Panchayat with Formal Panchayati Raj System in Managing Community Affairs (Monograph), Gandhigram, Rajiv Gandhi Chair for Panchayati Raj Studies, 2003.
54. Palanithurai, G, Panchayats, Communities and Social Development (Monograph), Gandhigram, Rajiv Gandhi Chair for Panchayati Raj Studies, 2003.
55. Palanithurai, G, Change Makers at Grassroots: Leadership Matters Much, New Delhi: Concept Publishing Company, 2008.
56. Palanithurai, G, Dalits and Dalit Representatives in Rural Local Governance: Voices from the Field, New Delhi, Concept Publishing Company, 2013.
57. Palanithurai, G, Process and Performance of Gram Panchayat Women and Dalit Presidents, New Delhi: Concept Publishing Company, 2005.
58. Palanithurai, G, and Ragupathy. V, Functional Efficiency of Gram Sabha, New Delhi: Concept Publishing Company, 2008.
59. Palanithurai, G, Problems Faced by the Elected Women Representatives (Monograph), Gandhigram: Rajiv Gandhi Chair Panchayati Raj Studies, 2002.

60. Palanithurai, G, Role Perception of Legislators, New Delhi: Konark Publication, 1991.

61. Palanithurai, G, Uma, G and Vanishree, J, Networking of Elected Women Representatives at Grassroots, New Delhi: Concept Publishing Company, 2010.

62. Palanithurai, G, Vallinayagam, K, Chidambaram N.S, and Subramaniam K, Handbook of Panchayati Raj Administration (Tamil Nadu), New Delhi: Concept Publishing Company, 2007.

63. Phillips, A, "Representing Difference: Why it matters if women get elected: in A Coote (ed) New Gender Agenda London:!! PR, 2000.

64. Population Foundation of India, Empowerment of Panchayati Raj Institutions on Issues Related to Population, Health and Social Development, A Final Report, New Delhi: Population Foundation of India, 2001.

65. Rai, Manoj, Nambiar Mabini, Paul Sohini, Sangeeta Sing and Satinder S. Sahni (eds), "The State of Panchayats: A Participatory Perspective", New Delhi: Sanskrit, for PRIA, 2001.

66. Rajiv Gandhi Chair, Functional Efficiency of Gram Sabha: A Report submitted to II State Finance Commission, Gandhigram: Rajiv Gandhi Chair for Panchayati Raj Studies, 2000.

67. Rajiv Gandhi Chair, Problems faced by the Gram Panchayati Leaders, Gandhigram: Rajiv Gandhi Chair for Panchayati Raj Studies, 2000.

68. Rajiv Gandhi Foundation, Dialogue on Panchayat: Summary proceedings of four Regional Tripartile Interface Interactive workshops, New Delhi: Rajiv Gandhi Foundation, 1999.

69. Rajiv Gandhi Foundation, Panchayati Raj in India: Status Report, New Delhi: Rajiv Gandhi Foundation, 2000.

70. Rajiv Gandhi Foundation, Proceedings of the National Seminar on Panchayats, New Delhi: Rajiv Gandhi Foundation, 1997.

71. Rajiv Gandhi Foundation, Proceedings of the National Seminar on Panchayats, New Delhi: Rajiv Gandhi Foundation, 1993.

72. Rajiv Gandhi Foundation, Revitalisation of Panchayati Raj in India, New Delhi: Rajiv Gandhi Foundation, 1999.
73. Rajiv Gandhi Foundation, Voices from Below: Summary proceedings of Sub-Regional workshops on panchayats: Issues and Recommendations, New Delhi: Rajiv Gandhi Foundation, 2001.
74. Rani, Celine A, Women Leadership at Grassroots, New Delhi: Gyan Publications, 2004.
75. Robert, E. Goodin, Innovating Democracy: Democratic Theory and Practice after the Deliberative Turn, United Kingdom: Oxford University Press, 2012.
76. Rukmani, R., Panchayati Raj Institutions in Tamil Nadu: A Historical Review, Chennai: Madras Institute of Development Studies, 1996.
77. Rural Development Department, Democratic Decentralisation: Panchayati Raj System in Tamil Nadu, Chennai: Rural Development Department, 1999.
78. Santha, E.K, "Political Participation of in Women in Panchayati Raj: Haryana Kerala and Tamil Nadu", New Delhi: Institute of Social Sciences, 1999.
79. Sarasvathi, The Madras Panchayat System Vol. I. A Historical Survey, Delhi: Impex India, 1973.
80. Sekhon, Joti, "Democratic Theories and Women's Practices" Canadian Journal of Development Studies", XXII (special issue).
81. Sekhon, Joti, "Engendering Grassroots Democracy: Research, Training and Networking for Women in Local Self Governance in India" NWSA Journal Vol. 18: No. 2 (summer, 2006).
82. Shah, Ghanshyam, Caste Association and Political Process in Gujarat, Bombay: Popular Prakashan, 1975.
83. Siddartha, Sivaramakrishnan, Discussion: Challenges and Opportunities for Panchayati Raj, New Delhi: World Bank, 1999.
84. Siddartha, Sivaramakrishnan, Panchayati Raj Institutions in India - A Society Study for the World Bank, Washington DC: World Bank, 1999.

85. State Finance Commission, Summary of Recommendations of the State Finance Commission for Local Bodies, Chennai: State Finance Commission, 1966.

86. State Planning Commission, Report of the working group on Decentralised Planning and Panchayati Raj, Chennai: State Planning Commission, 1997.

87. State Planning Commission, Report on the Entrustment of Powers to Panchayats, Chennai: State Planning Commission, 1997.

88. The Catalyst Trust, Citizens Audit of Basic Services in Tamil Nadu, Chennai: Catalyst Trust, 2008.

89. The Hunger Project, Report on the workshop on Panchayati Raj: Trials and Triumphs, Gandhigram: Rajiv Gandhi Chair for Panchayati Raj Studies, 2003.

90. The Hunger Project, Thus Spoke the Press: Select Articles on Elected Women Leaders in Village Panchayats, New Delhi: The Hunger Project, 2006, 2007 and 2008.

91. The Hunger Project, Thus Spoke the Press: Select Articles on Elected Women Leaders in Village Panchayats, New Delhi: The Hunger Project, 2006, 2007, 2008, 2009 and 2010.

92. The Hunger Project, Women and Panchayati Raj The Pathway to Social Transformation and a New Future for India, Bombay: The Hunger Project, 1999.

93. Verba Sidney, Nie Norman H and Kim o K, Participation and Political Equality: A Seven Nation Comparison, London: Cambridge University Press, 1978.

Appendix - I

ICSSR Sponsored Project on Critical Mass to Critical Action: A Study of the Process of Empowerment Interview Schedule

Location Details

1. Name of the Hamlet/Village :
2. Name of the Panchayat :
3. Name of the Union :
4. Name of the District :

Mailing Address

Respondent Details

1. Name of the Person :
2. Age
   (a) 20 yrs and below
   (b) 21-30
   (c) 31-40
   (d) 41-50
   (e) 51 and above
3. Marital Status
   (a) Married
   (b) Unmarried

(c) Widow
(d) Separated

4. Religion
(a) Hindu
(b) Christian
(c) Muslim
(d) Others

5. Community
(a) BC
(b) MBC
(c) SC/ST
(d) Others

6. Educational Status
(a) Illiterate
(b) Upto V
(c) VI to VIII
(d) IX to X
(e) X to XII
(f) Graduate
(g) Above

I. Agency Indicators:

Material Assets: Ownership of land and housing status

7. Housing Status

Own House			Rented House		
Hut	Tiled	Others	Hut	Tiled	Others

8. Landholding
(a) Upto 2 Acres
(b) 2 – 5
(c) 5 and above
(d) Nil

9. Landholding on your Name
   (a) Upto 2 Acres
   (b) 2 – 5
   (c) 5 and above
   (d) Nil
10. Do you have toilet facility in your house, Yes/No
11. What is the primary source of drinking water?
   (a) Public tab
   (b) Tab connection in the house
   (c) Public well
   (d) Hand Pump
   (e) Others
12. What type of lightings in your house?
   (a) Electricity
   (b) Solar
   (c) Kerosene, gas
   (d) Others

Financial Assets: Occupation, Income and Expenditure Level

13. What is your occupation?
   (a) Farmer
   (b) Coolie
   (c) Private employee
   (d) Small business
   (e) Business
14. How would you categorise your employment status?
   (a) Employed on contract
   (b) Monthly Salary
   (c) Self Employed
   (d) Unemployed
   (e) Others

15. What is your monthly family income (In Rs)
    (a) 1000 - 1500
    (b) 1500 - 2000
    (c) 2000 - 3000
    (d) 3000 – 4000
    (e) 4000 and above
16. Do you feel economically secure in your present / occupation? Yes/No
17. Have you borrowed money from another person / institution? Yes/No
18. Did you borrow money from the banks for any purposes? Yes/No
19. What is the total monthly expenditure?
20. How much money is being spent in a month for the following:
    (a) Food
    (b) Education
    (c) Health
    (d) Rent and housing costs
    (e) Others
21. Did you handle money for the election expenses on your own? Yes/No

Support Structure from Family / Society

1. Who has motivated / encouraged you to contest in election?
    (a) Family Members
    (b) Relatives
    (c) Community
    (d) Friends
    (e) Others
2. Have you mobilised and used your friends for the election campaign? Yes/No
3. Are you continuously getting support from any external agency for your functioning? Yes/No

4. Do your family members allow you to travel alone? Yes/No
5. Do your family members extend their full support to you on your independent functioning? Yes/No
6. Are you getting support from any external institutions/ organisations to perform your functions effectively? Yes/No

   If yes, what kind of support?
7. Do you contact the trainers regularly to get ideas and guidance to bring changes and development in the community? Yes/No

   If yes, explain in what ways?
8. Do you contact any institutions / organisations / universities towards transfer the technology for the development of your village panchayat? Yes/No

Informational Assets: Awareness level on Issues and Access to Information

1. Are you aware of the opportunities for women empowerment? Yes/No
2. Are you aware that Panchayats can work for gender justice? Yes/No
3. Are you aware that Panchayat can work for women component plan? Yes/No
4. Are you aware that Panchayat can work for gender budget? Yes/No
5. Are you aware that Panchayat can stop violence against women? Yes/No
6. Are you aware that Panchayat can be made as pro women panchayats? Yes/No
7. Are you aware that Panchayat can work for gender equality? Yes/No
8. Are you aware of the health conditions of women in the rural areas? Yes/No

9. Are you aware of the health conditions of the children in the rural area? Yes/No
10. Is your village easily accessible to the outsiders / visitors? Yes/No
11. How often do you watch television?
12. Do you listen radio? How often?
13. Do you read newspapers regularly? Yes/No
14. What type of programmes you watch, listen and read?
    (a) politics
    (b) current affairs
    (c) cinema news
    (d) sports
    (e) novels
    (f) films
    (g) others
15. In a year how many times Gram Sabha has to be convened?
16. Do you know the quorum for Gram Sabha meeting? Yes/No
17. Do you know how to conduct the Gram Sabha meeting? Yes/No
18. Do you know how to implement the decisions of Gram Sabha? Yes/No
19. Do you know the quorum for panchayat council meeting? Yes/No
20. Do you know how to conduct the panchayat council meeting? Yes/No
21. Do you know the planning exercise at the panchayat level? Yes/No
22. Do you know the procedure to prepare the budget? Yes/No
23. Are you aware of tracking panchayat finance? Yes/No

Laws and Regulations

1. Have you read the Panchayati Act of Tamil Nadu? Yes/No
2. Are you aware of rules of the panchayats? Yes/No
3. Are you aware of the schemes of rural development? Yes/No
4. Are you aware of the reservation policy for women? Yes/No
5. Are you getting the Government Orders properly? Yes/No

Organisational Assets: Membership of Organisation / Political Party and Group Leadership

1. Are you affiliated with any political party? Yes/No
2. Is your husband or family members affiliated with any political party at State / National level? Yes/No
3. Have you ever given chance to meet the political party leaders? Yes/No
4. Have you participated in civil society organisation activities? Yes/No
5. Are you a member of any social organisation? Yes/No
6. Are you a member of any society just like SHG? Yes/No
7. What is your position in the organisation?
   Leader / Member
8. How are the leaders and members in group selected?
9. How effective is the group leadership?
10. As a member of the group, do you get benefit individually? Yes/No
11. Are you involved in SHG movement in Tamil Nadu? Yes/No

Skill / Training / Capacity Building / Self Confidence

1. Do you take decisions on important matters on your own? Yes/No

2. Did you ever dream of your village development? Yes/No
3. Are you thorough on your responsibilities? Yes/No
4. Did you go to offices far and near on your own? Yes/No
5. Did you speak to the officials on your own? Yes/No
6. Did you speak in the public meeting? Yes/No
7. Did you attend training programme? Yes/No
8. Do you think, the trainings have enhanced your capacity and leadership quality? Yes/No
9. Do you have administrative manual? Yes/No
10. Did you make promise to the people to seek their votes? Yes/No
11. Did you participate in all the meetings along with men? Yes/No
12. Are you satisfied with your present post? Yes/No

II. Opportunity Structure

Politics and Administration

1. Is your panchayat reserved for women? Yes/No
2. Have you attended any political party meeting? Yes/No
3. Did you make political campaign for your election? Yes/No
4. Will you contest in MLA election? Yes/No
5. Duration of Gram Sabha meeting?
   (a) 1 hour
   (b) 2 hours
   (c) 3 hours
   (d) 4 hours
   (e) 5 hours
6. Total member attended
7. Total members participated

8. Duration of Panchayat Council Meeting?
   (a) 1 hour
   (b) 2 hours
   (c) 3 hours
   (d) 4 hours
   (e) 5 hours
9. Total members attended:
10. Total members participated:
11. Who is the chairperson of the Gram Sabha?
12. Who presides over the panchayat meeting?
13. How many of the members in Gram Sabha would speak?
14. Do the ward members pay attention to your words? Yes/No
15. Do people actively participate in the Gram Sabha meetings? Yes/No
16. Did you identify yourself with political parties for the election? Yes/No
17. Are you meeting government officials directly? Or with the assistance of your male member of your family? Yes/No
18. Have you approached government officials to solve the problems in your panchayat area frequently? Yes/No
19. Are they positive to your requests? Yes/No
20. Do you have the practice of approaching the officials regularly? Yes/No

If yes, who are the officials?
   (a) Project Officer
   (b) BDO
   (c) Health Officials
   (d) Agriculture officer
   (e) Education officer
   (f) Others Sectoral Officials

21. What kind of support you get from the officials for panchayat work?
22. Are you ensuring maximum presence of women in the Gram Sabha meeting? Yes/No
23. Who are the speakers in Gram Sabha?
    (a) Women
    (b) dalit
    (c) higher caste
    (d) men
24. Which are the issues predominant in Gram Sabha?
    (i) Women
    (ii) Children
    (iii) Public Services
    (iv) Health
    (v) Education
    (vi) Road
    (vii) Water supply
    (viii) Agriculture
    (ix) Livelihood
    (x) Social Issues
    (xi) Electricity
    (xii) Public distribution
25. Who are managing the commons?
26. Who prepares agenda for Gram Sabha meeting?
    Government / Panchayat Leader / Panchayat Council
27. Which are all the department you approach the government for panchayat development activities?
28. Do you have contact with sectoral department for rural development activities? Yes/No
29. How many accounts you have in your panchayats?
30. Are you sufficiently informed about your roles? Yes/No
31. Do you send letters to District Collector? Yes/No

32. Have you ever visited Anganwadi? Yes/No
33. Have you ever visited PDS shops? Yes/No
34. Do you ever visit schools? Yes/No
35. Did you attend school functions? Yes/No
36. Did you involve in Admission drive for public schools? Yes/No
37. Do you find the strong presence of traditional panchayats? Yes/No
38. Do you find the parallel bodies presence in your panchayats? Yes/No
39. Are you involved in the functioning of parallel bodies? Yes/No
40. How do you sort out the problems you gather from Gram Sabha?
41. Are you attending all the official meetings? Yes/No
42. Are you going to panchayat office regularly? Yes/No
43. Where you maintain your official records?
    In your office / In your personal custody

Service Delivery

1. Are you able to deliver the services effectively on your own? Yes/No
2. Who makes important decisions about the public services in your panchayat?
3. Do you contact / invite any health professionals to provide healthcare to the people? Yes /No
4. Do you pay attention to the education and training services? Yes/No
5. Have you ever made a complaint to the authorities regarding the delivery of services? Yes/No
6. How many times have you made complaint?
7. Do you feel the complaint was successfully resolved? Yes/No

8. Are the people satisfied over the delivery of services? Yes/No

Justice and Redressal Mechanism

1. Are you attending social justice activities? Yes/No

   If yes, what kind of activities?

   Removing untouchability / temple entry / removing two tumbler system
2. Are you attending gender justice activities in the panchayats? Yes/No
3. Do you ensure maximum justice to the women and dalit? Yes/No
4. Are the women members of Gram Sabha permitted to speak out women issues? Yes/No
5. Are the Dalit women member of Gram Sabha permitted to speak out their issues? Yes/No
6. Do you have any experience in organising people for common problem redressal? Yes/No
7. What are all the mechanisms used in your area to achieve justice?
8. Have you ever used these systems to seek redressal / access justice? Yes/No
9. Do you think women and men get better, equal treatment in the system of justice? Yes/No
10. Are you effectively using the system of justice? Yes/No
11. Have you ever approached free legal aid cell to redress the grievances? Yes/No

Achievements and Actions Taken

1. What are the measures you have taken to put forth on your panchayat to become a model panchayat?
2. Have you created any opportunity for the women, youths and dalits to engage in income-generating activities? Yes/No

   If yes, what are they?

3. Are you aware about the awards of the government for the performance of the panchayats? Yes/No
4. Have you received any award / reward from the government for the outstanding performance of your panchayat activities? Yes/No

   If yes, mention below.
5. Have you created any common assets for the public? Yes/No

   If yes list them out.
6. Have you created any revenue generating avenues for your panchayats? Yes/No

   If yes mentioned them below.
7. Have you been invited for public function as president? Yes/No
8. Have you ever visited other states? Yes/No
9. Have you ever visited abroad? Yes/No
10. Did you disseminate the knowledge gained in the trainings to the people? Yes/No
11. Did you conduct any awareness programmes to the people? Yes/No

    If yes, mention the details of the programme.
12. Are you comfortable in crowd management? Yes/No
13. Have your family workload reduced? Yes/No
14. Are the schools in good condition? Yes/No
15. Are the water supply schemes working well? Yes/No
16. Are the streets clean and neat? Yes/No
17. Are the PDS functioning well? Yes/No
18. Is the ANM regularly visiting the village? Yes/No
19. Are the teachers coming to school in time and regularly? Yes/No
20. Are the roads in good condition? Yes/No
21. Are the benefits of the government schemes reaching the needy? Yes/No

Problems faced by the Respondents

1. Do you have problem in family front? Yes/No
2. Do you have problem in community front? Yes/No
3. Do you find problem in your party? Yes/No
4. Do you find problem in offices of the government? Yes/No
5. Do you find problem in panchayat council? Yes/No
6. Do you find problem in managing the vice-president? Yes/No
7. Have you faced problems from the family and community while contesting in the election? Yes/No

Specific Development Activities

1. Sanitation
2. Water Supply
3. Health of Women
4. Health of Children
5. Social Justice
6. Gender Justice
7. PDS
8. Connectivity
9. Streetlight
10. Commons
11. Technology Adoption
12. Innovation
13. Resource Mobilisation
14. Livelihood

Unique Achievements

S.No.	*Major Activities*	*Amount Spent*			
		I year	*II year*	*III year*	*IV year*

Resource Mobilisation

S.No.	*Resource Mobilised*	*Amount*
1.	Central Government	
2.	State Government	
3.	Own from panchayats	
4.	Others	
	Total	

Appendix-II

Capacity Building Exercises Done by Rajiv Gandhi Chair for Panchayati Raj Studies

My vision for Rajiv Gandhi Chair for Panchayati Raj Studies in Gandhigram was that it should emerge not only as a world class centre for research on decentralised governance but also as an outstanding leadership school. It must take up research, training, and policy advocacy. Hence steps were taken to prepare tools for training, training ambience and master trainers. First, we identified experts with rich experience in rural local governance. While fixing those resource persons, we made it a point that those experts had proper perspectives on and commitments towards new Panchayati Raj. Quite often in India, we come across knowledgeable people who are insensitive and not willing to come off their pedestal. Ultimately, they end up being uncommitted to the issues of the poor. We are wary of such people, and let them remain asleep.

Once the resource persons are identified, we had to prepare training modules and manuals. We conducted series of workshops to prepare both training modules and manuals inviting different stakeholders. Based on the above exercises we have prepared training modules and manuals. We have developed modules for training rural local governance leaders of all the three tiers. We have specific modules prepared for training women leaders for local governance.

Yet another module was prepared to train dalit elected representatives. All the modules were published and widely circulated among various training institutions. Most of our publications remain copy left. Except a few publications brought out by publishers investing their money, we do not hold any copy right because our purpose is dissemination even beyond our reach.

Government training institutions have also prepared such modules for conducting training programmes. We reviewed them to find out if they could be used in our training programmes so that we need not reinvent the wheel. But, we found them very much general or non-specific. Moreover, we find many of them adopt an instructive-mode which pedagogically we call: Do's and Don'ts Type. In other words, they prescribe what to do and what not to do. They tend to focus more on official / bureaucratic rules and procedures, rather than best practices with a developmental perspective. The specific aspects on dalits, or women get marginalised in such works. We make a difference by custom-designing our works with sufficient sensitivity for dalits, women, youth and so on. Organisations which conducted training programme for dalit leaders have used our training modules. Organisations which have conducted training programme for women leaders used our training module. All the modules are updated periodically.

After preparing the training modules, manuals have been prepared so as to give them as an operational tool or guide to the leaders who participated in our training programmes. We have prepared comprehensive manual for rural local governance meant for all the three tiers of rural local governance. Apart from the comprehensive manual, specific manuals were also prepared. Manual for Ward members of Gram Panchayat, Manual for Gram Panchayat Presidents, Manual for Block Panchayat Council members, Block Panchayat chair persons, Manual for District Panchayat chair persons. Moreover, we have prepared manual for Gram Sabha members and committee members of various sub-committees of the Panchayats. All the manuals have been published through various agencies. Apart from reading the material for semi-literature we have also prepared audio and video material. Video CDs and audio cassettes have been prepared and produced material in large scale for distribution. While preparing such training tools we have involved a whole array of stakeholders. We have involved gender specialist, specialist on marginalised, communication specialist, specialist on administration in all our exercises.

Preparation of all these materials was viewed not merely as an intellectual exercise. It was a soul satisfying experience that we were putting in our efforts, time and intellect for the benefit of empowering the rural community in Tamil Nadu. For preparing and publishing training tools three institutions have supported the Rajiv Gandhi Chair for Panchayati Raj studies. Rajiv Gandhi Foundation supported for production of comprehensive of training module and manuals for Panchayati Raj training. The Hunger project helped us to produce training modules and manuals for training elected women representatives and elected women dalit representatives. Population Foundation of India supported us for preparation and production of video and audio training material.

These raining materials were used in a series of training programmes we conducted later on. Although our focus was Gram Panchayat leaders, we have conducted training for leaders and potentials leaders of all the three tiers in the Panchayat set up. This is because we have a perspective that if a transformative leader is shaped for Gram Panchayat, the Gram Panchayat areas can be transformed very easily by the transformative leader. We believe that electing a leader is not in our hands, but shaping a leader can best be done in our hands. Hence preparing transformative leaders for Gram Panchayat was our target.

The Government of Tamil Nadu has developed a perspective that of the three tiers, Gram Panchayat has to be strengthened for effective service delivery at the grassroots level. Hence powers have been accorded to Gram Panchayat more than the other two tiers. In the party-based political marketplace, Gram Panchayat was to a considerable extent free from the party-based contest. In this regard working with Gram Panchayat was much easier apart from conducting training programme for Gram Panchayat presidents. We conducted a series of training programmes for the elected representatives of rural local governance, with the financial support of the Ministry of Rural Development and Panchayati Raj Government of India, the Government of Tamil Nadu, The Hunger Project, and Population Foundation of India.

Over a period of 15 years the Rajiv Gandhi Chair has trained more than 150 master trainers and 18000 elected representatives of rural local governance of all the three tiers. We used the Krishi Vigyan Kendra (KVK) as our training centre to conduct such training over a period of time. The resource persons Mr Vallinayagam, Mr N.S. Chidambaram and Mr S. Subramaniam, Mr Krishnamurthy have been with us for over fifteen years, now. They are retired Additional Directors of the Department of Rural Development, Government of Tamil Nadu. Apart from conducting the training programmes, we have organised many refresher programmes for the Panchayat leaders of the three tiers. These refresher programmes were organised only for clarifying doubts, and offering practicable suggestions for moving forward in Panchayat activities.

Rajiv Gandhi Chair did not stop with the capacity building exercises of its own. It went to support many of the organisations which conducted capacity building exercise for different stakeholders at Panchayat level.

Table 138

S.No	*Name of the District*	*Total No. of Presidents*			*No. of Presidents attended the training*			*Percentage of Panchayat Presidents*		
		Men	*Women*	*Total*	*Men*	*Women*	*Total*	*Men*	*Women*	*Total*
1.	Pudukkottai	326	172	428	275	140	415	84	81	83
2.	Dindigul	200	105	305	191	100	291	96	95	95
3.	Thiruchirappalli	275	132	407	255	131	386	93	99	95
4.	Sivagangai	292	153	445	242	112	354	83	73	80
5.	Ramanathapuram	282	147	429	229	116	345	81	79	80
6.	Theni	82	48	130	66	43	109	80	90	84
7.	Karur	109	49	158	91	49	140	83	100	89
8.	Virudhunagar	303	144	447	245	103	348	81	72	78
		1869	950	2819	1594	794	2388	85	84	85

Evaluation Report of the Training Programme submitted by the Former Director General of National Institute of Rural Development, Hyderabad

Dr.T.C.A.Srinivasaramanujan
Old No.12/New No.15
Sundararajan Street,
Abhiramapuram, Chennai-600 018

Phones: 24995700/24995050
e-mail: tcasr@yahoo.com
18 July 2003

Dear Sri Srinivasan,

Sub: Submission of two Reports-Concurrent Evaluation and Final Evaluation and TA claim

In connection with the assignments given to me, I had already submitted the following two Reports on 18-6-2003:

1. Tank Development Programme in Kottampatti Block proposed by Madurai District Tank Farmers' Federation
2. Individual Rain Water Harvesting System in 10 villages proposed by Centre for Women and Child Development, Parthibanur

In case the two Reports have not been received, I can send copies.

I am herewith submitting two more Reports as below:

1. Concurrent Evaluation of Capacity Building Exercise for Gram Panchayat Leaders implemented by Gandhigram Rural Institute
2. Final Evaluation of Renovation of Tank and Formation of Tank Users' Association implemented by Sri Ramakrishna Sarada Trust, New Edaikkal, Ulundurpet

I am also submitting my TA claims for all the four Reports. I had not claimed TA for the first two Reports sent on 18-6-2003.

Thanking you,

Yours sincerely,

[T.C.A.Srinivasaramanujan]

To
Sri P.N.Srinivasan
Member Convenor
CAPART
Regional Centre[South Zone]
NIRD Campus
Rajendra Nagar
Hyderabad-500 030

Dear Dr. Palanithurai,
Very Good.
Congratulations
16/10/2003

Dr. T.C.A. Srinivasaramanujam IAS(Rtd)
Old No.12 / New No.15
Sundararajan Street,
Abhiramapuram, Chennai – 6000 018

Phones:
24995700/24995050
e-mail:tcasr@yahoo.com
18 July 2003

Dear Sri Srinivasan,

Sub: Submission of two – Reports Concurrent Evaluation and Final Evaluation and TA claim

In connection with the assignments given to me, I had already submitted the following two reports on 18-6-2003:

1. Tank Development Programme in Kottampatti Block proposed by Madurai District Tank Farmers' Federation
2. Individual Rain Water Harvesting System in 10 villages proposed by Centre for Women and Child Development, Parthibanur

In case the two reports have not been received, I can send copies.

I am herewith submitting two more reports as below:

1. Concurrent Evaluation of Capacity Building Exercise for Gram Panchayat Leaders implemented by Gandhigram Rural Institute.
2. Final Evaluation of Renovation of Tank and Formation of Tank Users' Association implemented by Sri Ramakrishana Sarada Trust, New Edaikkal, Ulundurpet

I am also submitting my TA claims for all four reports. I had not claimed TA for the first two reports sent on 18-6-2003.

Thanking you,

Yours Sincerely,
[T.C.A. Srinivasaramanujam]

To
Sri P.N. Srinivasan
Member Convener
CAPART
Regional Centre [South Zone]
NIRD Campus
Rajendra Nagar
Hyderabad -500 030

Panchayat Training Programme – Gri Concurrent Evaluation

Introduction

The broad particulars about this Report are as below:

Name of the Evaluator	Dr T.C.A. Srinivasaramanujam
Name of the Project Holder	Gandhigram Rural Institute, Gandhigram
Name of the Project	Capacity Building Exercise for Gram Panchayat Leaders
Reference of Assignment	ORP/TND/14/6/2002 dated 28-5-2003
Dates of Visit	30-31 May 2003

Project

CAPART sanctioned to Gandhigram Rural Institute, Athur Block, Dindigul District, a Project entitled, "Capacity Building Exercise for Gram Panchayat Leaders". The sanction was communicated vide ORP/TND/14/6/2002 dated 25-7-2002. The cost sanctioned is Rs 9,27,500 for a period of two years. The project covers Madurai, Ramnad, Sivagangai, Pudukkottai, Tiruchi, Karur and Dindigul districts, excluding Vadamadurai and Kujiliamparai Blocks. The sanctioning order mentions that there will be training to 35 batches, each batch having 30 participants. Cost is estimated as below:

Item	Cost
	[In Rupees]
Boarding and Lodging @ Rs 150 per day for 3 days for 30 participants	13,500
Resource Materials @ Rs 200 for 30 participants	6,000
Resource Persons	3,000
Hall and Public Address System	1,000
Stationery. Postage and Miscellaneous	3,000
Total for one batch	26,500
Total for 35 batches	**9,27,500**

In the letter No.OPR/TND/14/6/2002 dated 28-5-2003, Member Convener, CAPART Regional Centre [South Zone] had asked me to make concurrent evaluation of the training programme slated from 31-5-2003 to 2-6-2003. The specific terms of reference for concurrent evaluation are:

(1) Quality of the Study Material
(2) Quality of the Resource Persons
(3) Response, experience and reactions of the participants
(4) Involvement of the State Government

Methodology

I followed the following methodology in this study:

(1) Study of training schedule
(2) Study of course material
(3) Participation in training sessions
(4) Discussions with participants
(5) Discussion with Course Director and Resource Persons
(6) Study of the Training Department

Training Schedule

The information given at the Gandhigram Rural Institute was that so for 14 training programmes have been completed as below:

(1) Tiruchi – 3
(2) Pudukkottai – 3
(3) Sivagangai – 3
(4) Ramnad – 2
(5) Dindigul – 3

The training under evaluation is 15th in the series. It is the third programmes for Ramnad.

CAPART gives grant for training for three days. Gandhigram rural institute coordinates with collectors of the districts from which participants come and adds two days to cover social development issues. Thus, each training is for a duration of five days; CAPART funds the first three days and collectors the last two days.

The training under evaluation was scheduled as below:

Duration [Minutes]	***Subject***
	First Day
60	Principles of Decentralisation 73rd Constitutional Amendment
60	Tamil Nadu Panchayat Act 1994
150	Gram Panchayat Administration: Duties, Responsibilities and Powers Discussions; Questions – Answers
30	Gram Sabha and People's Participation
30	Review
	Second Day
120	Multilevel Planning in Gram Panchayat: Discussion
90	Integration of Panchayat Plan and Sectoral Programmes Discussion Question – Answers
120	Common Property Resource Management Protection of Natural Resources Discussion question - answer
	Third Day
90	Financial Management Finance and Financial Resources Discussion Question – Answers
120	Maintenance of Accounts and Records and Audit Procedure Discussion Question - Answers
90	Social Development and Social Justice Discussion Question – Answers
90	Vision Building Exercise Discussion Question – Answers
60	Leadership Building
	Fourth Day
90	Status of Indian Women / Rural Women -Social Citizenship -Society and Family related issues faced by women

	-Problem – solving process -Gender equality role of individuals
120	Total Rural Sanitation
90	Social Development -Listing of issues -Role of Women in Social Development -Role of Panchayat in Social Development
75	Reproductive Child Health
75	Role of Panchayat in Economic Development
	Fifth Day
240	Computer orientation
120	Exposure visit to Gram Panchayat using Computer

The trainees are divided into three groups of which one is exclusively of women. Sessions are held simultaneously for the three groups. Resource persons rotate between the three groups. The advantage is that the classes are smaller. The disadvantage is that the resource persons have to repeat themselves thrice.

Forty four participants reported on the first day, 31st May, 2003. Of them 14 were women.

Course Material

All participants are given two printed books in Tamil:

(1) Panchayati Raj in Tamil Nadu – Acts, Rules, Schemes

(2) Supervision of Panchayats – An Explanatory Manual

The first book is a compendium of 763 pages. The book incorporates all Acts and Rules relating to Panchayati Raj and all Government Schemes implemented at Panchayat level. The second book is a handy manual giving information about rules and procedures applicable to Panchayats.

The course material has great reference value. When the elected Panchayat Presidents go back to their jobs, they will have ready reference to all information relevant to their functions.

The elected functionaries need all information in the books to be effective. Most of them are new and inexperienced. The system itself is new and as yet untested. Most functionaries are not fully aware of their powers and methods for exercising them. They are at the mercy of officers and do not always get good guidance. The course material will fill this gap in knowledge.

Training Sessions

I attended the training sessions for all the three groups. Elected Panchayat Presidents were the main participants. Besides, Government officials dealing with Panchayats and Development at the Block level participated.

Most of the elected functionaries were not aware of the legal framework of Panchayati Raj. Their ideas about their powers, responsibilities and charter were limited. They were also pessimistic about their potentials and overawed by the control by government officers. For them, the training was an opportunity to know all about their duties and obligations. They expressed surprise to learn that their potential was greater than what they thought. The questions put by them suggested that the information given in the training was an eye-opener to them. Some of them felt that they ought to have been given the training much earlier.

Surprisingly, the government officers also seemed as unaware of the legal framework as the elected persons. Most of the Acts and Rules are not available in field offices. Even circulars were not within their knowledge. The questions put by them and information given to them in the training sessions revealed that they were not uptodate in their knowledge.

The participants were given a questionnaire to assess the training. Their views are sought on the following:

- Course Material
- Each Resource Person
- Their training style
- Class arrangement

- Lodging
- Food
- Cooperation of training institution
- Duration

Except for duration, they were asked to assess on the scale of very good, good and satisfactory. For duration, the scale is sufficient, should be increased and should be reduced.

There are questions to test the grasp of the participants of the board subjects covered in the training. The questionnaire also seeks to draw the socio-economic profiles of the departments.

The questionnaire gives a good feedback about the training. I saw several reports of previous training programmes and found them informative.

Resource Persons

For conducting the CAPART training programmes, Gandhigram Rural Institute draws on the services of the following four retired Government servants of Rural Development Department:

1. Sri K. Subramanian, retired in 1998 as Additional Director in DRDA office at Chennai.
2. Sri N.S. Chidambaram, retired in 1996 as Principal, Rural Extension Training Center, Bhavanisagar.
3. Sri K.Vallinayagam, retired in 1992 as Additional Director, Rural Development.
4. Sri S. Krishnamoorthy, retired in 1993 as Assistant Director, Rural Development.

All the four are consultants in State Institute of Rural Development at Maraimalainagar. They have painstakingly collected all latest orders on Panchayati Raj. They have prepared detailed training modules. They have also learnt modern techniques of training pedagogy. Their expression and interactive style are effective.

The institute has many in-house experts to takes sessions on Sanitation, Childcare and Women Development, Leadership Qualities, vision Building and Computer Orientation. They have considerable research and teaching experience on the subject.

Training Department

Rajiv Gandhi Chair for Panchayati Raj Studies in the Department of Political Science and Development Administration of Gandhigram Rural Institute is the Training Department for this training. As an institution, the Training Department has emerged as a Resource Center of Excellence in Panchayati Raj. It has conducted many training Programmes for different levels of Panchayat functionaries. It has organised or participated in seminars and conferences relating to Panchayats. It has undertaken studies on the role of Panchayati Raj Institutions in population, health, ecology, gram sabhas, and sanitation, water supply and gender issues. These studies were financed by various agencies. It has published many books, monographs, articles and reports on Panchayati Raj. I was Director General of National Institute of Rural Development, Hyderadad, where there is a Center for Panchayati Raj Institutions. Its resource base in Panchayati Raj is impressive. What I found in the Rajiv Gandhi Chair for Panchayati Raj Studies is that it is very much stronger than the NIRD center. The chair is much more actively involved in grassroots study and has direct field exposure. Its database is very strong.

Dr G. Palanithurai is the head of the Rajiv Gandhi Chair for Panchayati Raj Studies. He is professor and Head of the Department and Dean. He has completed many projects and published several books and articles on Panchayati Raj. He is guiding all training programmes, which are underway all round the year. Being professor of a deemed university, he has research and teaching duties to back up his training and project work. I found him remarkably well informed on every aspect of Panchayati Raj –legal, administrative, social, political, planning, and developmental. He is an expert and a doyen among the scholars of Panchayati Raj.

The Rajiv Gandhi Chair has other experts also and they have made significant contributions in training and research.

With such resources, the Rajiv Gandhi Chair for Panchayati Raj Studies is a strong Training Department for the CAPART – assisted training programmes.

Conclusions

Based on the above analysis, I make the following evaluation about the training Programme, Capacity Building Exercise for Gram Panchayat Leaders, held from 31st May to 2nd June, 2003 at Gandhigram Rural Institute:

- The training module is comprehensive
- The training schedule is well planned
- It is imaginative to dovetail CAPART funds with grants from collectors and increase the duration by two days to include social development issues
- The training is well attended
- Course materials is useful
- Resource persons are knowledgeable
- The training is needed for both the elected and government functionaries
- The Training Department is a Centre of Excellence
- It has a rich experience in conducting the training.

The project is successful. CAPART can continue to support Gandhigram Rural Institute for future training programmes.

Place : Chennai
Date: 18 July 2003 [T.C.A. Srinivasaramanujam]

Training Session as in Progress

Capacity Building Exercise to Local Body Leaders

Index